"Mr Fussell's Steel and Plate Mill" - the Upper Works in Wadbury Valley, Mells (page 29).

Men of Iron

The Fussells of Mells

ROBIN THORNES

With a foreword by
Lord Rees-Mogg of Hinton Blewitt

Frome Society for Local Study

Frome, Somerset
2010

To Vivienne and Anna

Frome Society for Local Study 2010

ISBN 978-0-9565869-1-9

Designed by Nick Wigzell
Typeset in 11point Minion Pro

Printed and bound by Butler Tanner & Dennis, Frome

Contents

Acknowledgements

Special thanks are due to Michael McGarvie for his unfailing help and encouragement, to my mother Joan Thornes for the translation and interpretation of medieval documents, and to Nick Wigzell for designing the book. I am grateful to William Rees-Mogg for kindly agreeing to write the foreword, and to Frome Society for Local Study for its support and for publishing this book. I should also like to extend my thanks to David Rawlins, Alastair MacLeay, Derrick Hunt, Clive Wilkins, Joyce Jefferson, Charles Daniel, Ingrid Sofrin, The Earl of Oxford and Asquith, Philip Nokes, Hazel Tovey, Peter Williamson, Tristram and John Powell for their assistance. Finally, I would like to thank the staff of Frome Library, Downside School, Hampshire Museum Service, Bristol Record Office, Wiltshire Record Office and the Somerset Record Office.

Foreword

In the early 1960s my family took on the task of restoring Ston Easton Park, perhaps the finest Palladian house on Mendip. There was a trunk of dry rot, at least 70 feet high, from the basement to the roof. When working on the roof, our builders, Haywood and Wooster of Bath, found a chisel which they gave to me. The chisel had the name of Fussell stamped on it.

From this new book on the Fussells, Men of Iron, which Robin Thornes has written, I take it that the chisel, which I later used for opening packing cases, would probably have been made by Fussells of Mells in the early years of the nineteenth century. As the Fussells had no less than six edge-tool works under their family control, it is not possible to identify the particular works in which the chisel is most likely to have been made.

I now live in Mells itself, in what is very much Horner (now Asquith) territory. The use of the Mells river to turn various mills goes back well behind the Fussell family, into the period when Mells was a property belonging to Glastonbury Abbey. The house in which we now live is a Glastonbury-built house, with the arms of Glastonbury in the porch. It was apparently used as the miller's house at the time of the dissolution of the monasteries. Indeed the miller in the 1530s was married to Alice Whiting, the niece of the last Abbot of Glastonbury.

Robin Thornes traces iron work in Somerset further back than the dissolution of the monasteries. "The earliest iron worker to whom Somerset lays claim is St. Dunstan of Glastonbury. Dunstan was born in Baltonsborough around the year 909 and took holy orders in 943, after which he turned to Glastonbury where he practised the craft of metalworking. The story has it that while working at his forge one day he was visited by the devil, whom he seized by the nose with red hot tongs."

The end of the Fussell story can be taken as the winding up of the limited company of J.I. and J. Fussell, which came on 29 August 1900. After that there are still family reminiscences but nothing to compare with the nineteenth century glories of the business which for a time made East Mendip one of the national centres of the edge-tool trade.

The iron works of East Mendip and Somerset extend almost exactly 1,000 years from Saint Dunstan to the eventual closure of an insolvent company. The growth and prosperity of the Fussells' enterprise and its contribution to local prosperity are the proper subject of this excellent industrial history.

William Rees-Mogg

Introduction

The historical importance of an industry is often only recognised when it is on the verge of extinction. This was certainly true of edge-tool making in the East Mendips. In the early 1930s Dr R.D. Reid visited and photographed a small works at Gurney Slade that had recently closed. The site was the last one in the area to retain its water-powered machinery, which, in his opinion, made it of special value, and he hoped "that something will be done to preserve them, as they are on the point of collapse".[1] Unfortunately, by the time he paid a second visit in 1933 the buildings had been demolished to make way for a water treatment plant. Five years later the same works were immortalised by Dom Ethelbert Horne of Downside Abbey in his book *Somerset Folk*. The main character in the story is Jerry, a deaf and irascible shovel maker who runs a decrepit forge single-handed - working to his own rhythm, keeping time with his great hammer "which strikes its ponderous blows at a pace that is above hurry".[2] In an age of mass production Jerry and his real life counterpart, Arthur Steeds, were already anachronisms, their antiquated working practices of interest only to those who wished to commemorate their vanishing world.

Reid's account of the Gurney Slade works was published in the *Somerset Yearbook* of 1935. Coincidentally, another article about edge-tool making had appeared in the same publication a year before. Written by Edward Tylee of Chantry, this focused on the edge-tool making activities of the Fussell family of Mells.[3] Tylee had lived in Chantry for 30 years and drew on the reminiscences of former Fussells' employees. It was not until the 1960s that a fuller and more academic account of the Fussells' businesses was published in Robin Atthill's *Old Mendip*. In recent years interest in the edge-tool industry of the East Mendips has continued to centre on the Fussell family businesses. The Fussells have been the subject of articles, monographs, museum displays, exhibitions, and even a song. There is now a Fussell Society, and the Mells area has even been referred to as "Fussell Country".

The Fussells were not great industrialists, innovators or inventors, and their influence and historical significance is local rather than national. Why then have they and their businesses attracted the attention of historians? The answer lies, in part, in the fact that their businesses lasted for more than 150 years, spanning the period of the Industrial Revolution. They made their appearance in the historic record in the time of water-powered craft industry and their exit in the age of steam-powered mass production. In that same period the Fussell family made the transition from village craftsmen to prosperous "men of business", and finally to gentlemen with country estates and mansions.

My interest in the Fussells and their businesses began when I came to Somerset in 1994 and found that the house I was living in was on the site of the family's Stoney Lane edge-tool works at Chantry. I asked who the Fussells were and was pointed to Robin Atthill's *Old Mendip*, the book that has done more then any other to kindle my interest in this subject. Atthill rightly declared that to "know and to love one's countryside, one must continually be asking questions".[4] His book answered my first question, and also provided information suggesting other lines of inquiry. In the early stages of my research it was my intention to write a short document that would be of interest to visitors to our house and, hopefully, to subsequent owners. However, the scale and variety of their activities, and the timescale in which they occurred, meant that what had started as a few notes soon grew to become the makings of a book.

Like all men, the lives of the Fussells reflected the times and places in which they lived. With this in mind I have sought to place the Fussells in the broader contexts of the history of the East Mendips and of the landscape they played their part in shaping, and on which they have left their mark. It was tempting to tell their story in the manner of a classic tale of the rise and fall of a family dynasty, although the truth, as is often the case, is both more complex and interesting. The impact of the Fussells on their small part of Somerset was such that even in their own lifetimes they and the tools they made took on a mythical quality. It is the task of the historian to separate myth from reality, while not losing sight of the fact that myths themselves, and the beliefs and circumstances that gave birth to them, are a crucial part of the story. Researching and writing this book has been a hobby, an intellectual challenge and at times a source of consolation. I will miss it now that it is completed, but know that the experience has enriched my appreciation of the valleys of the East Mendips and those who lived and worked in them through the centuries.

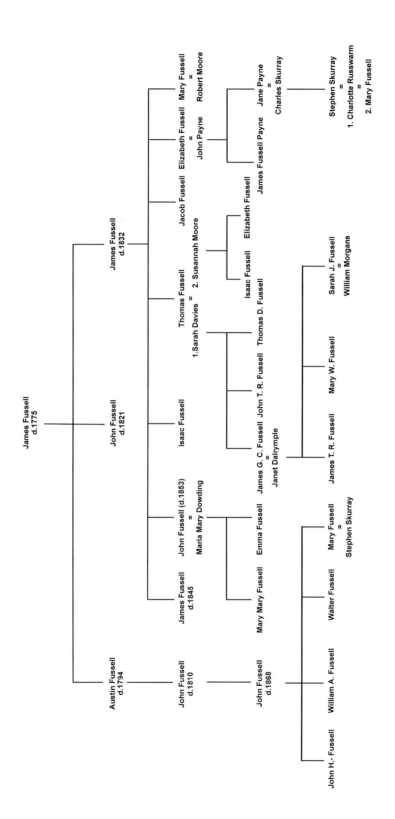

Family tree of the Fussells showing members mentioned in this book

The Iron Industry of the East Mendips before the Fussells

The Middle Ages

The earliest iron worker to which Somerset lays claim is St Dunstan of Glastonbury. Dunstan was born at Baltonsborough around the year 909 and took holy orders in 943, after which he returned to Glastonbury and is said to have built himself a small monk's cell where he practised the craft of metalworking. The story has it that while working at his forge one day he was visited by the devil, whom he seized by the nose with red-hot tongs. Hearths uncovered during archaeological excavations indicate there was an iron industry in Glastonbury in Dunstan's time, while a century later the Domesday Book recorded the presence of no less than eight smiths.

In the Middle Ages iron was made wherever suitable pockets of ore were found. This was raised from pits close to the surface and smelted in small charcoal-fired furnaces, known as bloomeries which produced 'blooms' of malleable iron. Iron is found in many parts of the Mendips in the forms of deposits of nodules of yellow ochre and thin veins of haematite washed into fractures in the limestone. The red-coloured haematite, in particular, can be seen in many quarries in the area. The archaeological evidence for iron working in the area is equally widespread, iron slag having been identified in fields in Stoke St Michael, Downhead, Leigh-on-Mendip, and Holcombe. There is also ample field and place name evidence for iron extraction, including Great Iron Pits and Little Iron Pits at Stoke St Michael, Irepitts at Ashwick, Iron Pits and Cinder Hill in Holcombe, Orrpitts Farm at Lypeate, and Orrpitt Lane, Babington.

Documentary evidence for the presence of the iron industry in 11th century Somerset is provided by the Domesday Book, which lists a number of places where rents were paid to the lord of the manor in blooms of iron.[1] There are indications that iron was being sought in the Mendips by the 13th century, the Bishop of Bath obtaining permission in 1235 to mine for iron ore in the royal forest of Mendip and to make iron from the ore raised.[2] At the east end of the Mendips there is evidence for the presence of iron makers, then referred to as smiths, by the end of the century - a perambulation of Elwood Forest in 1298 mentioning the settlement of "Smethwek", now Smithwick, in Marston Bigot.[3]

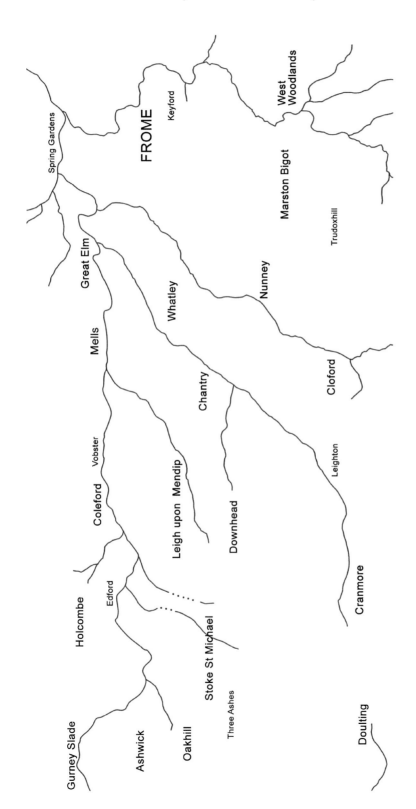

The East Mendips showing the principal settlements of the area and the rivers and streams that drain it.

In this period a number of Glastonbury manors still had several tenants paying iron rents, these including East Pennard, Ditcheat, Mells and Pilton. The iron was paid in the form of "vomers", which translates as ploughshares. Abbot Amesbury's survey of Mells in the middle of the 13th century records that "Elias de la Mare holds one crofter and pays thereof 2 vomers a year at the feast of St. Michael". In the same period the rent of the manor of Stoke St Michael – then administered from the neighbouring manor of Downhead - included 50 vomers. An early 14th century survey of the Glastonbury manor of Doulting lists among its assets 50 vomers of iron from the lord of Downhead worth 25 shillings.[4] By then Mells had for some time been receiving vomers from Doulting, the accounts of the manor for 1259 recording that 11 had been received from that manor. The Mells accounts continued to include vomers from Doulting until the early 14th century, the number received varying and declining in latter years to three in 1301 and five in 1305. It seems likely that the vomers were, in reality, bars of iron, evidence for this being found in the Mells accounts which on one occasion changed the usual heading of "vomers" to "ferrum" (iron) and describes the amount due as two pieces of iron. By the early 15th century this rent was still being paid, although as a cash payment of 2s 6d rather than in iron.

There is evidence for smiths working with, and possibly making, edge-tools in the East Mendips by the 13th century. Abbot Amesbury's survey of Glastonbury Abbey, made in the middle of the century, recorded that Henry the Smith of Mells was paying a rent of 12 pence for something called a stangrist.[5] The term stangrist has been taken to mean a blacksmith's grindstone, but appears to have also been applied to a water-powered mill for the grinding of tools. It is significant that in a document of 1265 Henry the Smith's stangrist was described as a "mill for smith's work" ("Molendino Fabrili"). Half a century later, in 1315, Thomas Hyleberd of Mells paid 40d for a "stangrist and smith's workshop lately raised". Further evidence for stangrists being buildings is provided by a lease of 1348, which required William Badecoke to "newly roof and repair the said stangrist at his own cost".

That the Mells stangrists were driven by water-power is indicated by the fact that all known examples were described as being on watercourses. For example, Thomas Hyleberd's stangrist was said to be "on the water course of Wulewellsyche (Wulwell Stream) near the fulling mill", while in 1314 William Daunt took over the lease of a stangrist with pond and water formerly held by his father Henry. By the early 14th century there were two stangrists on the edge of Mells village, both of which were described as being situated on part of the stream then known as Peter's Pool. One of these was William Daunt's, which was on or near the site of what became Bilboa corn mill.[6] Evidence for stangrists having millponds and purpose-built dams is provided by

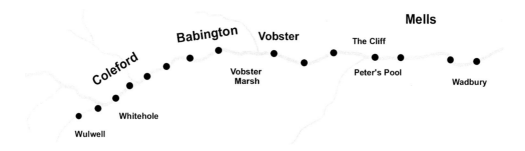

Water-power sites in the manors of Mells, and the adjoining manors of Coleford and Babington (1250-1650).

a reference in 1366 to Nicholas Aleyn of Babington paying 6d to Mells for permission to anchor the weir of his stangrist on the south side of the Mells Stream. The fact that stangrists had mill ponds seems to have tempted their occupants to illegal fishing and in the 1340s two tenants, John Batyn and William Daunt, were accused of setting fish traps without the permission of the lord of the manor.

Such water-powered tool grinding mills are known to have existed in France by the early 13th century, where they were known by a variety of names, including "molendena ad cultellos" (a mill for cutlery) and "molendenum . . . ad quod ferramentur molentur" (a mill that is for grinding ironwork).[7] The presence of the Mells Stangrists indicates that the technology may have been introduced into England not long after its adoption in mainland Europe and been well established by the mid 12th century.[8] By the early 14th century there were no fewer than three stangrists in the Manor of Mells, one at the west end of the manor at Wulfwell leased by Robert the Smith and his brother Adam and two close to Mells village on a stretch of the stream then called Peter's Pool.[9] In 1301 the latter two were reported to be untenanted and in 1303 one of these was described as "fallen down", while the tenant of the other had, it was said, died and "there is no one to look after it".

However, within a few years there seems to have been a revival of interest in running stangrists and in the course of the next fifty years the two on Peter's Pool appear to have been in fairly constant use. When the Black Death struck Mells in the summer of 1348 it claimed the lives of around half the population - 44 out of the manor's 83 males over 16 years of age being listed as dead in the autumn of that year. Surprisingly, at least one vacant stangrist was re-let soon after the first onset of the pestilence - William Badecoke taking over the running of the stangrist formerly leased by William Daunt in 1349. Badecoke ran the stangrist until 1367, when he was accidentally killed by a scythe (or sickle), possibly while grinding it. The incident was recorded in the Mells hallmote since the tool that caused his death was forfeit to the lord of the manor - a fine known as a deodand. Within months of William's death his widow, Joan, remarried and her new husband, Henry atte Slade, took over the running of the stangrist in the following year.

By the early 15th century the situation had changed again, however, all three stangrists in Mells being out of use for want of tenants. In 1516 the Abbot Beere's Terrier of the manor records that there was only one working stangrist rented by John Young, alias Smyth, said to have been formerly held by William Badecoke and Henry the Smith. By then this stangrist was over 200 years old, its former tenants including Henry Daunt, William Daunt, William Masmyrdry, William Badecoke and Henry atte Slade. The sites of two other stangrists in Mells village were occupied by fulling mills, of which there were by then no fewer than seven in the manor. That water-powered sites formerly occupied by stangrists were being reused for fulling mills provides evidence that the woollen industry had been expanding, while that of iron working had declined.

Forges and Furnaces

Towards the end of the Middle Ages innovations had been made which were to change the nature and scale of the iron industry. One of the first of these was the introduction of forges with water-powered tilt hammers, these being used to work reheated blooms into bars of malleable iron. There is evidence for water-powered forges having been established in the area by the end of the period. In 1544, following the dissolution of the Carthusian monastery of Witham Friary, part of the estate was granted to Sir Ralph Hopton, including a corn mill and an iron mill.[10] The iron mill seems to have been located on the River Frome at Witham Hole, close to the present "Iron Mill Bridge" and slightly upstream from Smithwick. It appears to have ceased working before its acquisition by Sir Ralph, this being indicated by an account written by Francis Thynne in 1583.

> In Trottoxhill in Nunney parish (as my brother Mawdlye, Lord of Nunney, being LX years of age herde olde menne before report) there were thre smythes that kept pretenses [apprentices] dwelling with them who wrought the yrone maille at the yrone mill standing therebye & not far from Frayrye to ewe bridge & so to frome [the River Frome].[11]

Given that Thynne's brother - who was 60 at the time of writing - had heard the story when young from men already old, implies the mill had become disused before the middle of the 16th century. The "ewe" bridge mentioned is identifiable as the present Iron Mill Bridge, which was formerly known as Yewe Bridge and Yeowe Bridge, the River Frome being known as the River Yeo at that time.[12]

Smiths' Coal

It is likely the smiths of the Mendips used local coal, as well as charcoal, to heat the iron they worked. By the early 14th century coal was being mined in Mells, the manor's accounts recording in 1301 that 18 quarters of coal were raised and used for the burning of lime. The full extent of mining is hard to gauge, since it is clear that not all coal appeared in the manor's accounts. For example, in 1340 William Esey and Galfrido Atte Clyve were fined for digging coal without the lord's permission.[13] In many years no coal was sold, the accounts giving the lack of buyers as the reason. The Mells Terrier of 1516 mentions that "William Feyerman" had a 12-year lease of the nearby common at Whitehole to work "the coal pits without damage to the ground within the manor of Mells". A memorandum attached to the Terrier also noted "That there has been for some time mining for smiths' coal in Melcomb Wood, on the lord's common there, and also that the trial digging began in the thirtieth year of the lord Richard Beere, abbot [1522/3]".[14] In this period Mendip coal was still only of relatively little importance economically, and it is significant that as late as 1586 the coal of the nearby manor of Stratton was said to be used only by smiths for iron working.[15] The coal of the southern coalfield was, indeed, particularly suitable for use by smiths in their forges, a factor which may have encouraged the development of an edge-tool industry in the area. Writing in 1795 John Billingsley of Ashwick noted that it was "excellent for the forge",[16] and in 1840 Richard Boodle of Radstock confirmed that Vobster coal was "of superior utility for smith's work, which is proved by the fact, that in all the smiths shops in our own Coal works, they use Vobster small Coal instead of their own".[17]

Decline

The dissolution of the monasteries led to profound changes in the life of the country, not least of which was the transfer of the huge monastic estates such as Glastonbury into private hands. In the East Mendips, one of the principal beneficiaries was the Horner family, who purchased a number of estates, including the manor of Mells with Leigh-on-Mendip. Landlords like the Horners now owned and controlled much of the land, together with its associated water and mineral rights. Anyone wanting to establish mills, mine coal, make charcoal, or work iron, could only do so with the approval of these landowners and by paying them for the privilege.

By this time the English iron industry was suffering from the effects of foreign competition, Bristol and Somerset merchants importing significant quantities of bar iron from Northern Spain. These imports reached a peak in the 1530s, by which time it is estimated that around 3,000 tons were entering the port annually. The Bristol records show that the average size of a shipment of iron was around 10 tons. In his will of 1504 Thomas Upcot, a Dunster merchant, bequeathed to the church of St.

George "10 tons of iron coming in a ship of John Cokkys" and to his daughter "10 tons of iron coming with John More of Stokgursi (Stogursey) from parts beyond the sea if they duly come and in peace and safety".

One Bristol merchant who was heavily involved in the iron trade with Spain at this time was James Smyth. Smyth exported woollen cloth bought from local clothiers and imported woad, wool oil, wine, and iron. His ledger book, which survives, records that individual consignments of iron bars could be in excess of 100 tons. These were then sold on to other merchants, and also direct to iron workers. Among his customers were smiths in Bruton, Shepton Mallet, Wanstrow and Warminster, these buying his iron bars in quantities of around half a ton. The iron came in the form of 22-24lb bars, a size suitable for being handled and moved by packhorse.

The extent of the penetration of imported Spanish iron into local markets in this period indicates that the local industry had decayed, possibly to the point of collapse. There is, however, evidence that there were men still actively seeking local sources of iron. Writing in the 1530s, Leland noted that "Iren owr found a late in Mendipe, and yren made ther" (iron ore had been found of late in the Mendips and iron was made there).[18] Interest in locating new sources of iron was given a boost when relations with Spain began to deteriorate following the accession of Elizabeth I. It has been estimated that by the late 1560s Spanish imports had declined to under 1,000 tons per year, falling to less than 500 tons around the time of the Armada. The decline in imports, coupled with increasing demand for iron goods, resulted in a steady rise in the price of iron. This encouraged landlords and merchants to invest in the development of the domestic iron industry in England and Wales. As a result, the country became almost self-sufficient in iron by the end of the sixteenth century, a situation that lasted for almost 50 years. The new iron industry of this period was very different from that of the Middle Ages in terms of technology, scale and organisation.

One important change was that an increasing amount of the iron produced was made using blast furnaces - large and relatively permanent structures, each of which was capable of producing hundreds of tons of iron a year. These were expensive to build and maintain, consumed large amounts of iron ore and charcoal, and needed water power to work the huge bellows that provided the air blast that gave them their name. Moreover, the new ventures required considerable capital to build, equip and run.

The coming of the blast furnace also led to the emergence of the "iron master", a new breed of man who combined technical knowledge with organisational and business skills. It is significant that there are no recorded examples of blast furnaces having been set up in the Mendips in this period. The area had adequate sources for charcoal, and suitable sites for water-powered furnaces. What it lacked was sufficiently large deposits of iron ore to keep furnaces in blast for weeks or even months on end. The other major problem was the area's poor communications, there being no navigable waterways and only roads of poor quality.

Lady Hopton's Forge

The blast furnace may have revolutionised the iron industry, but it had one major drawback in that it produced cast iron, often known as pig or sow iron, rather than the more useful wrought iron. Before 1700 few articles were made of cast iron, the most important being fire backs, cooking pots, and cannon. As a result, the greater part of the cast iron produced by the furnaces was sent to forges for conversion into malleable iron. In the forge, the iron was first melted in a "finery" hearth to remove the majority of the carbon. The resulting bloom of malleable iron was then hammered out into a bar using a water-powered tilt hammer, the metal being reheated in a "chafery" hearth at intervals during the hammering process.

The only known example of such a forge in the East Mendips was that established around 1600 by Rachel, Lady Hopton, at or near the site of the earlier forge owned by Witham Friary. In May 1619 the manager of Lord Boyle's Cappoquin furnace in County Waterford, Ireland, wrote to one Thomas Smith asking him to "procure a guide to the Lady Hoppens Fordg. Called Wittham, which is about 20 myles from Bristoll".[19] Smith was also asked to find out where the Hoptons bought their "sow iron", assess the state of the business and the likelihood of it continuing, and attempt to "deale with Sir Robert or my Lady Hoppen for a hundred or half a hundred tonn of sow iron."[20] Smith was instructed that "The lowest price that his lordship will sell a tonn of sow iron for is five pound sterling delivered on the key at Bristoll, or four pound ten shillings sterling delivered on the key at Yoghall, free of all charge."[21]

In the event, the Hoptons came to an agreement with Lord Boyle, buying more than 40 tons of sow iron from his furnace. These transactions are recorded in the accounts of Boyle's Bristol agent, John Doughty, which include entries for the purchase, storage, weighing, and carriage of a number of consignments of iron. The business relationship was to prove short-lived, for on 17 February 1620 Boyle received a letter from Doughty informing him that the Witham forge had closed. He reported that Robert Hopton had asked him to sell 20 tons of iron he had ordered since "he hathe wrought out his and purposeth to doe no more". He also passed on an offer from Hopton "that yf your Lordship wante a hammer mann you may have his, the which is as good as any is in England, he thinketh."[22]

The former existence of the Witham forges was not forgotten locally, for as late as 1751 Wells Assizes indicted the parish of Nunney for failing to keep up the road between Nunney Pound and Trudoxhill ironworks.[23] Today, the iron industry of Witham is commemorated in the names Iron Mill Bridge, Iron Mill Farm, and Iron Mill Plantation. Iron slag has been found at Witham Hole, and excavations on the site of Witham Friary in the 1960s exposed a road metalled with slag that had been built across the site after the Dissolution.[24]

The records of the Hoptons' dealings with Lord Boyle provide a valuable insight into the iron industry in Somerset in the early 17th century. The first point of interest is that the Hoptons' forge was converting cast iron into wrought iron, presumably for use in tool making and for general blacksmiths' work. The second point is that the correspondence confirms that the industry was dependent on imports of iron coming in through Bristol. The fact that the Hoptons were using imported iron in their forge indicates that local iron was either not available or too expensive to be worth using. The iron they bought from Boyle was shipped from Youghal to Bristol, from where it was brought overland by wagon or packhorse. The very fact that the Witham forge was using iron brought in via Bristol means that local iron workers could equally well buy their iron from any other region that shipped iron to Bristol, Wales, the Forest of Dean, or, increasingly, the Baltic.

Blacksmiths and Edge-Tool Makers

The identification of early edge-tool makers is difficult, many being described simply as "smiths", a term applied to any craftsmen who made or worked iron. In the Middle Ages iron workers in the larger towns and cities became increasingly specialised, and at the beginning of the 15th century the branches of the metal working trade of the city of Bristol formed themselves into a guild of "farriers, smiths, cutlers, and lockyers". Such guilds rigidly enforced specialisation by regulating the training of apprentices and the types of work their members could undertake. In rural areas, on the other hand, village smiths remained free to shoe horses, make and mend implements, and take on any task that required the working of iron. An exception to this rule was the manufacture of edge-tools, which was emerging as a separate and specialised rural craft by the end of the period.

An indication that some of the smiths mentioned in the documents of the time were tool makers is the fact that there were more of them in some villages than was necessary for general blacksmithing. In Mells, for example, in the 1680s there were no fewer than four smiths – John Smith, John Budd, Thomas Maynard and James Everett. What is clear is that whether described as smiths, cutlers, or edge-tool makers, the trade of tool making was well established in the villages of the East Mendips by the mid 17th century.

The earliest reference to the trade of edge-tool maker in the area yet found is provided by a Diocese of Salisbury marriage licence granted in 1633 to John Smith (alias Singer) of Nunney giving him permission to marry Joan Bryant of Steeple Langford, Wiltshire.[25] The first specific reference to an edge-tool mill appears in an inquisition taken at Wells in December 1583 after the death of James Pewe, yeoman of Stoke Lane (Stoke St Michael). This states that Pewe held a corn mill [molendium bladum] called an "edgetolemyll" now in the tenure of Robert Toplyffe and Joan Townsend.[26] The mill appears to have been on the stream at East End and was probably a grinding mill not dissimilar to the stangrists of previous centuries. The Toplyffe family were still engaged in the trade half a century later, James Topley of Stoke Lane being described as a "cutler" in the list of the county's Royalist supporters made in 1655.[27] The term cutler was then used to describe craftsmen who made or repaired cutting tools, and was often applied to men who a century later would describe themselves as edge-tool makers. Eight years later in 1663, a lease was granted to Roger Clarke "cutler" for a cottage in Mells, the first firm evidence for a specialist edge-tool maker in that village.[28]

The Everetts of Vobster

The late 17th century saw an expansion of the edge-tool industry in Mells. Under a lease of 11th February 1688 James Everett of Vobster, "Blackesmith", was given permission to erect "a house & shop, wheele & grindstone and other things for the forgeing, or

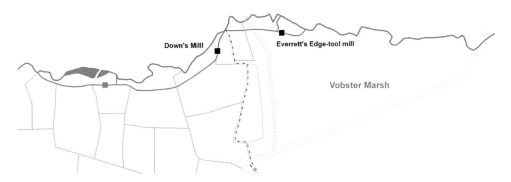

The position of Joseph Everett's edge-tool mill at Vobster.

making of any Manner of Iron Worke Relating to the trade of a blacksmith, and also to sett up a pond there." Everett's mill is mentioned in a memorandum written in the 1760s, which is more specific about its purpose - describing it as for the grinding of edge-tools.[29] The exact location of this mill is not known, but the wording of the lease makes it possible to determine its approximate position. It is described as being in Vobster Marsh and on a watercourse "which comes from Downes Mill tayle". Vobster Marsh was a large area of common land at the west end of Mells Parish, and "Downes Mill tayle" was the tail race of the corn mill of that name in the adjoining parish of Leigh-on-Mendip.

The Everett family were working as smiths in Vobster by the mid 17th century. James Everett's father, also James, had "a house or shopp neere the Gate at Vobsters Marsh" which had been granted to him by Sir John Horner in 1651.[30] In 1660 James Everett senior, together with John Butcher, Robert Clarke, John Griffin, and Henry Ashman, entered into a bond with George Horner which appears to relate to a lease to work coal in the Vobster area. Henry Ashman of Kilmersdon, described as a "coalman", may well be the same Henry Ashman who was later recorded as having the lease of a coal pit from George Horner "by virtue whereof he did worke the same upon some part of this land".[31] Robert Clarke and John Griffin, both from the adjoining parish of Babington, were also coal miners.[32] John Butcher is described in the document as a clothier of Mells, although a number of Mells leases show that he lived in Vobster and at one time occupied the fulling mill downstream from Vobster Bridge. That he too was involved in the coal industry in this period is recorded in an "information of wrongs and trespass" laid against him and his brother Gabriel in 1655. In that year an unnamed informant wrote to Sir John Horner accusing them of having "landed and sold many sacks of cole on the marsh yr worship having no share therein and I being desirous to know why they did so they told me that I ought not to speake of it or meddle with it".[33] Further weight to the idea that this was a mining partnership is provided by the fact that the previous lessee of the coal at Vobster, John Salmon, died in 1659, only a few months before the bond was signed (see chapter 10). James Everett's involvement in the venture indicates that he was a man of some substance, and explains how his son would, in the course of time, be able to expand the family business by building an edge-tool mill.

James Everett senior died in 1687 or 1688, and in the latter year his son James erected his mill on Vobster Marsh and was granted the cottage and four acres of land occupied by his mother Elizabeth. James Everett junior may have died in 1711, for in that year his son Joseph leased the mill. Following Joseph's death the mill passed to George Snook, described in the lease of 1721 as a blacksmith of Vobster.[34] In 1755 it was leased to John Nuth, a coal driver of Babington - the property being described as a "mill upon Vobster Marsh…formerly in the tenure of Joseph Everett, late of George Snook & now of James Nuth".[35] The mill was still in existence in 1769 when Nuth, who was by then described as "yeoman", took out a new lease. It is unlikely that he took over the mill with the intention of operating it himself, and it may be that it was disused by this time or that Snook continued to work it as a sub-tenant or employee. What is certain is that the Snook family were still living and working locally in 1774, for in that year the local magistrate, Thomas Horner, dismissed a "complaint made by one Snook a blacksmith of Vobster against the village inn-keeper, Harry Austin, for keeping ill orders in his house, suffering gaming".[36] The mill was still in existence in the 1760s, when a memorandum written at that time describing the watercourse between Coleford and Vobster stated that it was "now remaining." By this time the tail race of the mill was supplying water to a "coalwork" of Mr Horner begun in

A late 19th century photograph of Bridge Cottage, Mells, believed to have been the property leased by Richard Hoddinott in 1689 (Michael McGarvie Collection)

1763. The mill is mentioned in another lease granted to Nuth in July 1769, but is not referred to thereafter and is not shown on Samuel Donne's map of the manors of Mells and Leigh made in 1779.[37]

This was not, however, the end of edge-tool making in Vobster, for by the mid 19th century Robert Cook and his son John were running a small tool making and general blacksmiths business in the village. In 1851 Robert described himself as an "Edge Tool Maker and Smith", while John was listed as "Edge Tool Maker". They also appear in the census of 1861, by which time Robert was 53, but not in that of 1871.

The Hoddinotts of Nunney and Mells

Within two years of James Everett setting up his edge-tool mill at Vobster, a Nunney edge-tool maker called Richard Hoddinott moved into the parish of Mells. In a lease of a cottage in Leighton granted in September 1688 Richard was described as a blacksmith of Nunney,[38] but in another for two cottages in Mells in August the following year was called an "edgetoolmaker". The location of the Mells property was described as follows:

> Scituate [sic] in Mells aforesaid adjoyneing to the howse Late of John Yeoman on the west side and standinge neare to Hills Mill on the south parte… together with a Little plot of ground where the sawpit was lyeing before the said

dwellinghowse on the east side for a garden; Leaving out sufficient wayes for horses and men to travel on all sides.[39]

This seems to have been the building now called Bridge Cottage, the position of which closely matches the description in the above lease, allowing for the fact that the rights of way mentioned above were later moved to their present position on its eastern boundary. The surviving leases make no mention of a workshop, although the proximity to what is described as "Hills Mill" raises the possibility that this may have served as a grinding mill.

In 1690 Mary Hoddinott gave birth to a son, Simon, and in October of that year a new lease was granted which added his name and removed that of Joseph. Simon was born in Nunney in 1690, suggesting that the Hoddinotts were not living in Mells for some months after the granting of the first lease. In this second lease the property is described as "all that Old Cottage or dwellinghowse with a new Chimney erected and a Little garden".[40] Richard Hoddinott seems to have been living in Mells by 1706, when he is recorded as a churchwarden.[41] However, by 1717 he may have moved back to Nunney, for in that year he was granted a lease of a property called Nichol's Temmes on Nunney Brook to the north of that village (the present day Combe Farm). Richard died in 1733 and was succeeded in the business by his son Simon. It appears that the Hoddinotts continued to lease the property in Mells after the Nunney lease was granted in 1717, a presentment to Mells Court Baron in 1720 requiring that a stay be put "at the farther bridge called narrow bridge being the bridge that leads from Rich Hodinots to the way that goes to little green".[42] It is possible that the Mells cottages were held by the Hoddinotts until the 1730s, a lease of the property in 1738 to a clothier called James Clark describing it as "late in the possession of Simon Hoddinott of Nunney Edgetool Maker". For the property to have been in the possession of Simon Hoddinott, he must have continued the lease after his father's death in 1733.

In 1751 Simon died and was succeeded by his son Richard (1727-1760), the last Hoddinott to run the family edge-tool business. In the following year John Theobald recorded that the Nunney Brook powered "shearmills for grinding the Clothiers Shears and other edge tools, called Hoddinott's Mill, as being on Lands belonging to one of that name".[43] The shears in question were large, heavy iron implements with long angled blades used to trim the nap of woollen cloth, this having first been "raised" by brushing with teazles set in frames. The process was essential to the finishing of the types of woollen cloths made in the district, and in 1800 there were 146 shearmen in the town of Frome alone.

Theobald's description of the Nunney mill as a "shearmill", and his mention of the grinding of clothiers' shears as being its primary purpose, indicates that the

Hoddinotts may have been involved in shear grinding as well as edge-tool making, or have rented the use of their grindstones to others for this purpose. Another piece of evidence that connects the Hoddinotts with the business of shear grinding is to be found in their relationship with the Hooper family of Nunney. In his will of 1760 Richard Hoddinott named Benjamin Hooper, "sheargrinder", as one of his executors.[44] The two families were related by marriage, Benjamin having married Mary Hoddinott in 1740, while their son William was Richard's godson and a beneficiary of his will.

The death of Richard Hoddinott in 1760 brought to an end that family's involvement in edge-tool making, but created an opportunity for another family of edge-tool makers, the Fussells, who were by then established in Mells and already looking for opportunities to expand their growing business.

The Fussells Come to Mells

The Fussells were established in Stoke Lane by the mid seventeenth century, the name James Fussell appearing on the first page of the parish register in 1646. It is not known when they first began making edge-tools, but in 1702 George Horner leased to Isaac Fussell, his wife Anne, and Isaac their son, "a new Erected dwelling house and Smith's shop at a place called the Three Ashes in the Parish of Stoake Lane."[1] In this lease Isaac is described as a blacksmith, but in a subsequent one of 1712 as an "edgetoolmaker".[2] In the same year William Fussell also leased land at Three Ashes, including fields formerly held by his father John in 1662.[3] These subsequently passed to Josiah Fussell and then, in 1734, to another James Fussell. Among other things, the lease by which James occupied the holding gave him permission to:

> Erect build and set up a new mill house and mill wheel in any convenient part
> of the stream called Worms Stream . . . and also to make any sufficient ponds
> or mounds upon the said stream with necessary banks ditches or flood gates
> for baying or penning up the water for the use of the said mill . . . which mill
> when so erected built and set up shall be made use of for grinding of edgetools
> and such like implements and not other without the consent of the said Thomas
> Strangeways Horner.[4]

Worms Stream has been identified as the small watercourse that runs through the property from a spring above. This is a relatively poor water-power site, having a small and erratic flow, although possibly sufficient to turn grindstones.

Ten years later, in 1744, James entered into an indenture with John Horner for a site "over and in the river running between Wadbury and Haydon in the parish of Mells at a place where a mill formerly in possession of one Nailor stood".[5] The mill may well have been a fulling mill, since there was a fuller by the name of Stephen Naylor living in Mells in the 1630s.[6]

This earlier mill would appear to have been abandoned before 1682 because a plan of Mells made in that year clearly shows a leat at Wadbury but no mill building. The Fussells' Upper Works were later built beside this leat, indicating that it was on this site that their Mells operations began. This is confirmed by a plan of the Manors of

Mells and Leigh in 1779, which shows "Mr Fussell's" mill as being at that location.

The indenture recording the 1744 lease stipulated that within twelve months James Fussell was to build "a Good Firm and Substantial Mill or Mills for Grinding Edge Tools and Forging Iron Plates."[7] The document, which is dated 25 December 1744, states that the lease was for the lives of James, his wife Barbara, and their oldest son Austin. In other words, it would end when the last of the three died. The annual rent was fixed at £1 10s, to be paid on the Feast of St Michael the Archangel, and a further 10s on the Feast of the Annunciation of the Blessed Virgin Mary. It seems very likely, however, that James Fussell was occupying the mill prior to 1744, since the manor rent roll for September 1738 includes the entry: "James Fussell for the mill 10s." - the same rent charged for the Wadbury Mill under the terms of the 1744 indenture.[8] Moreover, the indenture stated that it related to a grant made by Thomas Strangeways Horner, Esq., who died in 1741. It seems likely, therefore, that in 1744 James was already running the mill under an earlier grant, and sought a new agreement in order to add the life of his son, Austin (born in 1737) to the lease. If James was already renting the Wadbury mill by 1738, what had become of the one at Stoke Lane? It is always possible that after having obtained permission to build his mill at Stoke, James changed his mind and decided to build instead on the more promising site in Mells.

James Fussell's edge-tool works at Wadbury as depicted in Samuel Donne's 1779 map of Mells.

What is certain is that the Wadbury Mill occupied a far better water-power site than that at Stoke Lane, one capable of turning larger wheels and driving heavier machinery. It is significant that whereas the lease of the Stoke Lane mill restricted James to the "grinding of edgetools", that of Wadbury permitted both grinding edge-tools and "Forging Iron Plates". The latter process involved the working of heated pieces of bar iron under a heavy, water-powered trip hammer, and it may be that the move to Wadbury was made in order to make this possible. This is the first evidence for the use of a trip hammer in an edge-tool works in the area, and its importance is underlined by the 1779 map of Mells, which described the Wadbury site as "Mr Fussell's Steel & Plate Mill". Steeling was the name sometimes given to the process by which the steel that formed the cutting edge of the tool was forged welded between two pieces of bar iron under a heavy trip hammer known as a steeling hammer. This description of the mill shows that the Fussells' mill was using water power for both

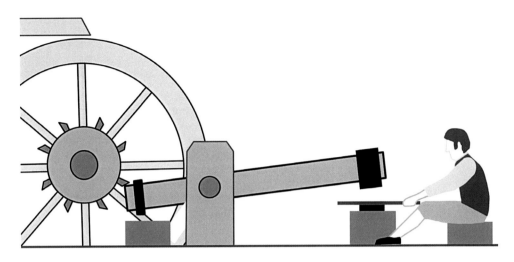

A simplified drawing of a water-powered trip hammer.

this process and the subsequent one of working the iron and steel bars into the shapes required using the plating hammer.

In January 1754 James Fussell was granted a new lease on the mill "lately erected and now used by the said James Fussell for Grinding Edge Tools on ye River running between Wadbury and Haydown in the Parish of Mells".[9] The new lease was sought in order to add the life of James's second son John, then aged 13, to the agreement. By then the Fussells were firmly established in Mells, James holding various parish offices, including churchwarden, and becoming a trustee of the village's workhouse.

From the time of their arrival in Mells the Fussells displayed signs of the driving ambition that was to set them apart from other edge-tool makers in the area. In the 1760s James Fussell bought the Nunney edge-tool mill, following the death of Richard Hoddinott. The running of this business was entrusted to his son John, who was occupying the mill by 1766. John Fussell was to manage the Nunney works for more than half a century, in which time he became a major figure in the village - buying property, establishing a charity, and playing a full part in parish affairs.

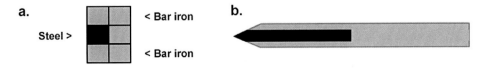

Section through a sandwich of bar iron and steel before forging (a) and after (b).

One of the few documents referring to the Nunney business in this period is the justice's diary of Thomas Horner, which on 21st February 1774 records that he had that day "granted a warrant on the information of John Fussell of Nunney edgetoolmaker, against Cornelius Russell labourer, on suspicion of his having stolen four hatchets the goods of the said John Fussell and Partners in Nunney aforesaid". Russell was brought before Horner and evidence given that he had "sold several hatchets of 2s a piece value for 8d each". In other words, he had disposed of them for less than they were worth because they were stolen. Horner committed Russell - whom he judged "a most daring rogue" - to Ilchester Gaol and bound John Fussell and his witnesses to prosecute him at the next quarter sessions.[10] This incident is of particular interest because it shows that John, his father and brothers were running the business as a partnership by this date.

At this time the Fussells do not seem to have been the only family operating an edge-tool business in Nunney. The Hoopers, who had been so closely associated with the Fussells' predecessors the Hoddinotts, continued to run their shear grinding business, the Universal Directory of 1793 listing Joseph Hooper of Nunney as "Share [Shear] Maker", while one of his grandsons, Charles, went on to establish a shear grinding business at Spring Gardens, Marston Bigot, in the 1820s.[11] By the late 18th century the traditional method of hand-shearing cloth was under threat because some woollen manufacturers were seeking to mechanise the finishing process by introducing water-powered mechanical shear frames. The Somerset shearmen resisted this threat to their livelihoods, just as their Yorkshire counterparts, the Luddites, were to do twenty years later. Shearmen were relatively well paid and had a reputation for riotous behaviour. They were also well organised and committed to maintaining a closed shop and resisting the mechanisation of the trade. On a Thursday night in December 1797 between 200 and 300 hundred men with faces blackened "entered the house of a shear grinder at Nunny and demolished about £30 of shears belonging to the manufactory of Messrs. Bamford, Cook & Co".[12] The Bamfords had recently installed shear frames at their mills at Twerton, near Bath, and it is interesting that they sent the shears all the way to Nunney to have their blades sharpened. That they did so suggests that the sharpening of the long heavy blades required specialised skills and that cloth finishers were prepared to send their implements considerable distances to get this work done.

In 1775 James Fussell died and the running of the family businesses passed to his three sons, Austin, John and James, all of whom had been trained up by their father to be edge-tool makers. As oldest brother, Austin took over the running of the Mells works, while John, the second son, was already established at Nunney. The youngest

A photograph of the Upper Works, Mells, taken in the late 19th century

of the brothers, James, had no obvious managerial role in the business, but more than made up for this disadvantage by a combination of energy, determination, and business acumen. In 1781 he leased a water-power site at Wadbury, downstream from that operated by Austin. Under the terms of the lease from Thomas Horner he was permitted "to erect and build a New Mill for Grinding Edge Tools and for other purposes". The mill was to be built within one year and four months on a piece of ground "demised to contain thirty six feet in length and thirty feet in breadth". The indenture mentions that Thomas Horner had supplied James with 30 pounds worth of oak timber for use in the construction of the mill. The accompanying lease, which is dated 18 November 1781, was for 99 years determinable on the lives of James Fussell (33) and his brother John (41). The lease would, therefore, be deemed to have expired on the death of the last surviving of the two brothers. In the event, this was James Fussell, who died in 1832, a date which came to have considerable importance for both the Fussells and their landlords, the Horners.

The new works at Wadbury, like the family's existing one close by, was built on the site of a former fulling mill, in this case Gunnings Mill. In the mid 17th century the mill had been occupied by Robert Gunning, who died in 1659 and was described in his will as "Fuller of Mells".[13] Shortly after the death of Robert, his widow Mary was involved in a legal dispute with the occupant of a neighbouring mill, Thomas Redman. Redman later confessed that on 14 October 1659 "a pig belonging to Mary Gunning having come into his mill he threw a hammer and killed it, and then dressed it; but it was the first he ever served so, and it should be the last."[14] This was not Redman's last brush with the law, for in 1673 he was one of five millers of Mells accused of overcharging their customers.[15] Two years later the manor court heard that his mill was "not yet repaired" and demanded that "he doe repaire it before the next court upon the payne of XLs. [£2]."[16] Mary Gunning continued to run the mill and in 1662 took over the lease of "that one tucking [fulling] mill and outhouses plots and gardens thereunto." In 1673 the Gunnings Mill was one of two surviving fulling mills in the manor, the other being held by John Butcher of Vobster.[17] Widow Gunning is recorded as doing homage at the Court Baron in 1678, but in 1696 her name was entered and then crossed out, presumably because she had died. Her descendants continued to occupy the mill into the 1740s, William Gunning paying 9s rent for it in 1742.[18]

Gunnings Mill seems to have been abandoned some time in the next two decades, but in 1769 was leased to James Edgell, a gentleman of Frome. Under the terms of the 20-year lease, Edgell was "to put the mill into repair within three months" and "make a good road for carriages from the mill now in the tenure of James Fussell".[19] The lease also gave him the right to "dig, raise, land and carry away the marble" found in a vein on Vobster Tor and to "square, scaple or part the same". The marble was said by Edmund Rack to be "ash coloured . . . streaked with red" and "receives a fine polish & is used for chimney pieces".[20]

The intention may have been to convert the mill into a marble works, for the agreement states that Thomas Horner would provide rough timber for the repair of the house and mill and for "any necessary buildings for sawing the stone". James Edgell was a man of many interests, and a keen inventor. A year after leasing the Wadbury mill he patented a mechanical chaff cutter, for which he was awarded a purse of 20 guineas. In 1771 he went on to invent "a cheap and simply constructed water engine . . . which will throw a constant stream of water with great force and at a great distance",[21] and in 1799 patented a process for producing iron "of a peculiar quality, and great strength".[22] It is not clear how long Edgell occupied the Wadbury mill, or indeed if he ever did. It is significant that the mill is not shown on the map of the manor of 1779, suggesting that it was unoccupied when James Fussell leased it in 1781.

By 1791 the scale of the Fussell brothers' edge-tool business was large enough to be thought "worthy of remark" by John Collinson in his *History and Antiquities of*

Somerset. In the entry for Mells he noted that "there are two iron forges" which were "carrying on a trade, little inferior, in point of extension, to those in the northern parts of this Kingdom."[23] This account was, in fact, written by Abraham Crocker of Frome, whose original version is slightly longer than Collinson's and provides more detail.

> It is worthy of remark that in this sequestered vale there are two large iron forges which at this period are carrying on a trade little inferior in point of extension to those in the northern part of this kingdom. All western England are supplied by these manufacturers with spades, hooks, hatchets, scythes and every other iron implement of husbandry. The connections even extend to the European and American continents.[24]

It is clear from this description that the business had been able to expand because it now had a large market for its products. The demand for edge-tools was growing as English agriculture boomed. A rapidly increasing population, combined with rising prices, new farming methods and an increase in the average size of holdings, was creating a new breed of farmer with both the desire and the money to invest in improved stock, buildings and tools. From the middle of the century this process was given a further boost by the enclosure movement, which greatly increased the acreage of land under cultivation. The effects of these changes were felt in the Fussells' adopted village of Mells, where the medieval open fields disappeared and the commons of Haydon and Vobster Marsh were enclosed. To the west of the village even greater changes would follow when the enclosure of the Mendips transformed a large tract of moorland into a landscape of cultivated fields and hedges.

Another important factor in the expansion of the market for edge-tools in this period was the improvement in communications resulting from the development of the network of turnpike roads, which made road haulage easier and reduced travel times. The Frome Trust was established in 1757 and began work on improving local roads, including a branch to Mells from the Frome–Wells road.[25] The statement by Collinson that Fussells tools were being exported to the Americas indicates that the brothers had by that time formed links with merchants in Bristol and/or London. This is reinforced by evidence that by the early nineteenth century the Nunney business was making plantation hoes and sugar bills for export to the West Indies and blubber knives for the whaling industry, some of which found their way to New England.[26]

A year after Collinson's account was published, the business was further enlarged by leasing a mill in the neighbouring village of Great Elm, which brought the number of edge-tool works under the family's control to four. The Great Elm site, formerly known as Curtis's Mill, was leased from Sir Henry Strachey, the agreement being signed on 12 March 1792. Formerly a corn mill, it had previously been operated by the Curtis family. In July 1775 "William Curtis of Elm, Miller" was summoned before the magistrates to answer for an assault committed on Hester Cray, also of Elm. The charge against Curtis being proved, the bench asked him to "make some small satisfaction", and when he "obstinately and rudely refused" they ordered him to appear before the next quarter sessions to answer for the assault.[27] After this incident, William seems to have gone downhill and died a pauper in May 1786.[28]

Once in possession of the mill, the Fussell brothers adapted it for edge-tool making. It is not known which parts of the manufacturing process were done there, but by the late 19th century it seems to have specialised in the forge welding of bar iron and steel ready for working into tools at the Wadbury works. The evidence for this is provided by Edward Tylee who had been told "At Great Elm they beat out the bar iron and split it, and put steel in the centre for making scythes, reaphooks, & Co., in the old fashioned way."[29] The surviving fabric of the works shows that during its lifetime there was at least one major rebuild which included the resiting of the waterwheels.

In the early 1790s the four works were still run as a single concern, described by the *Universal Directory* of 1793 as "Austin, John & James Fussell, Edge Tool Makers, Mells", the three brothers' names being listed in order of seniority. When Austin died in the following year his place at the Upper Works was taken by his son John, while James continued to run the Lower Works, and John the Nunney business.

Of the three, it was James who seems to have been the most active and energetic, although some of his business transactions were very questionable and one resulted in legal action. In November 1792 the Mells maltster, John Bradley, made a will in which he named James Fussell, Henry Austin, and William Brown as trustees of his estate. The three trustees were all relatively prosperous local tradesmen, Henry Austin being the innkeeper at Vobster, and William Brown the tenant of Bilboa corn mill in Mells. On his death Bradley owned a number of freehold properties in the area, including an estate at Tadhill, a field in Mells, and two tenements in Bristol.[30] In October 1795 James Fussell bought the Bristol properties, one of a number of transactions that resulted in legal action being taken against him by Robert White, a distant relation of Bradley.[31] The claim made was that James and his fellow trustees had abused their position to obtain some of Bradley's land and property "at a great under value and for considerably less than the same were formerly worth to be honestly sold by public auction".[32] In the best tradition of the Court of Chancery, the suit relating to the Bristol properties continued for many years and in 1829 James was still in possession, selling them in that year to a haulier called John Hemming.[33]

These were not, however, the only properties bought from Bradley's estate by James, another being a large field adjacent to Mells Park. This field, called Huntleys, was one of the few pieces of land in the manor of Mells not owned by the Horner family.

Colonel Horner watched the case with interest and in December 1814 obtained a legal opinion that "the lands bought by the trustees themselves will in due time be ordered by the court to be resold - you will then of course have an equal chance with other individuals to purchase the same." This view turned out to be over-optimistic, the case dragging on inconclusively and Huntleys remaining in the hands of the Fussells, a seemingly small victory that would in time prove to be of central importance to the future of their edge-tool business.

Canals and Inventions

I n the 1790s James Fussell became involved in the canal mania of the period, investing in the proposed Dorset and Somerset Canal. This venture had its origins in a meeting at the Bear Inn, Wincanton, on 10 January 1793, held "for the purpose of taking into consideration the propriety of an Inland Communication between Poole and Bristol".[1] As originally conceived, the proposed canal was to follow a route from Widbrook on the Kennet and Avon to the English Channel at Poole, with a branch serving the Mendip collieries in the Nettlebridge Valley. From James's point of view the benefits of the family's Mells and Great Elm works being linked to the national canal network were clear, while the possibility of a dividend on shares provided an additional incentive to invest.

In 1793 the canal's surveyor, William Bennett, proposed a route for the branch that would run on the level from a basin near Edford as far as Upper Vobster, then descend into the valley of the Mells River, which it would follow to its junction with the main line of the canal at Orchardleigh. From the Fussells' point of view the route chosen had particular advantages, not the least of which was that the canal would pass through the two Wadbury works and close to the Great Elm works. Coal could be brought down the valley from the collieries in the Nettlebridge Valley and iron up the canal from Bristol, while the tools they made could be distributed using the inland waterways network and exported overseas from Bristol.

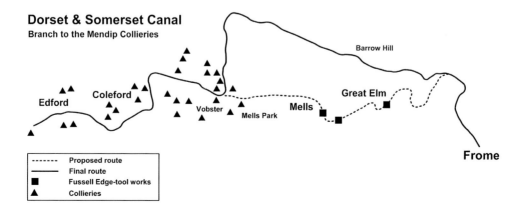

Unfortunately for the Fussells, the route proposed passed close to Mells Park, leading to strenuous objections from Thomas Horner.[2] Horner was determined to keep manifestations of industry in any form as far as possible from his house and park at Mells. On coming into the property in 1758 he had embarked on a major programme of enlargement and improvement, which included closing footpaths through the park, building a wall around it, and planting screening trees. His scrapbooks record ideas for hothouses, follies, grottos and temples, rustic cottages, hermitages and Turkish tents, lakes, plantations, and various eye-catchers, most of which never came to fruition. Humphrey Repton was consulted by Horner, who also subscribed to his *Sketches and Hints on Landscape Gardening* (1794). In 1768 he closed the corn mill in the Park, offering the miller Bilboa Mill on the edge of Mells village in exchange.[3] Thomas Horner was also concerned to prevent any noisy and or unsightly activities in close proximity to the park. To this end, he added a clause to coal leases granted in the 1780s and 90s stating that the partners should not "sink any pitt or land any coal earth on any of the closes . . . which can or may be seen from the house of the said Thomas Horner in Mells Park."[4] Interestingly, in 1779 there was what was described as "a large coal work", complete with leats and water wheel, on the very edge of Mells Park in the area known as Lully Batch. It is possible that this pit was screened from the park by trees, or it may have been that the restriction on siting was added to the leases in the early 1780s precisely to prevent a repetition of this intrusion.

Portrait of Thomas Horner (1737-1804) in Mells Park, a landscape he sought to make a private space insulated from the effects of industrialisation (reproduced by kind permission of the Earl of Oxford and Asquith).

It is not surprising, then, that Thomas Horner insisted on the proposed canal being kept as far from his park as possible. Eventually, a compromise was reached whereby the canal would be diverted well to the north of Mells village, running on the level to Barrow Hill from where it would descend to the valley of the River Frome.[5] Horner's objections deprived the Fussells of the possibility of canal wharves within their works.

It also presented the promoters of the canal with the daunting engineering problem of finding a means of raising boats 264 feet in less than one mile, the technical difficulties and cost of which sealed the fate of the venture.[6]

Thomas Horner's attitude to industrialisation, like that of so many country gentlemen of the period, was one of increasing ambivalence. In the winter of 1780 he made a tour from Edinburgh to the Midlands, in the course of which he visited the Carron Ironworks. England was at war and ironworks were recognised as vital to national defence, Carron becoming famous for manufacturing a type of heavy cannon for the navy officially called a carronade but nicknamed the "smasher". Works like Carron were the wonders of the age and an attraction for the curious gentleman tourist, as Horner well knew, and recorded in his journal:

> To come so near to so capital a place of Carron & not give it a minute inspection would have been unpardonable, this I did, & the pleasure we had in view made us overlook the wretched accommodation of the Ale House for I cannot call it an Inn - We were so lucky as to meet with one of the Partners who most obligingly conducted us through every part.[7]

Of the blast furnaces he wrote "nothing but the Craters of Etna or Vesuvius can be more tremblingly Horrid" - a description combining awe and revulsion that was typical of the tourists of the period. It is interesting to note that when the poet Robert Burns tried to visit the works seven years later in 1787, he was refused admittance by the porter, probably because he was not deemed to be a gentleman. Burns took his revenge by returning to the inn, almost certainly the one Horner thought so little of, and wrote the following verse on the window of his room with a diamond he had recently acquired.

> We came not here to view your works
> In hopes to be more wise,
> But only, lest we go to hell,
> It may be no surprise.
> But when we knocked at your door
> The porter could not admit us
> So may, should we to Hell's gates come,
> Your fellow Satan serve us.[8]

As far as Thomas Horner was concerned, it was one thing to admire such manifestations of industrialisation and applaud their contribution to the nation's security, but quite another to want such intrusive excrescences on his own doorstep. Nonetheless, as a landlord with minerals on his land, he was interested to find out

Reconstruction of cross-section through James Fussell's balance lock, designed for use on the Nettlebridge Branch of the Dorset & Somerset Canal at Barrow Hill, Mells.

the details of leases by which the ironstone was mined, and obtained specimens of the ore.

The act for the construction of the Dorset and Somerset Canal, which received royal assent on 24 March 1796, specified that the branch from Frome to Nettlebridge should be completed before work began on the main line of the canal. Despite the setback of not having the canal pass through his works, James Fussell invested £1,000 in the venture and became a member of the committee. With attention focused on the Nettlebridge branch, it became the practice for the committee to meet at the Talbot Inn, Mells, although general meetings continued to be held at Wincanton. Tenders for the work of building the branch were let at the Talbot, and plans, sections and specifications for the work were available for view by would-be contractors at the house of the engineer, William Bennett, at Stoney Lane, and at the George Inn, Frome.

The committee soon addressed itself to the problem of raising boats to the summit level at Barrow Hill, which would have required a flight of approximately 30 conventional locks. It was thought the answer lay in the use of canal lifts, possibly the caisson lock invented by Robert Weldon proposed for use on the neighbouring Somersetshire Coal Canal. However, the committee deferred making a decision on adopting this type of lock until it had a chance to judge how well it worked. Work began on the coal canal's locks in 1797 but problems with their construction meant they were not ready for demonstration until April 1799.

In the meantime James Fussell, who had ideas of his own, went ahead and invented an alternative type of canal lift, the balance lock, which he patented on 24 December 1798. As its name suggests, the lock used counterbalancing as its operating principle. The structure of the lock comprised a large masonry chamber divided into two sections. Into these were put two tanks full of water, each long enough to contain a canal boat. A central dividing wall ran the length of the chamber, on top of which was mounted a pair of large iron wheels. The tanks were attached to each other by chains that passed over the wheels so that when one tank was level with the bottom of the canal the other was level with the top. The tank weights were adjusted to be equal, so that they were in balance and could be moved up and down with little effort. At the end of each chamber was a sliding panel that could be raised to allow boats to be floated in and out. With the boats in the tanks, the panels were closed to seal the ends of the canals and the tanks. The lock-keepers would then use a crank handle and brake to raise the boat in one tank while lowering the boat in the other.

There was a flaw in the design that James may have sought to rectify with a second patent in 1799. As originally conceived, the raising and lowering mechanism seems to have relied on conventional chains passing over large, grooved iron wheels. The problem with this arrangement was that any slippage in one of the chains would cause the tanks in which the boats rested to tip forwards or backwards. The new patent was described as being for "An Improved Apparatus Composed of Chains, Wheels, Rollers, and Conductors, for the Purpose of Lessening Friction in Raising, Lowering, Driving, and Conducting Heavy Bodies and Applicable to other Useful Purposes".[9]

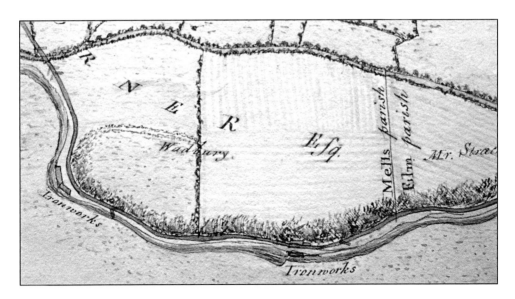

Detail from the original survey for the Nettlebridge Branch of the Dorset & Somerset Canal showing the proposed route running past the two Fussell edge-tool works at Wadbury (reproduced by kind permission of the Earl of Oxford and Asquith).

The patent was for a sprocket chain, in essence a large version of the modern bicycle wheel. The use of a chain with sprocket wheels would have prevented the slippage that could have occurred with the original design.

This patent was taken out in the names of James Fussell of Mells and James Douglass of Christchurch, Surrey. It is not known how Fussell and Douglass got to know each other, or when they began to collaborate. In his patents, of which there are a number, Douglass describes himself as a "Machinist", but he may once have been a clockmaker, since a clockmaker of that name is recorded as living in that part of Surrey from 1768 until he went bankrupt in 1791. In the same year that James Fussell patented the balance lock, Douglass obtained a patent for "An Improved Apparatus or Machinery for Shearing or Cropping of Woollen Cloth with Shears, Knives, and Cutters, put in Operation by various Powers now in Practice". It is interesting to note that an illustration attached to their joint patent for the chain shows it driving Douglass's shear frame.

A trial balance lock was built at Barrow Hill and demonstrated in September 1800, followed by a public exhibition on 13 October 1800. The glowing reports on the latter occasion must have been gratifying to James Fussell, as well as pleasing to his fellow promoters who were seeking the investment needed to complete the canal.

A public exhibition of Mr. Fussell's balance lock on the D & S canal, was again
made, and laden boats with great facility, transferred to and from the upper to

the lower level, in manner that gave great satisfaction to a numerous company of noblemen, gentlemen, and others, who were assembled on the occasion. The locks were continued in action two hours, that the ingenuous might have ample testimony of its principles and utility, which are now fully established and admitted, not only by committees of canal companies, but also by the ablest mechanics, who have given it their inspection. There seems no doubt that the balance lock will be brought into general use in all canal undertakings, where the saving of water is an object of consideration.[10]

The committee was pleased with James Fussell's system and at a general meeting in Wincanton on 1 December 1800 agreed to erect five similar locks between Mells and Frome.

The Fussell balance lock was also viewed with interest by the directors of the neighbouring Somersetshire Coal Canal, who were looking for a replacement for the caisson lock, which had not proved a success. By 1800 the committee were reviewing a number of options, one of which was James Fussell's lock. In April 1800 William Bennett submitted a report that approved of the balance lock but recommended that any decision on adopting it should be deferred until after the proposed public trials by the Dorset and Somerset.[11] Unfortunately, these did not take place until September and October, by which time the coal canal had made the decision to use an inclined plane on the Dunkerton branch and to link the Radstock branch to the main line using a section of horse-drawn tramway. In the event, neither of these solutions proved satisfactory, the Dunkerton inclined plane being later replaced by a flight of conventional locks and the entire Radstock branch relaid as a horse-drawn tramway.

Construction work on the Dorset and Somerset continued along the length of the branch throughout 1801, but the financial situation of the company was deteriorating and a report presented to the committee on 21 March 1802 stated that £18,000 more would be needed to complete it. To raise morale and attract investors, another demonstration of Fussell's balance lock was made in June 1802, but in the following year the company finally ran out of money and construction work ceased. On 30 March 1803 a meeting of the proprietors was held at the George Inn, Frome "for the purpose of taking into consideration the situation of the said undertaking."[12] The meeting was called by the management committee, of which James Fussell was a member, to get agreement that a new act of parliament should be obtained to give the company powers to raise additional capital. On 20 June the House of Lords select committee heard the application for the new act. The application succeeded, and on 4 July 1803 the act was passed enabling the company "to raise a further sum of

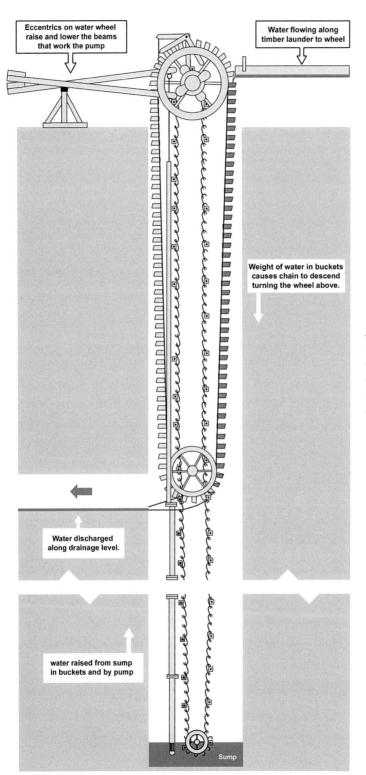

Eccentrics on water wheel raise and lower the beams that work the pump

Water flowing along timber launder to wheel

Weight of water in buckets causes chain to descend turning the wheel above.

Water discharged along drainage level.

water raised from sump in buckets and by pump

Sump

James Fussell's invention for draining mines using a combination of water-driven buckets and pumps (1803).

money towards completing the said Canal".[13] It also granted the company powers to construct a railway rather than a canal on any part of the line if they so chose. Despite this success, additional finance was not available and the committee resolved "to suspend the works until more auspicious times arrived".[14]

The failure of the Dorset and Somerset left the Mendip collieries without the promised access to the inland waterway network. Meanwhile, to the north, work continued on the two branches of the Somersetshire Coal Canal, and by 1805 the pits of the Paulton and Radstock area were linked to the Kennet and Avon Canal at Limpley Stoke. Around this time a plan was put forward to give the collieries of the southern coalfield access to the coal canal by making a branch from Radstock south to Kilmersdon, terminating at a basin at Owl's Nest near Babington (NGR 3687

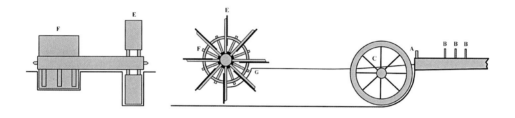

James Fussell's invention for "preventing water wheels from being flooded" (1803).

1513). The evidence for this scheme is provided by a document found in the Mells Archives which gives the distances from each of the then extant Mendip collieries to Owl's Nest, a field near the head of the stream running south from Kilmersdon towards Mendip.[15] The purpose of the exercise seems to have been to demonstrate that all of the collieries were less than four miles from that location. The document, entitled "Distances from intended canal", is undated but appears to have been prepared between 1800 and 1805. An examination of the topography of the route shows that the canal branch would have been three miles long with a fall of 150 feet from Owl's Nest to the coal canal's Radstock basin, necessitating between 15 and 20 locks. There seems to have been some thought of providing a coal wharf at Kilmersdon, since the document also gives the distances from the eastern collieries to the bridge by the village school. The proposal came to nothing, possibly because the Radstock branch of the Somersetshire Coal Canal was itself in difficulties. The need to tranship coal from the branch onto the tramway at Midford and then back onto the main line of the canal proved a serious handicap, and by 1810 traffic on the branch had virtually dried-up. The problem was not solved until the canal branch was replaced by a tramway in 1815. It is possible that thought was given to laying a branch of this tramway up the valley to Owl's Nest, but no evidence has been found for such a scheme.

James Fussell retained his shares in the Dorset and Somerset Canal, hoping they might be turned to advantage at some point in the future. The Fussells also came into possession of a memento of the scheme in the form of the date stone of the Coleford Aqueduct, which is now in the village of Chantry, preserved in the grounds of the former Fussell house of that name. The demise of the canal project did not, however, curb James Fussell's interest in inventions. In 1803 he was granted a patent for a number of inventions, all of which were connected with industries in which he had business interests.

One of the inventions was a water-powered chain bucket pump suitable for draining coal mines. James Fussell had by then been involved in the local mining industry for more than twenty years, having taken a one-sixth share in a partnership working coal on Thomas Horner's land at Vobster in 1781. James's partners in that venture included Thomas Charles (the landlord of the Talbot Inn, Mells), William Tarrant (a cooper of Frome), and Walter Beacham (a coal miner of Babington and probably the manager of the venture). The partnership was typical of the period, being made up of local tradesmen, most of whom had no practical experience of coal mining. The lease gave the partners the right to work coal along the valley bottom between Coleford and Vobster, where pits were very prone to flooding (see Chapter 10).

James's invention was different from traditional water-powered pumps in that the waterwheel was positioned over the shaft, being used to turn a continuous chain with buckets attached, as well as conventional cylinder pumps. The pump needed water to turn the wheel, and a sloping site so a drainage adit could be created to carry away both the water raised up the shaft by the buckets and pumps, and that which had gone down the shaft after passing over the wheel.

The same patent also included an invention for "preventing water wheels from being flooded".[16] Accumulation of water in wheel pits and the backing up of water in times of flood could reduce the efficiency of the wheels themselves. Like all those who operated water-powered mills, the Fussells went to great lengths to construct the tails so as to prevent water accumulating in the wheel pits. James Fussell's invention involved placing a second waterwheel downstream of the main wheel, which was driven by a leat running parallel to the tail. The purpose of this wheel was to turn a paddle wheel in the tail that pushed water downstream, thereby preventing it from accumulating in the pit.

Seven years later, in 1810, James obtained his last patent, which he described as "An improved method of making and working forge and other bellows". In the specification for this invention he stated:

> I have several pairs now at work by means of water wheels, for forges and foundery [sic], and find they will bear a much greater force than any other I have seen, without the least injury. The bellows discharge one third more air at least than those made in the usual way of the same size.[17]

James's reference to his using such bellows in a foundry – a place where iron is melted and cast in moulds - is interesting because it is the only evidence that the business may have had one in this period. It may also be significant that in his patents James Fussell describes himself as "Iron Manufacturer" rather than the more usual "Edgetool Maker", suggesting that he may have had ambitions to develop his business into a full-scale ironworks. By 1812 James Fussell's patent forge bellows were being manufactured under licence by the Bristol firm of Thomas Harding & Son, who made the following claims for them:

> The Patent Bellows will not take more than half the room of the common sort, require less strength to work them, and not so liable to get out of repair, on which account they are more valuable. They may also be fixed with as much ease and nearly at the same expense.[18]

Four years later Harding & Son were still manufacturing the bellows, which they argued were so designed as leave "little doubt of their superseding the use of common Walking and large Foundry Bellows."[19]

In July 1808, a damaging hailstorm hit Dorset, Somerset and Gloucestershire. A great deal of damage was reported, some claiming that the largest stones were around 11cms in diameter. Reporting on the storm, the *Monthly Magazine*, carried an account of it written by James Fussell.

> From the village of Mells, another correspondent (Mr Fussell, the eminent manufacturer of iron instruments) gives me the following particulars; the storm, he says, began at half-past seven, coming from the SW that it was not more than seven minutes continuance at his house, but at other parts of the parish more than half an hour: the hail-stones from four to nine inches circumference: the intermissions between the flashes of lightning could scarcely be perceived; at every place where the violence of the storm was felt, the effects were truly

astonishing. Wheat, oats and barley entirely destroyed; as were all the garden vegetables; unmown grass beaten down flat; the roads and lands strewed with leaves and branches of trees: wherever a hail-stone struck a tree or large branch, the bark was struck off: every pane of glass exposed to the storm, was broken to pieces. Two days after the storm, hail-stones were taken from a ditch, which measured from six to seven inches in circumference.[20]

In reporting the effects of the storm on his village, James exhibited the same spirit of scientific curiosity he brought to his work as an inventor, positioning himself in the tradition of the scientists, engineers and industrialists of the Enlightenment; men such as Joseph Priestley, James Watt, and Josiah Wedgwood, whose interests in science and technology extended beyond its immediate practical application to the getting of wealth.

War and Peace

In the year that James Fussell patented his lock, the country was faced with the threat of a French invasion. On 2 May 1798 a meeting of householders was held in Frome at which a "Military Association" for the defence of the town was formed, this to comprise a corps of 100 volunteer infantry and one of 60 volunteer cavalry. Among those who subscribed to the volunteer cavalry were James Fussell and his sons James and John. At a second meeting a week later Thomas Strangeways Horner was asked to accept the command of the Association. It was disbanded when an uneasy peace was concluded with France in 1802 but was reformed as the Frome and East Mendip Regiment of Volunteer Cavalry when war broke out again in May 1803.[1] Colonel Horner was again made commandant of the new force, two of the troops of which were stationed at Mells.

Richard White, the son of a Mells farmer, recalled in his memoirs that "the squire had great power and knew how to use it. As he was Colonel of the North Somerset Cavalry every tenant had to join the force."[2] Despite this edict, the names of the Fussells are not to be found among those who served in it. However, not to be outdone by his landlord, James Fussell made his own patriotic gesture, which was reported in the *Bristol Journal* on 6 August 1803.

> At this eventful and momentous crisis, when the heart of every Briton beats high with true loyalty and patriotism, we feel pleasure in recording the spirited offers made to Government for the defence of the country. Mr James Fussell of the Mells Iron Factory, near Frome, has offered to prepare (gratis) 1,000 pikes, and afterwards to supply Government with 2,000 weekly as long as they may be wanted.

The article says that the first 1,000 pikes were to be supplied free of charge, but is not clear whether he expected payment for subsequent consignments. This raises the possibility that, with an eye to business, James was hoping to join the ranks of those iron companies making large profits from government armament contracts.

One important result of the war with France was its effect on the nation's currency. On 26 February 1797 the Bank of England was ordered to suspend the convertibility of coins and notes into gold. The country was also suffering from an acute shortage of coins, to which the government responded in March 1797 by lifting restrictions on country banks issuing small denomination banknotes. Faced with a growing need to provide local means of payment for their goods, a number of manufacturers went into banking and began to issue their notes. Licences to print notes were issued by the Board of Stamps, and in 1813 licensees included a number of iron manufacturers among which were Dowlais and Penydarren in Glamorgan, Wilkinson of Bradley and Brymbo, Bowling Iron Company at Bradford in Yorkshire, and James Fussell & Sons of Mells.[3]

During the invasion scare of 1804, inventories were made of both the Upper and Lower Works as part of a survey of resources available to the government in the event of a French landing. These provide a valuable insight into the two Wadbury businesses in this period. The inventory for Lower Works lists "1700 dozen scythes, 500 dozen reap hooks, 80 tons of old iron, 25 tons of bar iron, 9 water wheels and forges, hammers and other machinery".[4] That of the Upper Works lists "160 dozen spades and shovels, 12 dozen hooks and axes, 12 pairs of bellows, 12 anvils, 2 water wheels and forges, hammers and machinery thereto, 30 tons of bar iron, 60 quarters of coal, and 60 dozen spade and shovel stems".[5]

It is clear that the Lower Works was by then much the larger of the two, with nine waterwheels to the Upper Works' two. It can also be seen that the Lower Works was mainly engaged in the manufacture of scythes and reap hooks, while the Upper Works was concentrating on the manufacture of spades and shovels, the products it was to specialise in until its closure almost a century later.

It is also noticeable in the inventory of the Lower Works that it had many more scythes than reap hooks in stock, holding 20,400 of the former and only 6,000 of the latter. In this period the scythe was beginning to replace the hook in the harvesting of grain. Until the mid 18th century the use of the scythe was restricted to the mowing of grass and cheaper cereal crops such as oats, the sickle being preferred for harvesting of wheat because it made a neater cut and spilled less grain.

Reports on scythes being used to harvest wheat were made as early as the 1760s, but it was not until the early 19th century that the practice became common. In this period tool makers in Sheffield and the West Midlands dominated the manufacture of scythes, James Fussell being the only major manufacturer of them in the South West.

The inventories also show that, in addition to buying bar iron the Fussells also possessed a large quantity of scrap iron ("old iron"). The Fussells' businesses, in common with other local ironworks, bought scrap iron and would later employ a man whose job it was to weigh and price it. What the inventories do not mention is steel, an important and relatively expensive component in edge-tools requiring a sharp blade, such as scythes and reaphooks.

Orchardleigh and the Montagues

In the early 19th century James Fussell further expanded his edge-tool business by leasing an edge-tool works called Kirty's Mill on the River Frome at Orchardleigh. The mill was owned by the Champneys family and formed part of their Orchardleigh estate. It had been an edge-tool mill for some time before the Fussells leased it, for in 1793 Thomas Swymmer Champneys let it to an edge-tool maker called William Montague of Elm.[6] William Montague

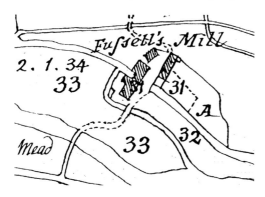

was born in Mells and seems to have been a former employee of the Fussells. His father, also called William, was an edge-tool maker who had moved to Mells from Tisbury, Dorset, around 1750. There is a reference to an edge-tool mill in Tisbury in 1706, when John Osborne leased one.[7] In November 1754 William senior married Margaret Penny in Mells, and their son William was born in Mells in 1760. Young William followed his father into the works and learned the trade of edge-

Kirty's Mill at Orchardleigh, leased by William Montague in 1794 and later occupied by James Fussell.

tool making. In 1789 he married Ann Cayford, daughter of John Cayford of Egford House, Whatley.[8] Four years later William leased Kirty's, which comprised the edge-tool mill, a house and garden. The lease was granted for the lives of William, his infant son William, and brother-in-law John Cayford of Whatley.[9] William does not appear to have made a success of the edge tool business, because the mill had been re-let to James Fussell by 1809.

Around this time the Montagues, together with Ann's brother John, emigrated to the United States. They would appear to have left the country in or before 1809, for in that year the will of Ann's father included bequests of £100 each to his son John, and daughters Mary Sly (or Sleigh) and Ann Montague, on the condition that they "come to England to collect it within two years of the testator's death".[10] There is a family story that Ann Montague went back to England after her father died to try to get her share of his estate but was denied it by her brothers.[11] This may well be true, the reason for their refusal being that she had not fulfilled the terms of the bequest by arriving within the time stipulated.

On arrival in the United States, the Montague family settled at Boston but then moved to the nearby town of Roxbury, where William was employed at a Mr. Faxon's trip hammer shop. There he made spades, shovels, and scythes, reputedly the first that were ever made by that business. After a while he moved from Boston to Biddeford, Maine, where he ran the blacksmith's shop at the shipyard of Thomas Coutts. Following the outbreak of the War of 1812 between Britain and United States, Englishmen were forbidden to live within forty miles of any navigable stream. Unable to stay at Biddeford, William and his family moved first to Albany, New York, and then to Canada, where he enlisted as armourer in the 49th Regiment. After the war he returned to Albany, but in 1816 moved back to Canada, settling in the township of London, Ontario, where he remained until his death in September 1822.

Kirty's Mill was still being described as an edge-tool mill in 1824, when a conveyance made by the Champneys to pay off debts mentioned "an iron edge tool mill called Kirty's mill".[12] It is not clear if it was still in use at that time and, if so, who was operating it. Today the former existence of the mill is commemorated in the names Iron Mill Farm and Iron Mill Lane.

Kirty's Mill does not seem to have been the only edge-tool works in the vicinity, the Orchardleigh map of 1816 showing a second building, labelled Iron Mill, to the west of Kirty's in a small detached portion of the parish of Marston Bigot. Little is known about this works, although it is possible that it may have been occupied by Charles Hooper, an edge-tool maker of Marston Bigot who was declared bankrupt in 1824.[13] Hooper was in fact a great-great-grandson of the edge-tool maker Richard Hoddinott, and a grandson of the shear grinder Benjamin Hooper of Nunney. It is not entirely surprising, therefore, to find that four years after his bankruptcy he had reverted to the family trade of shear grinding. In 1828 Charles, who was still living at Spring Gardens, Marston Bigot, patented an "improved machine for shearing and cropping woollen and other cloths".[14] His invention was not a new machine but an unusual design for the cutting element of existing ones "consisting of a rotary frame holding a series of steel blades which are placed in the form of a cone".[15]

The Stoney Lane Estate

The first decade of the 19th century saw James Fussell make the purchase that would, more than any other, influence his family's fortunes in the generations that followed. In 1806 he bought the Stoney Lane estate in the neighbouring parish of Whatley. Two years before, his older brother John had entered into a partnership with Jane Folliott of Nunney, the then owner of the estate. Under the terms of this, John Fussell would manage and improve the estate in return for half the profit on the difference between the price paid for it by Jane Folliott and the amount it was sold for, once expenses and reasonable interest had been deducted. In October 1806, they sold most of the estate to James Fussell for £8,916, the only parts excluded being a tenement called Clements and two fields called Lamberts and Pithayes. These were sold to a Kilmersdon farmer called Bryant, a transaction that would prove to be a source of acute embarrassment to James's descendents in two generations' time.

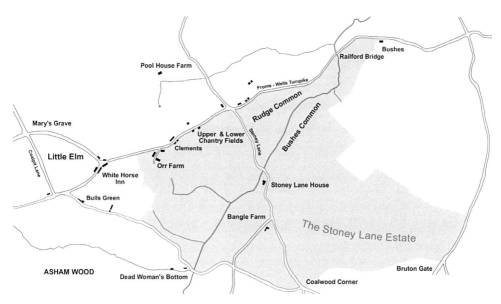

The Stoney Lane estate, Whatley, as bought by James Fussell in 1806

An important selling point for the estate, and one of which John Fussell would have been well aware, was that it came with a one-mile stretch of stream. Lying between the Mells Stream to the north and Nunney Brook to the south, it provided James with freehold land suitable for water-powered edge-tool factories, together with the necessary water rights. Equally importantly, it gave him the possibility of expanding his business empire without the need to do so through leases.

Unlike the neighbouring Mells Stream, where dozens of mills had been established over the centuries, there were few water-power sites in the valley. A possible explanation for this difference is that the flow of the stream is irregular and unpredictable, being fed by springs, which can fail in a dry summer.[16] There is evidence that months before purchasing the estate, James was already laying his plans. These included provision for the improvement of the flow of water through the valley by the creation of a conduit to convey water into it from Downhead. In January 1806 Edward Berkeley Portman granted him a licence for 21 years to make and use a watercourse from the tail race of a recently erected corn mill at Downhead to Barcombe Spring in Asham Wood.[17] The conduit crossed the Downhead fault, channelling water that would have otherwise gone underground in a sink, or "slocker", hole into the Castle Hill Stream, a tributary of the stream that ran through the valley.[18]

The building of the conduit may also have had the more immediate purpose of significantly increasing the flow of the Castle Hill Stream. Part of James's intention in making the conduit may have to been to make this stream a water-power site in its own right. What is certain is that by c.1810 a mill had been built on it at Dead Woman's

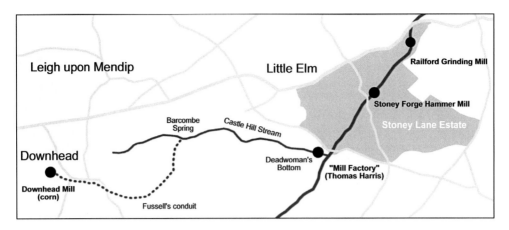

Watercourses and mill sites associated with James Fussell's Stoney Lane estate.

Bottom. This mill was still in existence in 1829 when James Fussell junior and a lace manufacturer called Thomas Harris jointly renewed the lease of the conduit. Harris appears to have been operating the mill at Dead Woman, which is described in the agreement as "mill factory". However, it appears to have gone out of use in the 1830s, since it is not mentioned in the Tithe Award of 1840.

It is not certain when James first established an edge-tool works in the valley. The survey drawings for the first Ordnance Survey map of about 1810 shows a dam in the valley to the west of Stoney Lane and a curious series of leats, one of which runs under the lane and then back into the stream. The works certainly appears to have been in existence by 1817, in which year James Rossiter, an edge-tool worker, was recorded as living in Stoney Lane.[19] Before coming there, James was employed at the Orchardleigh mill, the entry in the Elm parish register of his son James's baptism in 1815 giving Orchardleigh as his place of abode. James Rossiters's relocation to Stoney Lane may have been one of the periodic movements of staff that occurred within the business, but might be evidence that the latter mill had just opened and needed experienced workers. Five years later, Charlton's Map of 1822 shows the waterwheel symbol for a mill at the bottom of Stoney Lane, although on the opposite side of the road from the present ironworks site. Clear evidence for the works being in existence by 1828 is provided by an entry in the diary of the Reverend John Skinner of Camerton, who mentions that the Fussells were making edge-tools in Little Elm (the original name of the west end of the present village of Chantry). The first map to depict individual buildings is a survey of Whatley made around 1830, which shows both the Stoney Lane and nearby Railford works. The Railford works was so positioned because it was sufficiently far downstream from the Stoney Lane works that water from its dam would not back up and drown the wheels at the latter, although its proximity to the turnpike road at Railford Bottom must also have been a consideration.

The functions of the two mills are made clear in the will of James Fussell, made in 1831, the Stoney Lane works being described as a "Forge Hammer Mill" and the Railford works as a "Grinding Mill".[20] With the building of these two mills, the number of edge-tool works under the Fussell family's control increased to six, firmly establishing them as one of the leading manufacturers in the trade and a major employer in the area.

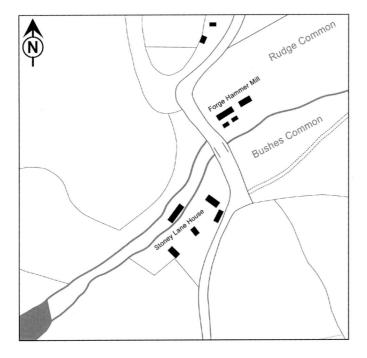

The Stoney Lane edge-tool works as depicted on an undated map of Whatley, probably produced around 1830.

Diversification and Litigation

The Chantry

By the beginning of the 19th century the Fussells were already seeking to raise themselves up socially as well as financially, using the time-honoured methods of advantageous marriages, education, and the purchase of land. In 1806 James Fussell sent his youngest son Jacob to Queen's College Oxford. On graduation he was ordained priest and became vicar of the nearby parish of Doulting in 1823, remaining there until his death in 1867. In 1821 James's older brother, John, died without a male heir, and so his second son, Isaac, took over the running of the Nunney works. His third son, John, seems to have worked in the Mells business, and also in the family woollen mills. Thomas, the second youngest son, concentrated his efforts on building up the Mells edge-tool business, styling himself "proprietor in the iron works" in entries in the Mells Parish Register.

In keeping with the usual practice of the time, it was the oldest son, James, who was to be the principal heir of the growing Fussell fortune, and for whom the conditions were created to ensure that the family would become established among the leading gentry of the area. The basis of this was the land his father had bought at Stoney Lane in Whatley in 1806, which was transformed into a landed estate fit for a gentleman. In the early 1820s James Fussell built a country house, The Chantry, at the north end of Stoney Lane, the name of the new house being derived from the fields on which it stood.[1] A compact and relatively modest building, it was designed by the fashionable Bath architect, John Pinch. In 1820 James Fussell's nephew, Henry Austin Fussell, had commissioned Pinch to design a house for him in Corsley, Wiltshire, and it may have been Henry who brought Pinch to the attention of his Mells kinsmen.[2] The exact date of the building of The Chantry is not known, although Greenwood's map of 1822 does show a building labelled Chauntry House on the site. Following its building, the old Stoney Lane House, later known as Manor Farm, was downgraded to a farmhouse, part of which was converted into cottages for iron workers.

The Chantry was built in spacious grounds and possessed a lodge, stable block, and walled kitchen garden complete with gardener's cottage. The hillside on which it stands was landscaped to create gardens and a deer park, while in the valley below is the lake that supplied the water power for the adjoining Stoney Lane Works. In its

The south front of The Chantry, designed by John Pinch for James Fussell and built in the early 1820s.

original form, the lake was considerably smaller than it later became, the dam being more than 100 metres further back up the valley from its present position. It seems to have been enlarged in the 1830s, presumably with the primary purpose of improving the supply of water to the works. The creation of such a large body of water also provided a landscaping opportunity that was not to be missed. James Fussell laid out a carriage drive along the north side of the lake, erected a boat house and built an elaborate network of grottos with water features fed by a pond behind. The house also boasted a large kitchen garden complete with hothouse, in which he grew, amongst other fruit, prize-winning pineapples and black grapes.[3] Describing a visit to The Chantry in the early 1840s, Thomas Bunn of Frome thought the grounds "a paradise without an Eve".[4] It was now one of the foremost estates in the area, and formed a suitable basis for establishing a dynasty of landed gentlemen. The problem was that James Fussell junior had neither wife nor children.

The first of the brothers to produce a male heir was Thomas Fussell, who had married Sarah Davies, the daughter of the Reverend George Davies of Flint. In 1813 the couple had their first child, James George Curry, and four years later a second, John Thomas Richardson. But in November 1819 tragedy struck, when Sarah died giving birth to their third son, Thomas Davies, who was baptised three days later by his uncle the Reverend Crewe Chetwood Davies. There are indications that Thomas Fussell was a difficult and unpopular man. The comments made by contemporaries,

The lake at The Chantry, looking towards the dam wall.

and his own actions, suggest that he was a single-minded, uncompromising man who cared little for the opinions of others. Nowhere was this more evident than in his religious beliefs. Despite belonging to a family that was deeply attached to the Church of England, and with a brother, father-in-law and brother-in-law who were ordained priests, Thomas went his own way and became a Methodist. The first evidence for this is as early as November 1819, when a "sermon occasioned by the death of the late Mrs. Fussell, wife of Thomas Fussell esq. (of Mells)" was preached at the Methodist chapel in Frome.[5] In his memoirs, Richard White, who was born in 1828 at Holwell Farm, Mells, remembered that Thomas "was a great supporter of Methodism" and that "He had an upper room fitted up as a chapel in a central position in the village where many attended". Another Mells resident, William Long, recalled that Thomas Fussell would ride in his carriage to the chapel "every Sunday morn and evening to the services as long as he lived".

Four years after the death of his first wife, Thomas Fussell married Susannah Chaffey Moore of West Coker. Susannah was a relation by marriage, Thomas's sister Mary having married John Moore, surgeon of West Coker. In 1824 Susannah gave birth to a son, Isaac, who died in infancy, and in 1832 to a daughter, Elizabeth Anne. Following Thomas's second marriage, their uncle James seems to have taken a part in the upbringing of his brother's sons by his first wife. When James George Curry Fussell was sent to Shrewsbury School in 1830, he was entered in the register as the son of James Fussell, Esq., a mistake that may have occurred because it was his uncle who had been in correspondence with the headmaster and who was taking care of his education.[6] Young James was destined to be his childless uncle's heir and was receiving an education fit for a gentleman.

Celebrated Makers

By the early 1820s the firm of James Fussell & Co. was firmly established and its tools now had a national reputation. It was particularly well known for its scythes, one publication of the period describing the company as "a celebrated maker of these and other articles", which it thought the "best known in the London market".[7] The high regard in which Fussell tools were held is reflected by the Reverend John Skinner of Camerton's account of a visit to the Nunney works in July 1828.

> I rose before seven, and walked with Richard Hoare to the Iron Works at Nunney to purchase a scythe for mowing the garden, as the best in the country, perhaps in the kingdom are made by the Fussells, who have mills at Mells, Nunney and Little Elm [Chantry], and have realised an immense property among the fraternity by their superior skills in hardening edged tools.[8]

His companion on this occasion, Richard Colt Hoare of Stourhead, was himself a customer of the Nunney works. Two years previously he had brought one of its products – a tree planting tool called The Perforator - to the attention of the Bath Agricultural Society.[9]

Some believed the superiority of Fussells' tools was partly due to the lime content of local streams. The *Outlines of British Geology*, published in 1850 asserted:

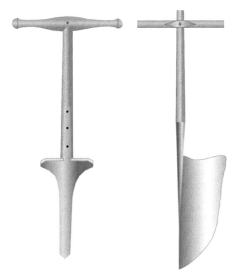

"The Perforator" (left) and a whaler's blubber knife (right) made by Isaac Fussell of Nunney

The manufacturers of edge tools prefer this water for grinding them, from its being less liable to rust them than any other, and the celebrated manufactory of scythes at Mells, in Somerset, is supplied by this water, to which they are supposed to own in part their excellent temper.[10]

Skill in tempering was said to be the mark of the expert tool maker and the precise methods employed were often closely-guarded secrets. There have been other theories about the secrets behind the Fussells' success, one of which was retold by Dr R. D. Reid in 1935.

> Mr Fussell apparently did his own smelting and it is said that he mixed the
> black oxide of manganese (fairly common on Mendip) with the iron ore, and
> that it gave a peculiar virtue to his iron. If so, he seems to have discovered the
> modern manganese steel alloy in very early days.[11]

This makes a good story but is almost certainly not true. It is highly unlikely that
the Fussells ever smelted their own iron, all the evidence pointing to their following
the usual practice of buying bar iron and steel from merchants and scrap iron from
local sources. By 1830 they were obtaining high-quality Swedish steel, of a type
known as Hoop L, from the firm of Joseph Sykes & Sons of Hull, the sole importer of
that product. In July of that year Sykes took an advertisement in a number of papers
to warn that lower quality steel was been passed off as this product, and announced
that to prevent this fraudulent practice continuing, they were limiting their sales of
the genuine article to 13 companies, from whom it could be obtained, one of which
was Messrs. Fussell Sons & Co. of the Mells Iron Works.[12] This advertisement is of

Farleigh Hungerford Mill, operated by James Fussell in the 1820s

interest not only because it provides the source of Fussells' steel at that time, but also because it reveals that they were reselling it to other businesses.

The real reasons for the Fussells' success were that they had a dynamic business that produced well-made tools, from good quality iron and steel, manufactured in large numbers, and sold at competitive prices. Some contemporary observers felt that the human cost of this success was very high. The Reverend John Skinner later described how, on a visit to the Nunney works with Hoare, they "saw two men grinding scythes, with their noses literally to the grindstone" and declared "if any of our West Indian slaves had been seen by any of our modern philanthropists in such a situation, the tocsin of anti-servial malediction would have sounded from John Groats to Lands End".[13] The Fussells' growing business empire was giving their part of rural Somerset a taste of what the process of industrialisation was doing to the North and West Midlands, and valleys of South Wales. It was not to everyone's liking, not least their landlord in Mells, Colonel Thomas Horner.

The Woollen Industry

James Fussell's involvement in the woollen industry had begun by 1809, when the partnership of Fussell & Charles was operating a fulling mill and factory at Marston Bigot.[14] By the 1820s James owned Farleigh Hungerford Mill, which he insured in 1821 for £4,230. At that time the main mill building housed 24 shear frames, seven gigs, and two pairs of fulling stocks. It was powered by two waterwheels and a steam engine. A separate dye house, which also contained four gigs, and a detached fulling mill stood nearby. By this time James had entered into partnership with his kinsman by marriage, John Payne of Nunney, who had married his daughter Elizabeth in 1798. The Paynes had been clothiers in Nunney for several generations, and operated Nunney Mill. In an insurance policy for the mill of 1808, John described himself as clothier of Nunney but by 1822 was living in Farleigh Hungerford, possibly managing the fulling mill. He did, however, retain ownership of Nunney Mill, which he let to another clothier called Patey. The partnership of Fussell & Payne was still in existence in 1824, when it is recorded as buying fulling soap from the Trowbridge firm of John & Thomas Clark.[15] Sometime in the 1820s John Payne appears to have got into financial difficulties, and in 1830 he sold Nunney Mill to James Fussell and moved to Cricklade in Wiltshire, where his son John Robert had opened a chemists shop. The following year James Fussell made his will, leaving his "clothing mill and factory" in Nunney "late in the occupation of John Payne" to his sons James, Isaac and John. By this time the local woollen industry was in the final stages of its long decline and the Fussells seem to have made no further investments, being content to rent out the mill until its eventual sale in the 1850s.

By the early 1820s James Fussell's second son, John, seems to have been actively involved in the family's textile business. In 1824 John, described as an "edge-tool maker of Mells", was awarded a patent for the invention of "an improved method of heating woollen cloth, for the purpose of giving it a lustre in dressing".[16] Unfortunately, two years later John's patent was successfully challenged and set aside on the grounds that the method he had patented was already in use by a number of other manufacturers, including Wilkins of Twerton, near Bath.[17] This reverse does not seem to have deterred him from following in his father's footsteps as an inventor, for in 1835 he obtained another patent, this time for "improvements in pumps".[18]

The Poor Law

In 1828 the Fussells found themselves the defendants in a legal action when the executors of Sir Henry Strachey took them to court for breaching a covenant made when they leased Great Elm Mill in 1792. Under the terms of this, they had undertaken to indemnify the parish "for any costs and charges resulting from them taking an apprentice or servant who should thereby gain a settlement within, or become chargeable to the parish of Elm".[19] In February 1827 William Lansdown, a workman hired by the Fussells in the previous December, began claiming poor relief from Elm Parish, thereby causing a breach of the covenant. The case is of particular interest because the arguments of the plaintiffs and defendants reflected a larger debate that was in progress on the suitability of the Poor Law to a rapidly urbanising and industrialising nation, a debate that would result in the New Poor Law of 1834.

The Poor Law as it then stood was based on legislation enacted in the reign of Elizabeth I, which laid down that every person had a parish of settlement and that parish was obliged to receive him or her back and maintain them if they could not support themselves. The major drawback was that it discouraged the rural poor from moving to another parish to find work. The economist Adam Smith, in his influential *Wealth of Nations*, argued the case against settlement.

> To remove a man who has committed no misdemeanour from the parish where he chooses to reside, is an evident violation of natural liberty and justice… There is scarce a poor man in England, of forty years of age, I will venture to say who has not, in some part of his life, felt himself most cruelly oppressed by this ill-contrived law of settlements.[20]

However, from the point of view of the ratepayers of the parishes there was no incentive to relax these restrictions, since this would increase the number of poor mouths they might be called upon to feed. In 1795 John Billingsley of Ashwick Grove summed up the views of many when he stated, "the poor's levy is a more alarming grievance than tithes".[21] Like the majority of ratepayers, he was concerned by the rapid rise in rate assessments, observing "Many parishes, which within twenty years past paid no more than 50l. per annum to the poor now pay 200l. and unless some plan of prevention be adopted, the evil is not likely to abate".[22] Billingsley attributed this increase to a combination of an increase in population, coupled with "a growing dissoluteness in the manners of the poor".[23] Thirty years later the situation was even worse from the ratepayers' point of view. Thomas Bunn of Frome, writing in 1836, claimed that in the time he had lived in the town its poor rate had increased from £1,966 to £11,723, and complained that "every idle, or drunken fellow had a right to maintain himself and his family from the income of his more industrious neighbours".[24] The wealthier ratepayers of Great Elm may well have been alarmed by the implications of the rapid growth of the population of their small village, which rose from 331 in 1801 to 449 by 1821 – an increase of 36%. This increase was almost entirely due to expansion of the Fussells' edge-tool business, a connection made by the Greenwoods in their book *Somersetshire Delineated* of 1822, which reported "Some extensive ironworks have been lately established here, which has increased the population considerably".[25]

The case brought against the Fussells first went to court in the Michaelmas term of 1828 and dragged on until the autumn of 1829. Their defence was that the covenant was illegal on three counts: "First, as being in restraint of trade; secondly, because it is unreasonable; and lastly as being contrary to the general policy of the poor laws."[26] On the first count they argued the covenant was in restraint of trade because it limited the persons whom the defendant could employ to those coming from a certain area.[27] On the second, they maintained that it was unreasonable for the lessor to attempt "to prescribe a particular mode in which a lessee is to carry on his business, or the servants he may choose to employ, or the parishes or districts from which they may be engaged". Lastly, it was their submission that the covenant was void because it was against the policy of the poor laws in that it prohibited the defendant from employing as many workmen as he otherwise would "by which the parish would be relieved from the burthen of maintaining such paupers as might enter into the defendants service".

At the end of the case the judge, Lord Chief Justice Tindal, found against the Fussells, declaring the covenant to be legal and binding. In his view there was nothing to prevent the "poor generally from being employed by the defendant." He stated they were at liberty "to employ as servants or apprentices the poor of the parish, who may be sufficient for the service of the mill", or could give jobs to "the poor who have settlements in other parishes, but who have certificates from those parishes".[28] Failing that, they could hire servants for less than a year "and thereby prevent them altogether from gaining a settlement".[29]

The Fussells must have felt the judge had no understanding of the realities of their business. The great majority of their employees were skilled workers who had served long apprenticeships and in small villages like Great Elm there was no pool of such men from which to recruit. It is true that many of their workmen were the sons of Fussell employees and were brought into the shops by their fathers as boys and trained up. However, when new hands were needed in a particular edge-tool works these might have to be brought in from another in a different parish. At this time they were operating in four adjacent parishes – Mells, Elm, Whatley, and Nunney. Moreover, in this period of expansion they needed to recruit edge-tool workers from outside the immediate area. Unfortunately for the Fussells, the Poor Law as it stood did not encourage such mobility, workers with families worrying that if they moved to another parish and then became unemployed, sick, or too old to work, they might be refused relief and sent back. As a result, it tended to be the younger workers who were prepared to take the gamble of leaving the relative security of their parish of settlement. One who took the risk was William Montague, who moved to Mells from his native Tisbury in the mid 18th century. Another was William Vickery, who moved to Nunney from Chew Magna in 1813. Montague was a bachelor when he came to work for James Fussell and Vickery had only recently married his wife Betty when he was offered a position by John Fussell. Both were skilled workers, having served apprenticeships before being employed by the Fussells. In this respect the Fussells were at a disadvantage compared to their competitors in large urban areas like Sheffield and Birmingham, who not only had abundant quantities of coal, iron and steel available to them, but also benefited from relatively large pools of skilled labour.

But if the Fussells lost the battle, they and their kind would win the war. Increasing dissatisfaction with the workings of the Poor Law led to the Poor Law Amendment Act, which was passed in 1834. The new Poor Law radically altered the administration of poor relief, one of its effects being to remove the restrictive law of settlement. The Fussells would later secure another victory in Great Elm by gaining control of the works themselves. In July 1858 it was advertised for sale by auction along with other Strachey lands in the village, the advertisement describing it as: "An IRON FACTORY and MILL, with water power, occupied by Messrs. Fussell & Sons". That the Fussells bought the works at this time seems certain, since it formed part of the family estate when it was offered for sale in 1895.

Railway Mania

In 1825 the British Government repealed the so-called Bubble Act of 1720, legislation which for over a century forbade the establishment of joint stock companies, except those authorised by royal charter. The result of the repeal of this legislation was a speculative boom that led to the floating of hundreds of joint stock ventures, including a large number of railway companies. One of the schemes projected at this time was for a railway from the mouth of the river Parrett in Somerset to Basingstoke in Hampshire. On 24 October a meeting of shareholders of the Dorset and Somerset Canal - or Dorset and Somerset Canal and Rail-Road Company as it was now calling itself - was held in Wincanton Town Hall. The advertisement for the meeting included the signatures of the main players in the company, James Fussell's among them. The purpose of the gathering was to consider "the propriety of forming a JUNCTION with the line of the PROJECTED WESTERN RAILWAY COMPANY, or of adopting such other measures, and coming to such resolutions, as may be deemed expedient for the general benefit of the shareholders, and of the public".[30] The new project was seen as a way of reviving the Dorset and Somerset Canal project, in which James still held a large number of worthless shares. At the meeting it was resolved the canal should be completed as quickly as possible, especially the branch from Nettlebridge collieries to Frome. A pamphlet outlining the advantages of completing the works either as a canal or railway was produced to support a new share issue. Thus it was argued "the extensive Iron-works at Mells and Nunney, which have justly acquired so high a reputation, would find a Canal or Rail-road invaluable to their purposes, both in receiving the raw materials and conveying their manufactured goods".[31]

The Western Railway scheme was soon abandoned, however, and replaced with one for a railway from Radstock to Poole Harbour. A public meeting was held at the Old Down Inn on 9 November 1825 to consider applying for leave to bring forward a bill "for laying down a RAILWAY from the collieries at Radstock and neighbourhood to Hamworthy near Poole Harbour". Some at the meeting argued the scheme would damage the Dorset and Somerset Canal, but the majority of those present were in favour of it and resolved accordingly. At a meeting at the George Hotel in Frome on 19 January 1826, a new committee of the canal company was elected that included both James Fussell and his eldest son, James Fussell junior. Another resolution passed at this meeting recommended there should be a new share issue and that existing debts be taken in shares. James Fussell agreed to the proposal, presumably because he recognised that the new venture provided a chance for him to recover the money he had invested in the canal scheme.

The boom conditions that created the first railway mania could not be maintained indefinitely and the collapse was every bit as spectacular as the boom had been. Between October 1825 and February 1826, 59 commissions of bankruptcy were issued against English country banks. The Radstock, Shaftesbury and Poole Railway scheme went the way of the majority of lines projected at that time, and it was to be another 20 years before railways would come to the East Mendips.

The Struggle for the Lower Works

The Fussells might have built up an impressive business empire by the end of 1820s but they had an Achilles heel - they did not own the freehold of the all-important Lower Works at Wadbury. It was by far the biggest of all the Fussells' edge-tool works and was of vital importance to the business and the family's prosperity. Unfortunately for them, the lease by which they held the works was due to end with the death of James Fussell senior, who was then in his seventies. The future of the business was, therefore, in the hands of their landlord, Colonel Thomas Strangeways Horner, a man who expected his tenants to know their place, do his bidding and show proper deference.

On Sundays he and his family would attend church at Mells, taking their places in a family pew fitted out with carpets, couches and a fireplace. In his memoirs written later in the century, Richard White recalled how after Sunday morning service in Mells "many of the parishioners used to wait in the churchyard making quite a row each side of the path, till the Col. and his family passed by, when the men did their most obeisance by holding the brims of their hats and the women did theirs by respectfully dropping their curtsies".[1] The colonel also required his tenants to follow him in their politics, as Richard White later recounted:

Colonel T.S. Horner (reproduced by kind permission of the Earl of Oxford and Asquith).

Colonel Horner was an out-and-out Tory. When the election came there was no canvassing of the farmers as it was understood that they had to vote with their landlord. Woe to him who dared to vote to the contrary, it meant their notice to quit. As the polling was at Wells, Colonel Horner, with his tenants riding behind him, went down in a body and voted.[2]

From the colonel's point of view the Fussells must have appeared to be over-mighty subjects, playing their part in parish affairs but not feeling the need to act in accordance with his wishes. Even Thomas Fussell's building of a Methodist chapel in the village was calculated to annoy the colonel, whose second son, John, was the parish priest. Richard White shared a commonly held belief that the Horners disliked the Fussells and wanted them out of Mells, believing this to result from Thomas Fussell having "often made himself disagreeable to the squire especially at the Vestry meetings".[3] For his part, Colonel Horner, aware of local gossip, wrote to the Fussells in May 1839 to deny that he bore them any ill feeling.

> It having been mentioned to me that you are impressed with the idea that I entertain a feeling of hostility towards you & a wish to put you out of the Parish & that the late disputes in Mells respecting the Poor Rates originated with me from ill-will towards yourselves & those rumours being contrary to the fact, I think it right to express to you my assurance to that effect.[4]

The dispute, which was over the recovery of poor rates, caused feelings to run high among the labourers in the village, their hostility being focused on the parish officers. One of the targets was John Fussell, whose plantation was damaged and one of his carts thrown in the river. Another was Joseph Rich, a former overseer of the poor, who had two heifers "maliciously shot".[5] Four months later, in September, a third officer, Richard Singer, was the target of a similar attack, one of his horses being shot and another having its throat cut.[6] This was not the end of the trouble, the *Bristol Mercury* reporting in November that a calf owned by a local farmer, Thomas Ponting, had been shot and that "no clue as to the perpetrator or perpetrators, to lead to detection, for either of the similar cases which have been committed in this parish within the last few months, has yet been discovered".[7]

Personal feelings aside, it was the issue of the ownership of the Lower Works that was the main source of conflict between the two families, clouding their relationship for over a decade. In an undated memorandum Colonel Horner confided, "The Fussells have for many years been endeavouring to persuade me to let them have the Mills but I always refused & said I could never part with them".[8] The Fussells, for their part, were equally determined to gain control of the Lower Works. The struggle began in earnest in the late 1820s and was to drag on until 1841. On the Horners' side the negotiations were conducted by Colonel Horner, his eldest son Fortescue and younger son the Reverend John Horner, rector of Mells. The Fussells were represented by Thomas Fussell and John Fussell, although at a later stage their cousin Henry Austin Fussell, a dyer of Corsley in Wiltshire, would be brought in to assist.[9] Of all the Fussell brothers it was Thomas who, as manager of the Mells, Elm and Whatley works, had the greatest interest in a successful outcome to the issue. It is significant that Richard White only ever mentions Thomas Fussell, indicating that he was, indeed, the most visible and active of the brothers.

The Fussells were anxious to resolve the matter of the Lower Works before their father's death brought matters to a head. In 1829 John Fussell wrote to the Horners expressing his desire that his father "may yet live to see us established upon a permanent and safe footing with our present means." The sticking point was that Colonel Horner was prepared to grant the Fussells a new lease but would not sell the freehold to them. The Fussell brothers, however, were not prepared to entertain the idea of a lease. John Fussell wrote to Colonel Horner on 4 December 1829 informing him that "after mature deliberation we are decidedly of the opinion that such a tenure may to us prove extremely unsatisfactory". The main thrust of John's argument in rejecting the proposal was that they needed to invest heavily in modernising the works and were not prepared to do so unless they owned the freehold.

> We must of necessity expend two or three thousands at the mills…for the improvement made to machinery by our competitors in the North have of late been so rapid and important, that unless we keep pace with them we may as well take the Articles of our Manufacture out of the Market.[10]

It was just this prospect of increased industrialisation of the valley that Colonel Horner was trying to prevent by retaining some degree of control over the Fussells' activities at Wadbury. On 12 December 1829 he wrote: "A lease will be better than

The Lower Works as depicted in the tithe map of Mells of 1840.

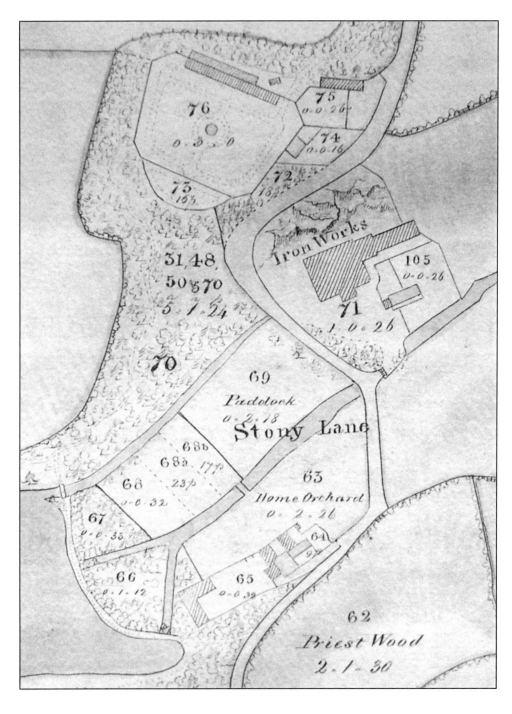

The Stoney Lane edge-tool works as depicted in the Whatley tithe map of 1840 (reproduced by kind permission of the Earl of Oxford and Asquith).

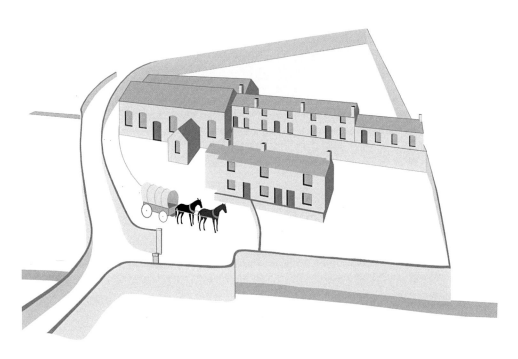

Reconstruction of the possible appearance of the Stoney Lane edge-tool works c.1840, based on the tithe map and archaeological evidence.

a Steam Engine, if I can secure the valley from being blocked up by buildings." The Fussells, who were still smarting from their recent defeat in court over their breach of the covenant in their lease of the Great Elm works, were in no mood to entertain an outcome that could curtail their freedom of action.

In April 1831 Colonel Horner wrote to Thomas Fussell renewing his offer of "a lease of 21 years of the mills now in his occupation to commence from the death of his father", but once again the offer was rejected. A month before, James Fussell had made his will, the terms of which set out how his property would be disposed of and the way the businesses would be structured after his death. As oldest son, James Fussell junior was to inherit the majority of the property, including the Stoney Lane estate and its two edge-tool works. Provision was also made for his clergyman son Jacob Fussell, whose inheritance included his father's shares in the highly profitable East Crinnis mine, in St Blazey, Cornwall.[11] Isaac, John and Thomas were made joint tenants for life of the two Whatley edge-tool works, the lease to end when the last of them died. This was how matters stood when James Fussell died on 18 February 1832 at the age of 84. This long-expected event brought the Fussell lease of the Lower Works to an end and left its future in the balance.

In the weeks that followed a number of letters were exchanged between the Fussells and Horners, those written by the brothers being on black-bordered mourning paper. On 7 March Thomas, John and James replied to a letter from Colonel Horner, in which he had suggested a meeting be held, as it seemed the matter could not be settled by correspondence. The brothers agreed they should discuss the matter in person but said they could not contemplate "entering into the subject personally except in the company of our solicitor". In a second letter to the Horners written on the same day, the brothers acknowledged their lease of the Lower Works had ended and asked if they could for the meantime "remain in possession of the property lately fallen in to him".

On the 19 April the colonel wrote to the brothers offering them a lease of one year while the matter was finally resolved, couching his concession in very polite terms.

> Feeling it may be a great inconvenience to them, taking the mill from them
> at this particular time of the year begs to say that if such is the case they are

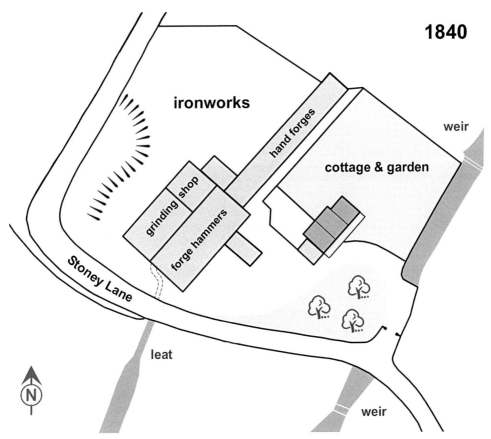

Plan of the Stoney Lane edge-tool works c.1840, based on the tithe map and archaeological evidence.

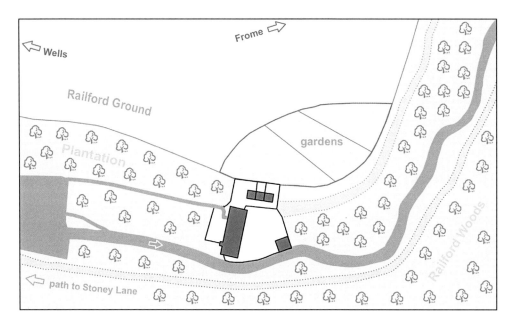

The Railford grinding mill redrawn from the Whatley tithe map of 1840. The garden above the works cottage was three allotments provided for the families who lived there.

> welcome to retain it for one twelve month from the day of the decease of their
> father being the 13th day of February last.

On 5 May the Fussells answered the colonel, acknowledging his right "to advertise the mills" if he so chose but taking up the offer to continue to occupy the works for a further 12 months. They added with ill grace that "in asking permission to do so, they feel that they are only requiring that accommodation which is invariably extended on the determination of an old lease".

One option available to the Fussells was to cut their losses and concentrate on developing the other works run by the business. At Great Elm they added a number of new buildings and may well have altered the arrangement of the wheel pits.[12] There is evidence, too, that they invested heavily in both the Stoney Lane and Railford works in this period. New buildings were erected at the Stoney Lane works in the 1830s and its dam enlarged. By 1840 it comprised a forge hammer shop, a grinding shed and a row of hand forges with rooms above. This works was very different in layout to the other Fussell sites, the forge hammer shop and grinding sheds being in wide, parallel ranges, forming a large, double-roofed building some 90 feet square. In design it was similar to the types of edge-tool works then being built in the Midlands and North of England. The presence of a scythe steeler, scythe shaper, scythe finisher, and scythe grinder in the Whatley census of 1851 indicates that Stoney Lane was a self-contained scythe works, carrying out every stage in the complex manufacturing

Left: chimney for the pumping engine at Railford Works. Right: detail of the dam at Railford.

process. Reaphooks also appear to have been made there, although on a small scale, since the census listed only a single reaphook maker among the inhabitants of the village. Writing a century later, Edward Tylee said he knew of a scythe and reaphook made in Chantry that were still in regular use.

Down the valley at Railford, the grinding shed was enlarged or rebuilt and a beam engine installed to pump water that passed over the waterwheel back into a sump so it could be used again. The dam also appears to have been enlarged at this time. The increase in the size of the dams at both works and the installation of the pumping engine are further indications that the stream was an unreliable source of water power, a problem which in the Fussells' eyes must have restricted the potential of the two sites for further development.[13]

From their point of view it was the Lower Works that was vital to the firm's prosperity and they remained committed to gaining control of it. The problem was that they had a weak hand and were desperately in need of a bargaining counter. By a twist of fate, this was provided by the field called Huntleys that their father had bought under such dubious circumstances more than thirty years before. Not only was Huntleys theirs to do with as they liked but it also adjoined and overlooked Mells Park. Colonel Horner later wrote his own account of what happened next.

> They [the Fussells] endeavoured to frighten me into letting them have them [the Wadbury works] by beginning works in a field called Huntleys, adjoining my park – these works were for a mansion for Mr. T. Fussell & a Forge, Steam

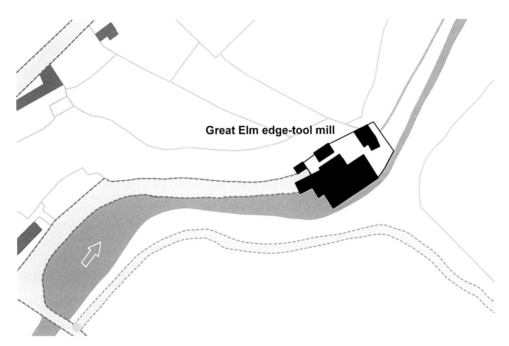

Great Elm edge-tool mill (redrawn from tithe map of 1839).

> Engine, Shops &c. &c. Still I refused parting with the Mills - tho an old copper
> was taken up there & hammered upon, for the purpose I presume of letting me
> know the sort of noise I had to expect.[14]

This clash of the village titans was now a major topic of conversation in Mells and
made such an impression on Richard White that he included the story as he had been
told it in his memoirs.

> Mr. Fussell was not a man easily daunted. As he owned land not far from Mells
> Park House, he soon set to work in building a high chimney (within sight of
> the house), afterwards getting all he required for carrying on his business. He
> also started a steam hammer which was used not only when required, but other
> times as well, making a tremendous noise which we could plainly hear at our
> house nearly a mile distant.[15]

It is interesting that the beating on an "old copper" of the Colonel's account is the
"tremendous noise" of a "steam hammer" in Richard White's. What is not clear is
whether the colonel was dismissively understating the event or White exaggerating
it. The problem with White's account is that it is unlikely that the Fussells possessed
a steam hammer at this time, since James Nasmyth did not invent it until 1839. It is
more likely that what was installed was a tilt hammer driven by a steam engine, an

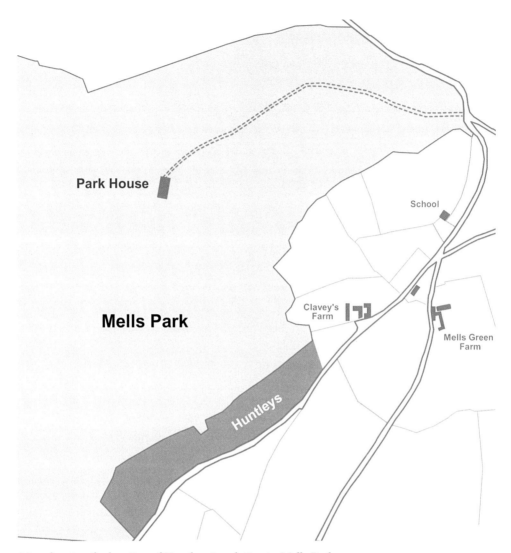

Map showing the location of Huntleys in relation to Mells Park.

arrangement that had been in use since James Watt built one for Wilkinson's Bradley Forge in Staffordshire in the 1780s. It may have been that the Fussells were obliged to install a steam-driven hammer because there was no usable source of water power in the immediate vicinity.

Huntleys was not a suitable location for an ironworks, as the Fussell brothers well knew and the Horners probably suspected. But the episode shows just how far the Fussells were prepared to go to secure the freehold of the Lower Works. As a strategy it was ultimately successful, the threat posed to the Horners' quiet enjoyment of Mells Park being a major consideration during the protracted negotiations. One tactic tried by the Horners was a suit in the Court of Chancery challenging the Fussells' title to

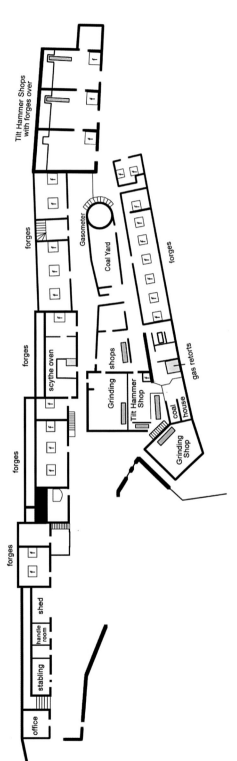

Tilt Hammer Shops with forges over

forges

forges

scythe oven

Grinding shops

Gasometer

Coal Yard

forges

gas retorts

Tilt Hammer Shop

coal house

Grinding Shop

forges

forges

forges

office   stabling   handle room   shed

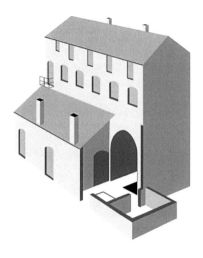

Above: reconstruction of the appearance of the hammer shop and forge building added to the Lower Works in the 1840s.

Left: ground floor plan of the Lower Works c.1850, redrawn from an original plan in Somerset Record Office.

the land, their counsel advising them: "The title of the plaintiffs to the land adjoining Mells Park proposed to be given in exchange is defective, the father of the plaintiffs having purchased that land whilst he held it as a trustee for sale." Unfortunately for them, they had no more success in Chancery than Robert White before them and the Fussells would remain in possession until the dispute over the works was finally resolved.

At various points in the negotiations one side or other would come up with a new proposal or demand. In 1834 the Fussells appear to have suggested that a new works might be built between the Upper and Lower ones, but this was ruled out by the Horners on the grounds that raising the water level downstream at the Lower Works to run wheels would "impede the working of the wheel of the upper." The Upper Works was by now occupied by Austin Fussell's grandson, John, his father having died in 1810. He seems to have been quite content to continue to lease the smaller Upper Works from the Horners and there is no evidence that it was actively involved in the negotiations. He is mentioned in a number of the letters exchanged between the two parties and the Horners claimed at times that they were acting in his interest.

The letters that passed between the colonel and his sons during the negotiations show that they felt themselves torn between a desire to act in the best interests of the family and their duty to act in what they perceived to be the best interests of the parish. Fortescue Horner summed up their dilemma in an undated letter to his father.

> On our individual account it seems to me it would in all respects be better to make the exchange . . . [thereby] . . . shoving the nuisance as far from us as possible - but for the sake of the parish I am very loth to part with the power of ultimately getting rid of what I cannot but deem an evil – I am therefore perfectly willing to abide the worst, and let the matter drop, as before proposed.

He admitted that he was in two minds and willing to go along with his father and brother John if they agreed to come to terms. In concluding this letter Fortescue admitted that he did not know what to do for the best but thought, "In my mind the matter seems to hinge on this: can Fussell establish a manufactory elsewhere in the parish? If he can, I would exchange – if not, I would not."

By June 1838 Fortescue had come round to the view that they should withdraw from the Chancery action, not just because of its expense, but also for the reason that the Fussells were withholding rent until the matter was settled. He also thought they should "revert to the original proposition of 'Huntleys for the Mills.' "[16] However, in a letter written from the yacht *Heron* in Weymouth Roads in September 1838, Fortescue had changed his mind again, arguing that in the interest of the parish the Fussells should not be allowed to gain control of the Lower Works.

The ruins of the hammer shop as they appear today, showing the arched bays in which the water-powered tilt hammers were housed.

> I have long ago made up my mind on the subject, and my conclusion is that I
> would rather the whole thing came to an end – letting him keep Huntleys and
> his other lands and we the mills. I am chiefly induced to come to this conclusion
> because I think the mills are very prejudicial to the parish and should it please
> god that any successor of yours should be a rich man, I should hope he would
> get rid of them altogether.[17]

1839 brought another change of heart, with the Horners now seriously considering letting the Fussells have the freehold of the works as part of an exchange of lands which would include James Fussell's house on the Island at Mells, Huntleys and a number of fields in Whatley.[18] While the negotiations dragged on the Fussells continued to occupy the works through a series of short-term agreements. On 27 July 1839 John Horner wrote to John Fussell of Nunney concerning one of these.

> I have consulted my father with respect to your proposition to continue in the
> occupation of the Mills & Houses for another month from 23 August and he

cheerfully accedes to it upon the understanding that possession be given up on 23rd September.

At one point in the negotiations Colonel Horner complained that James Fussell senior had "had possession of and worked the said mill for nearly <u>fifty</u> years without having <u>ever</u> paid me or my father one penny of Rent", and demanded, "before I say one word on terms, I insist upon the back rent since the death of the late Mr Fussell, be settled and paid up according to the Rent then agreed." The Fussells did, however, continue to occupy the works and at some point in 1839 an agreement was proposed by the Horners whereby they could continue to occupy it until Lady Day 1840 (25 March) on condition that they were to "immediately suspend all operations in Huntleys". The document also stipulated that if the exchange of properties was not effected by New Years Day 1840 the colonel would be "at liberty to offer the mills to any other person" and "Messrs Fussell & Co. to be at liberty to proceed with their works in Huntleys". This agreement, which may never have come into force, was an attempt to force the Fussells' hand by calling their bluff.

At various times in the protracted dispute each side accused the other of procrastination. In December 1839 Henry Austin Fussell wrote to John Horner: "I take the liberty to recommend you, to urge your father in the straight manner to make up his mind <u>finally</u> before the next meeting what <u>he will</u> – or <u>will not</u> concede to Mr Fussell."[19] The meetings between the parties also became heated on occasion, one meeting in Wells ending when John Fussell stormed out of the room. There were also hints of dubious practices, Fortescue Horner writing to his father that the Fussells' legal advisor "seems to have no very exalted opinion of his client" and had confided to him that "he would not be a party to any unhandsome proceedings on their part".

By 1840 there is evidence that the negotiations were drawing to a close and that the exchange of lands would take place. It is also clear that this agreement would provide Thomas Fussell with the freehold of land at Wadbury on which to build a house. These fields, then known as Grass Wadbury and Ploughed Wadbury, were on the hill above the Lower Works - the site of an Iron Age hill fort. At a meeting of Mells Vestry in 1840 Thomas asked for permission to stop up a right of way from Mells to Great Elm that passed through the fields, on the grounds that the presence of the nearby road made it unnecessary. The vestry approved his application on condition that he widened the road from Mells to Great Elm to 20 feet. Work seems have begun in the autumn, for on 1 October 1840 a neighbouring farmer wrote to Colonel Horner complaining that Thomas Fussell had cut back his hedges and "as usual treated me with a great deal of contempt".

Thomas's ambition to possess a country house of his own was a reflection of his social aspirations. Until the early 1830s he had always described himself as "Edge

Tool Maker" or "Proprietor in the Iron Works", but in 1832 he styled himself "gentleman" in the Mells parish register entry for his daughter's baptism.[20] Despite these pretensions, Thomas Fussell remained an industrialist to the core, taking it as a compliment when, in the same year, Colonel Horner described his brothers and himself as "men of business". Thomas's determination to site his new mansion as close as possible to the nerve centre of the business empire he managed also underlines where his priorities lay.

In March 1841 the future of the Lower Works was settled when an agreement came into force which transferred to James Fussell, as older brother, the freehold of the Lower Works, and to Thomas the land at Wadbury for his house. The hammer at Huntleys was to be stopped immediately. Richard White was probably reflecting local opinion when he wrote: "Mr Fussell played a trump-card and won, the chimney was taken down and everything removed back to the old site."[21] The Fussells were securely in possession of the Lower Works and free to make the investment they had been planning for over a decade. In the decade that followed the Fussell brothers invested heavily in the business – erecting new ranges of buildings, including a tilt hammer shop, gasworks, carpenter's shop, timber store, and a ropewalk for making the straw rope used to wrap the finished tools. By the early 1850s the Lower Works had four hammers, two grinding shops, and more than 25 hand forges. A plan of the works made at that time shows a large, sprawling complex of buildings approaching the scale that Thomas Horner had so feared when the struggle for control had begun more than 20 years before.

Wadbury House, Mells, designed by James Wilson for Thomas Fussell in 1841.

The Best Laid Plans

John and Thomas Fussell

Following the exchange of land with the Horners, Thomas Fussell lost no time in building the house at Wadbury he had so long desired. The architect was James Wilson, a competitor for the Nelson Memorial in 1838 and first recorded as working in Bath in 1840. Wilson's designs were completed in 1841, when he exhibited them at the Royal Academy.[1] Wadbury House is an Italianate villa, complete with campanile and porte cochere, and approached by a long carriage drive from an Italianate gate lodge. The builder was a Mr Davis of Bath, who greatly underestimated the cost of realising the project when submitting his tender. In November 1843 Thomas Bunn wrote to Thomas Fussell on Davis's behalf.

> I made application by letter to Mr. Fussell, a man of fortune for Mr. Davis a
> builder who erected for Mr. Fussell a handsome villa. At first Davis made a
> considerable error in his estimate which Mr. Fussell kindly allowed. Afterwards
> I wrote to request payment and Davis told me that Mr. F. on the next day paid
> him seven hundred pounds.[2]

Bunn visited the Wadbury House in 1845 following a mix-up at a local saleroom, some lots he had bought having been delivered to Thomas Fussell by mistake. What he saw impressed him greatly and he wrote his diary, "it delights me to see a taste for beautiful forms increasing in my semi-barbarous country". The house he thought "a charming residence" with a "fine rural location". The two men went on to exchange social calls, Thomas, Susannah and their daughter Elizabeth's governess dining with Bunn on one occasion. Recording the visit in his diary, he admitted he loved to flirt with governesses because they were "as handsome and delicate as other ladies, and usually better informed". Thomas Bunn also contributed to the growing mythology surrounding the Fussells when he retold as true a locally-held belief that Thomas's father James "began making tools as a labourer and subsequently by his skills and industry is understood to have acquired one hundred thousand pounds".[3] James may have amassed a fortune of this size but he did not start life as a labourer; he had grown up in a family that already operated two edge-tool mills and was ambitious to expand its business empire. That Bunn gave credence to the story is interesting in that it illustrates how the lives of the Fussells were already being exaggerated to reflect their increasingly larger-than-life status.

A year after his move to Nunney in 1831, John Fussell married Maria Mary Dowding of Westbury-on-Trym, daughter of Peter Dowding Esq. of Shirehampton. Their first son, John James Dowding Fussell, was born the following May but died six months later. A second son, John Norman, was born in 1836 and died in 1837. Their third and last son, Thomas Richard, was born in 1838 and survived until 1843. By then it must have been clear that there would be no male heir to follow John into the Nunney business. John and Maria also had two daughters - Maria Mary and Emma Eliza, born in 1834 and 1842, respectively. In addition to their own children, the couple also looked after a nephew, Richard, who was the oldest son of John's brother, Jacob. Richard was an invalid and on the 1 May 1837 Maria wrote from Penzance to her grandfather, John Prideaux in Shirehampton.

> You are aware that our much loved Nephew, Richard Fussell, who lived with us, and whom you may recollect to have seen at Nunney, has long been in an alarming state of health, and I grieve to tell you, we cannot hope he is better, or that his late voyage and stay at Lisbon, were any benefit to him.[4]

In the letter she asked her grandfather to send some of his mulberry syrup and guava jelly "by the Bath Weymouth coach directed Mrs John Fussell Nunney near Frome, to be left at Nunney Catch Gate". This may have been intended for Richard but, if so, it was too late. On the 19 May *The West Briton* carried the death notice: "At Penzance, after a long illness, on Sunday last, the eldest son of the Rev. J. Fussell".[5]

Although John Fussell managed the Nunney business and lived at Nunney Court, he does not seem to have possessed a share in the former or owned the latter. This was to change in 1846 with the death of his oldest brother James. In his will, James bequeathed to John "all that messuage or dwelling house called Nunney Court situate in the parish of Nunney aforesaid wherein he now reside" and also "all the moiety or undivided part to which I am entitled of and in the Iron Mills and Edge Tool Works situate [at] Nunney aforesaid".[6]

John was now firmly established in the Nunney business, but without a son to succeed him he seems to have become less and less interested in the works, which was by then only one of a number of his business ventures. By the late 1840s his business interests were more far-flung, including shares in the Australian Land Company and a directorship of the South Australian Banking Company.[7] His interest in South

Nunney Court, the residence of John Fussell (reproduced by kind permission of Charles Daniel).

Australia extended beyond the purely financial, for by 1845 he was also a leading member of the South Australia Society. In June of that year the *Morning Chronicle* reported on the society's annual dinner, noting that John Fussell was one of those seated within the "immediate vicinity of the chair".[8] John's interests in the Australian companies led to him spending more time in London, where he took a house off Grosvenor Square. He also began travelling abroad, spending periods of time in Paris.

Throughout the long struggle for control of the Lower Works, John and his brother Thomas had collaborated closely, not only in their negotiations with the Horners but also in a number of other business interests - from railway schemes, through insurance companies, to coal mining. The brothers' interest in railways seems to have begun in 1836, the beginning of what would become the second railway boom. John and Thomas bought shares in a number of other railway companies at this time, including the Devizes and Melksham Branch of the Great Western Railway, the Bristol and Gloucester Extension Railway, and London, Exeter and Falmouth Railway. In that year they joined the management committee of the latter company, Thomas subscribing £25,000 towards the scheme.[9] The Railway Magazine reported enthusiastically on the company's prospects.

> This magnificent undertaking is progressing with the speed of a locomotive
> engine, and such is the conviction in the public mind, of its expedience, utility,

and general success, that we are informed applications for shares are pouring in from all directions.[10]

The hyperbole did not prove to be justified, for the venture failed to achieve its objective. By late 1837 it was clear that many existing companies were over-extended and when a balance of payments deficit led to a rise in interest rates, the boom came to an abrupt end, leaving many of the serious investors badly burnt. Thomas continued his involvement in railway schemes, being appointed a director of the Bristol and Exeter Railway in 1846, a post he held until retiring in 1854.[11] It is significant that the railway projects in which Thomas and John Fussell invested were all ones designed to connect Somerset with the developing national network, although it was not until 1850 that Frome finally got a railway station.

Another major collaboration between the two brothers was the partnership they established to run coal mines at nearby Vobster and Coal Barton (see chapter 10). This began around 1838 but seems to have come to an end by 1847, when John Fussell renewed the lease as sole operator of Vobster Colliery. The business interests of the two brothers appear to have continued to diverge in the years that followed. In November 1850 the partnership under which they had run the edge-tool business of James Fussell Sons & Co. was dissolved[12] and Thomas was left in sole control of the company. Presumably, he must have bought out his brother, a costly exercise given the size and profitability of the business. It remains uncertain whether the ending of these partnerships was simply a matter of business or the result of disagreements between the two now elderly brothers.

The Next Generation

Another mystery of the story of the Fussell family in this turbulent period is that of the early lives of Thomas Fussell's three sons. The two oldest boys, James and John, both spent time at Shrewsbury School, receiving educations fit for gentlemen. There was then a gap of almost ten years before they went up to Cambridge. In December 1832 James was admitted to Trinity College, but then something interrupted his education and he did not resume it until his readmission in January 1841 at the age of 27. Similarly, John left Shrewsbury in 1834, but was not admitted to Trinity until 1844. It has been suggested the reason for the gaps could be that the brothers' educations were put on hold while the future of the Lower Works was settled, the time between James first going to Cambridge and finally beginning his university education corresponding with the period between the death of his grandfather in 1832 and the acquisition of the freehold of the Lower Works in 1841. The mystery might be partly solved if it was known what the brothers were doing in the years in between. One possibility is that they were put to work in the family edge-tool business, just as their own father had been. Given Thomas Fussell's commitment to the business, it would have been surprising if he had not wished at least one of his sons to follow him into it.

There are few indications as to what James, the elder brother, was doing in this period. Unfortunately the one document that might have shed light on this, the census for Mells in 1841, is no longer extant. The only clue to his whereabouts in the period is provided by the register of voters in the Frome Hundred of 1835, which lists him as living in Mells and having the vote for the Fussells' iron works in Great Elm. Two years later, when he subscribed for shares in the Bath and Weymouth Great Western Union Railway, he again gave his place of residence as Mells.[13]

Slightly more is known about James's younger brother, John Thomas Richardson Fussell. In 1841, at the relatively young age of 23, he married his first cousin Caroline Prescott Fussell, daughter of his uncle Jacob Fussell of Doulting. Shortly afterwards the Whatley census of 1841 lists John and Caroline Fussell as living at Egford House, Whatley, a property that would have been very suitable for a couple of their means and social standing.[14] In the census John is described as a "sythe maker" [sic], indicating that he was working in the family business at the time. Egford House is situated at the point where the turnpike to Mells branched off the Wells Road and is also close to a small lane leading to Great Elm. It would have been quite possible, therefore, for John to ride to the family works in either village.

Of the three brothers, it is the youngest, Thomas Davies, about whom least is known. In December 1838, at the age of 18, he lost his right arm as a result of a shooting accident, caused by climbing over a wall at the bottom of his father's garden while carrying a loaded gun.[15] The gun went off, shattering his wrist and causing such extensive damage that his arm had to be amputated below the elbow. Following this traumatic incident, Thomas seems to have gone into the family business, where he remained for the rest of his relatively short life. At the time of the 1851 census Thomas, then aged 31, was living at Cook's Cottage in Great Elm with two servants. In the census he was described simply as "Edge Tool Maker", a term which carries no indication of his position and responsibilities in the business. He died three years later in 1854 at the age of 35 and was buried at Holy Trinity Church in Chantry.[16]

The circumstances under which the oldest brother, James, resumed his academic career in 1841 are not known but, if he did so against his father's wishes, he must have been financially independent by this time, possibly assisted by his uncle James. Once back at Cambridge he demonstrated considerable academic ability, being awarded both the Brown Medal and Members' Prize for a Dissertation in Latin Prose.[17] He was awarded his BA in 1845 and in 1846 was ordained priest in the Diocese of Bath and Wells.

While James was at Cambridge his uncle James was actively engaged in persuading the Church of England to sanction the creation of the new ecclesiastical parish of

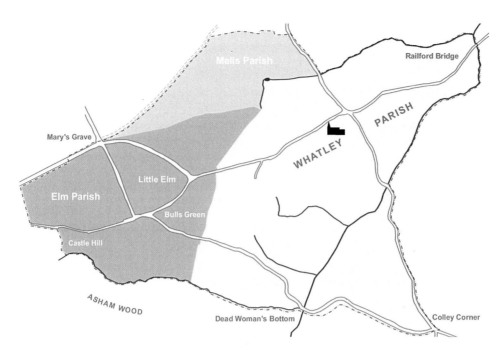

Map of the ecclesiastical parish of Chantry showing the portions taken from Elm, Whatley and Mells parishes to create it.

Chantry, the first incumbent of which was to be his nephew. The justification for the parish was the distance of the settlement of Little Elm from the parish church in Whatley. The ecclesiastical parish of Chantry was created by Order in Council, the greater part being carved out of Whatley parish, although it also took in land formerly in Mells and a small part of Elm. The parish church was built by James Fussell, who paid for it out of his own pocket. The building was designed by the architect Gilbert Scott, and erected by the Frome building firm of William Brown. Holy Trinity Church was sited close to The Chantry, reinforcing the close connection between the Fussells' estate and the parish they had created. Unfortunately, by the summer of 1845 James was bedridden with gout, and according to Thomas Bunn never saw the church he had built at such expense. *The Ecclesiologist* was critical of the new church because it thought the gothic details were "sadly overdone".[18]

On the death of his uncle James in 1845, James George Curry Fussell inherited the greater part of his estate, including his land and property in Whatley and the freeholds of the family's edge-tool works, together with his share in James Fussell & Co. Under ecclesiastical law clergyman should not carry on any trade for profit. There were a number of exceptions, one of which was if the business had been inherited, as in James's case. He was not, however, allowed to play an active part in the running

The Holy Trinity Church, Chantry, designed by Gilbert Scott and consecrated in June 1846

of the businesses, the law forbidding him to act as a director or managing partner, or carry on the trade or dealing in person.

As a possessor of a landed estate, a Cambridge degree and with no direct involvement in trade, he was now a gentleman in every accepted meaning of the term at that time. Moreover, he was about to become incumbent, as well as patron, of his own parish. The new church was consecrated on 4 June 1846 by the Bishop of Bath and Wells, with the Reverend John Horner of Mells, the Reverend Jacob Fussell of Doulting and James himself assisting.[19]

In April 1847 James married Janet Dalrymple, daughter of the late Major General Sir John Dalrymple, 5th Baronet of North Berwick. A marriage settlement was drawn up, under the terms of which most of James's property was transferred to its trustees, including much of the Chantry estate and its two edge-tool works and the Lower Works at Mells. A year after their marriage the couple's first child, James Thomas Richardson, was born and a new generation of Fussells began. Little is known about their early years at Chantry but it must be presumed that James attended to his duties as parish priest, owner of an estate and parent. In February 1848 he was elected a fellow of the Royal Agricultural Society and also joined the Royal Horticultural Society and the Somersetshire Archaeological and Natural History Society.[20] In short, he was fulfilling the destiny mapped out for him by his grandfather and uncle, as the gentleman who would place the family on an equal footing with their erstwhile landlords the Horners.

Like so many well-laid plans this particular one did not go quite as expected. At the time of the 1851 census James and his family were living in Paris, their house in Chantry having been let to Colonel Carlisle Spedding. The unlikely source of this information is the memoirs of Luigi Bianchi, an Italian political refugee who was befriended by James while living in France. Bianchi had been a Catholic priest but had lost his faith and joined Garibaldi's army in the defence of Rome during the insurrection of 1848.[21] Following the fall of that city to the French in July 1849 Luigi took refuge in the house of the British Consul, who provided him with a British passport. Fleeing the country he landed in Athens, where he became friendly with an English missionary who converted him to Protestantism. After more travels, which took him to Constantinople and Malta, he ended up in France. Shortly after arriving in Paris he was arrested because the owner of his hotel had entered his name in the register as Louis Blanc, the same as that of a leading French reformer who was wanted by the police. The mistake was soon recognised but he was told he must leave the country unless he could find someone to provide a letter of guarantee. Once again it was an Englishman who came to his aid – a clergyman called Chamier, who arranged for the British Embassy to provide the necessary letter. Chamier also arranged for Luigi to give Italian lessons and introduced him to his friend, James George Curry Fussell. Luigi later wrote about his new acquaintances.

> Among them was the Rev. J.G.G. [sic] Fussell, for whom I must ever retain an unabated regard. He treated me as a friend - nay, a brother; opened his house to me, and bestowed the utmost sympathy and friendship on me. He advised me in all my difficulties, and always with wisdom; his enlightened views and vast knowledge of Christianity, not merely as a science, but in the highest sense, were most useful to me. He laboured earnestly for my temporal advantage.[22]

Unfortunately for Luigi, James and his family returned to England towards the end of 1851, a parting which caused him great sadness, as he recalled in his memoirs. "I was much distressed at his departure, as his society and Christian conversation had afforded me much consolation. Up to the moment of his departure he neglected no opportunity of serving me, and left me fully occupied."[23] As things transpired the parting was not to be a long one, for in December 1851 Louis Napoleon expelled all political refugees from France and Luigi decided to move to England. Once in the country he called on his friend and patron James Fussell "who received me with the utmost kindness; and the anxiety he showed to procure me employment naturally inspired me with hope and confidence for the future".[24]

A major problem was that Luigi did not speak English, and so James made arrangements for him to attend a college in Birkenhead to learn the language well enough to be able to teach it.[25] Once back in London James found him pupils, Luigi remembering that he "received me at his house with the same frank kindness he always had shown me".[26] He would later move to Edinburgh, where he established himself as an Italian teacher. What happened to him after the publication of his memoirs in 1859 is not known, although it is possible he returned to Italy to take part in the war of liberation launched by Garibaldi when he landed in Sicily a few months later.

By 1852 it must have been clear to his family that James was not prepared to settle for the life of parish priest and village squire. Education was his principal interest and the field in which he wished to make his career. In that year he edited a new edition of Isaac Watts's *Divine Songs Attempted in Easy Language for the Use of Children*.[27] First published in 1715, it was one of the first books expressly written for children. Watts's songs, in the form of poetry, were regarded as less frightening than most religious materials of the time and were often given as school prizes. One of the best known songs in the book was an exhortation *Against Idleness*.

> How doth the little busy bee
> Improve each shining hour,
> And gather honey all the day
> From every opening flower!

This was famously parodied by Lewis Carroll in *Alice's Adventures in Wonderland*, in a verse that is now better known than the original.

> How doth the little crocodile
> Improve his shining tail,
> And pour the waters of the Nile
> On every golden scale!

James's next step was a more decisive one, his acceptance of the post of Assistant Inspector of Schools for the County of Middlesex on 16 October 1852.[28] This would require him to spend the greater part of the year in London and meant that he would no longer be able to serve as priest to his parish of Chantry. The problem was solved when James's younger brother John became his curate. John had followed James to Trinity College, Cambridge, in 1844 and was ordained priest in 1849. Following his appointment, John and his wife Caroline moved into the Parsonage at Chantry (now The Grange).[29]

At the time of James's appointment, school inspectors were not trained professionals but rather "able and promising university men". Writing in 1862, the poet and school inspector Matthew Arnold observed that at that time there were about 60 inspectors, all independent and with salaries like inspectors-general, but "not chosen with the care with which inspectors-general should be chosen".[30] However, whereas Arnold, on his own admission, did his job to finance his writing, James Fussell was undoubtedly committed to education and made his profession also a hobby, becoming actively involved in the educational activities of the Royal Society and being elected a fellow of the Royal Geographical Society in 1860.

The End of an Era

In June 1852 John Fussell made his will, in which he left his estate to his two daughters, held in trust for them by two executors - his nephew James Fussell and Frederick Dowding. Dowding, a successful Bath solicitor and a relation of his wife Maria Mary, was Mayor of Bath in 1850 and had the distinction of being the first to wear both robes and chain of office. Shortly before his term of office, Prince Albert visited Bath and was met by a group of civic dignitaries but was unable to identify the mayor because they were all dressed in a similar manner. As a result of this embarrassment, Queen Victoria decreed that mayors should wear a robe and chain.

In December 1852 John, for some reason, added a codicil in his will in which he revoked the appointment of his nephew James as an executor and trustee, replacing him with John Kent, the tutor and confidential secretary of the 4th Earl of Caernarvon. He had known Kent for over a year, having given him the use of Nunney Court during one of his periods of absence in 1851. How he became acquainted with Kent and why he changed his will to make him an executor is not known. The other members of the Fussell family were outraged and sought to have the codicil overturned by claiming John was insane. In January 1853 Thomas, his brother Jacob, and James George Curry Fussell petitioned the Court of Chancery for a commission of lunacy.

In a report on the opening hearing it was stated that John was "possessed of large property, some 500l. a year real estate, and about 200,000l. personal property" and "of a number of shares in the Australian Land Company, which had reached a high value in the market". It was also reported that he had "resided at intervals in Paris, but returned to England in the spring of 1852". This suggests that John and his wife were living in Paris at the same time as his nephew James. In August 1852 he was said to have suffered a "paralysis", possibly a stroke, that had affected his mental faculties and it was in this condition that he added the codicil to his will. This paralysis appears to have affected the hand with which he wrote, for he was unable to sign his name on the codicil and instead made a mark.

At the first hearing of the petition, the legal representative of John's wife and daughters said there was no question of wishing to have the custody of his person, only that "proper managers" be appointed to deal with his affairs. The Lord Chancellor responded that this was not possible unless John Fussell was found to be "irrecoverably of unsound mind".[31] Unwilling to have her husband declared insane, Maria Mary Fussell contested the petition. The case continued until March, several "very voluminous and contradictory" medical opinions and other testimonies being given. On 5 March the Lord Chancellor gave his verdict, rejecting the petition on the grounds that, while John Fussell "might or might not be of unsound mind", the court did not see "any adequate danger to his person or property to make it expedient in the present state of things to interfere".[32]

Throughout this time John Fussell remained in the care of his wife at their London house in Chapel Street, Grosvenor Square, where he died the following month. The entry in the Nunney Parish register describes him as being of Mayfair, London, while the death notice that appeared in the *Gentleman's Magazine* gives his residence as Nunney Court.[33] Following John's death, his wife and daughters continued to live in London, although they also appear to have continued to spend periods of time abroad.

On one of these trips the older daughter, Maria Mary, met and fell in love with a young officer, Pierre Phillippe Eugene de Grande, formerly of the 2nd Swiss Regiment at Naples. The two married at Dover in May 1858, Maria being 23 at the time and Pierre one year younger.[34] Maria tried to settle her fortune, then estimated at £40,000, on her husband but the trustees of her estate would not allow it. At her insistence Dowding and Kent did, however, allow her to give him £10,000.

Following the death of her mother in 1863, and of her younger sister Emma at Clarens near Montreux in Switzerland in 1865, Maria came into a larger fortune. It would appear from subsequent events that Pierre had married Maria for her money, as he "constantly annoyed her on the subject of the settlement" and had affairs with a number of women, until Maria sued for divorce on the grounds of his adultery and numerous acts of cruelty. Her petition was heard by Lord Penzance, who granted a decree *nisi* with costs in February 1871.[35]

After the divorce Maria reverted to using her maiden name and lived in Weston-super-Mare, Bath and Brighton. On her death in 1881 she was in possession of a fortune in excess of £100,000, which she left to the London Diocesan Home Mission.

Maria's bequest to the mission was so large that news of it even appeared in the *New York Times*.

> The London Diocesan Home Mission has been bequeathed £100,000 under the will of Mrs. Maria Mary Fussell, of Bath. Of this sum £60,000 will be available in about a year's time, and the remaining £40,000 will fall in by instalments on the deaths of certain annuitants.[36]

A plaque was erected to her memory in the crypt of St Paul's Cathedral in London by her lifelong friend, Sophia Crosland.

Thomas Fussell survived his brother John by two years, dying on 2 July 1855 at Wadbury House, aged 72. Unlike his brother's, Thomas's will was very short, his entire estate being bequeathed to his wife Susannah, whom he also named as sole executor.[37] His only surviving child by his second marriage, Elizabeth, had died the previous year, only months after her marriage to Frederick Brodie, the resident engineer at Esher Paperworks in Surrey.[38] Thomas Fussell's widow, Susannah, continued to live at Wadbury House until her death in 1859. It is clear that she shared her husband's commitment to Methodism, for in her will she left £200 to the Wesleyan Missionary Society. Following Susannah's death her executors sold Wadbury House and its contents at auction. The advertisement for the auction gives a picture of the interior of Thomas Fussell's mansion, the lots including "valuable and modern" furniture, more than 750 ounces of plate, cut glass, oriental and Dresden china, two pianofortes, engravings, about 400 books, and an "extensive cellar of choice old wines". There was also what was described as a "magnificent close carriage", a Brougham, a pony cart, and a pair of powerful carriage horses described as "fine steppers and perfectly gentle".[39] One of the selling points of the house was that it was "within 3 miles of Frome Railway Station", the railway that Thomas Fussell had worked so hard to bring to the area.

The deaths of John and Thomas brought to a close a chapter in the story of the Fussells, one which saw their business enter the industrial age and their interests expand to encompass the worlds of finance, mining, and railways. Born the sons of an enterprising Somerset edge-tool manufacturer, they rose to wield power and influence and lived to see their family established among the gentry of the county. The future of the Fussell businesses was now in the hands of a generation very different in outlook and ambitions.

Life and Work

In 1851 the firm of James Fussell & Co. was employing about 200 men and boys at Mells, Great Elm and Chantry.[1] They crowned this achievement by sending samples of their products to the Great Exhibition of that year. In comparison, John Fussell & Co. employed between 15 and 20 men at the Upper Works[2] and Isaac Fussell & Co. about 30 men at Nunney.[3] This made a total workforce of 250 people in the six works in the three valleys. In all, more than 1,000 men, women and children were now dependent on the Fussell edge-tool businesses. The size of these concerns set them apart from their competitors in south-west England, the majority of which were small-scale businesses employing between two and five workers – one of whom would usually be the owner. From time to time these small manufacturers might take on an apprentice and train him to be an edge-tool maker.

One such was George Steeds of Stoke Lane, who in 1815 took as his apprentice Bernard Swain, agreeing to instruct him "in the art of an edgetool maker". Under the terms of the indenture Swain was to be paid 3s 6d a week in the first year, rising in stages to 9s in the seventh and final year of his apprenticeship. Even when an apprentice had served his time and earned the status of journeyman there was no certainty that there might be an opening for him - in which case he would have to continue to assist a tool maker or move to another works if a vacancy arose. These young journeymen were the most mobile category of edge-tool worker, and it is no coincidence that those who came to work for the Fussells from outside the area in the 18th and early 19th century were all skilled men in their twenties. As has been noted, another reason for this was that young men without children were more likely to be prepared to leave the relative security of their parish of settlement. It was not until the new Poor Law of 1834 that this barrier to mobility was finally removed.

It was common for the sons of edge-tool makers to go into the same works as their fathers to learn a trade. One such was William Vickery of Chew Magna who was "at an early age taken to the shop to work with his father". As the Fussell businesses expanded they were able to recruit their growing workforce from the local community, particularly from among the sons of existing workers. The 1851 census for Mells lists a number of sons of workers of 13 to 15 years of age described as "helper". One result of this practice was that members of some local families worked for the Fussells for more than four generations. For example James Rossiter, who moved to Mells from Great Cheverell around 1800, had three sons and five grandsons who worked as edge-tool makers. Similarly, the Montague family provided workmen for the Fussells for 150 years. It is no coincidence that in 1851 no less than 12% of the edge-tool workers in Mells bore the surname Rossiter and 9% that of Montague. Other surnames that crop up again and again among the workforce in the 19th century are those of Cook, Wise and Baynton. The practice of bringing boys into the works and training them for jobs within their capabilities worked so well that when the business of James Fussell Sons & Co was at its peak in the 1850s, 95% of those employed were born within five miles of its four works. This situation did not change until the latter years of the business, when the proportion of locally born workers fell because workers with new skills were needed.

Despite the scale and large output of the Fussell businesses, they continued to depend heavily on the craft skills of their workers. With the exception of gaslighting, none of the changes made in this period were technologically innovative. The works continued to rely on water power, the new hammers being driven by waterwheels rather than by steam. The investment had been aimed at increasing the output of

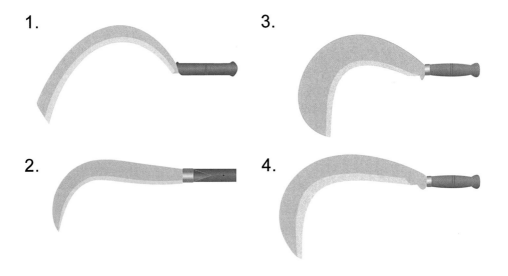

Examples hooks made to local patterns by James Fussell & Co. In the mid 19th century - 1. Speenhamland bagging hook (1854), 2. Chertsey brushing hook (1856), 3. Norton's furze hook (1864), 4. Hawkes bramble hook (1866). Redrawn from a pattern book of James Fussell & Co., formerly in the Curtis Museum, Alton, Hampshire and now held by Hampshire Museum Service.

Water-powered tilt hammer still in situ at Wadbury around 1900. Photograph reproduced by kind permission of Mike Booth.

the works by increasing its size without changing the processes and manufacturing techniques.

A major barrier to the mechanisation of edge-tool making in this period was the wide variety of tools produced, which prevented the makers benefiting from economies of scale. Nowhere was this more apparent than in the highly specialised area of hooks, where there was an extraordinary number of types and local variations. Fussell pattern books surviving from the mid 19th century are filled with the details of hooks with names such as Abergavenny Hedge, Basingstoke Eaves, Chertsey Withey, Cowbridge Bagging, Sherborne Reap, Tring Brushing and Warwick Bean. The patterns for hooks were usually provided by the ironmongers and merchants who ordered them, some of whom gave their names to the patterns, these including Albert Newton of Ringwood, Charles Simmons of Basingstoke and Theophilus Stephens of Chepstow. By the mid 19th century the Fussell business was employing a commercial traveller whose job it was to visit merchants and ironmongers and take orders. Between 1844 and 1864 James Fussell & Co. added around 100 designs of

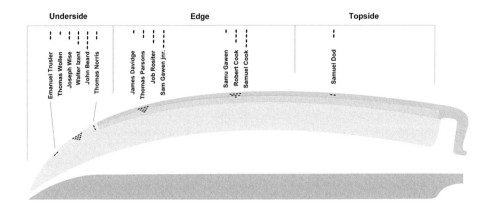

"Scythers" marks of the mid 1840s redrawn from a pattern book of James Fussell & Co., formerly in the Curtis Museum, Alton, Hampshire and now held by Hampshire Museum Service.

hook to their pattern books, of which 70% were for places in the South of England, half of them in Somerset and adjacent counties.

The numbers of a highly specialised local pattern tool to be ordered at one time would be very small and there was, therefore, no scope for mass production. When a traveller brought orders back the pattern books would be consulted and the tools made by hand. One of the few areas where mass production was possible, and where economies could be made, was the manufacture of spades and shovels, which could be stamped out or rolled by machinery.

The relatively large size of James Fussell Sons & Co did, however, encourage the development of specialisations that were not possible in smaller concerns. The core of the business was the skilled craftsmen who made the tools, such as the steelers and platers who forge-welded the iron and steel and shaped the blades under trip hammers, and the makers who worked the blades with hammer and anvil in hand forges. By 1861 there were more than 15 job titles that covered the various stages in the manufacturing process, from steelers and makers, through the temperers, grinders and finishers, to the packers and warehousemen. In 1861 there was even a scythe heater, whose job was to heat scythe blades in an oven. Some workmen specialised in the manufacture of particular types of tools which required particular skills, such as scythes, reaphooks, axes and spades. The steelers, platers, temperers, reaphookers and grinders all had their own marks, which were recorded in the company's pattern books. The men involved in these stages of the manufacturing process were pieceworkers, being paid so much for every dozen tools they worked on – the presence of their marks on the blades providing a record of their output. The marks were also used for quality control, as Edward Tylee pointed out: "Every workman had his own private mark that was placed on each tool – thus defects could be traced to the actual perpetrator".[4] The various stages of the manufacturing processes were overseen by the foremen, experienced and trusted workers who had come up through the ranks. The position of foreman was as high as a worker could rise within the business, management positions being reserved for family members and connections of higher social rank.

In the first half of the 19th century hours of labour for manual workers were long, a 12-hour day being usual and 15 not uncommon. William Vickery, for example, was said to have "often worked for 16 hours a day". There were, however, a number of factors which affected the hours worked. Trade depressions and seasonal fluctuations in demand for agricultural tools such as scythes and reaphooks could result in periods of short-time working and even lay offs.

The length of the working day in winter was also limited to some extent by the hours of daylight, although the introduction of gaslighting at the Lower Works in the 1840s made a longer day possible. The Fussell works were dependent on water power and a lack of water in dry months could bring the works to a standstill. The mills around Frome would send their workers home when there was insufficient water to turn the wheels, a practice that is commemorated in the following couplet, probably chanted as a children's rhyme.

> Slades and Nappers are shut down,
> there's no water up to town.

Steam was gradually introduced into a number of the Fussell works but all continued to rely on water power until the very end, the Upper Works at Mells getting a new wheel as late as 1883.

The strength and manual dexterity required to shape the tools could not be maintained into old age and it was not uncommon for older tool makers to move to less arduous but more poorly paid work, such as packing. There are examples of men still at work in their 70s, having been employed by the business for more than 50 years. Of all the manufacturing processes, the most unhealthy was that of tool grinding, the inhalation of particles of sand and iron during the process causing silicosis, also known as Grinder's Rot. The killer dust could be reduced by keeping the stone wet, a method used by most edge-tool makers - yet even then the average life expectancy was less than 40.[5] The conditions in which the grinders at the Railford Mill worked were described by Edward Tylee.

> The men who did the grinding lay straddled across a sort of "horse" like a vaulting-horse in a gymnasium, and wore a kind of large apron of woollen material…A former resident of this parish says he has a vivid memory of a beam-engine at work, the rows of tables or "horses" on which the grinders lay prone, with the grindstones just under one end of each table, revolving at terrific speed, the scythe or other tool held with both hands, and the sparks flying upwards."[6]

In cases of injury and illness the workers and their families might be attended by a village doctor, such as James Drake of Bilboa House in Mells. Richard White recalled that if his brothers were ill and Dr Drake was sent for, he would take their pulse, look up as if in "profound thought" and then invariably say, "Mrs. White, I must trouble you for a basin as I find it necessary to take away a little blood." His brother John would later joke: "If he had not been bled so much in his young days he would have grown up a finer man."[7] White also retold a popular local belief that the doctor's sovereign remedy for problems with legs was amputation, claiming, "there were a lot of one-legged men in Mells. When anything was the matter with a leg Dr. Drake was for having it off, as being in that case a perfect cure!"

In April 1846 the six-year-old son of one of Thomas Fussell's journeymen edge-tool makers, Ezekiel Baynton, injured his wrist and was treated by Dr Drake's junior colleague, Joseph Stringfield. Stringfield diagnosed a sprain and directed the arm be put in a sling and vinegar be applied to the affected area. Believing the injury was not healing as it should and might be more serious, Thomas Fussell sought a second opinion from Dr Harrison of Frome. Harrison's view was that the wrist had been dislocated rather than sprained, an opinion he expressed in a note to Thomas Fussell. On receipt of this Thomas wrote to Dr Drake in his usually forthright manner, declaring that he was "led to conclude that you or Mr. Springfield, or both, have taken a most erroneous view of the case, and treated it with equal want of skill". He went on to say the case had been referred to Dr Moon of Leigh-on-Mendip to get his opinion. Moon's reply to Thomas Fussell was cautious, suggesting the boy should be sent to the United Hospital in Bath for an examination. The surgeons at Bath agreed with the original diagnosis and said the bones were neither fractured nor displaced. James Stringfield then produced a pamphlet "to refute the charges of ignorance and incompetency preferred against me, which, if tacitly agreed to pass, may possibly inflict a serious injury on my reputation as a surgeon".[8] This small publication gives a rare insight into the lives of village doctors of the period, as well as providing more evidence of the uncompromising nature of Thomas Fussell's character.

In 1844 a friendly society was founded in Mells, a voluntary institution for the purpose of providing its members with financial assistance in times of sickness and in old age. The subscriptions were on a sliding scale, starting at 8 ¾d at the age of 15 up to 4s for a man of 50. In return, members received sick pay of 4s a week for the first 12 weeks and 2s thereafter. Those members who survived to the age of 65 received a pension of 4s a week.[9]

If a man were unemployed he would be paid an allowance from the poor rate but might be required to work on the parish roads. In times of economic depression other measures needed to be adopted, as in 1830 when Colonel Thomas Horner reduced his rents and allocated fields in Mells, Leigh-on-Mendip and Cloford for the cultivation of potatoes "to relieve the pressing necessities of the poor".[10] In some cases the unemployed or aged poor might be sent to the parish workhouse. A workhouse was established in Mells in 1763, Thomas Horner granting to the parish a house "for the reception, maintenance and employment of the poor of the parish of Mells". The property was transferred to trustees chosen from the principal inhabitants of the village, James Fussell being one of them. Mells workhouse continued in use until 1829 when it was resolved "that the present system of maintaining and clothing paupers in a Workhouse in the parish be discontinued at Midsummer next ensuing and allow them as a substitute a regular weekly allowance of cash".[11] Following the New Poor

Late 19th century photograph of Mells. In the foreground is Woodlands End, the part of the village closest to the two Wadbury works and the one in which many Fussell workers lived (Michael McGarvie Collection).

Above: workers' cottages at the entrance to the Nunney works. Below: a view of Great Elm c1900 with the workers' cottages on the right and the pond for the works in the foreground.

Law of 1834 Mells, Nunney, Great Elm and Whatley all became part of the newly created Frome Union, and from 1837 those who claimed poor relief might be sent to a new workhouse in that town. Those who remained in their home village bore the stigma of poverty, as in the case of 71-year-old John Ashman, who was described in the census of 1851 as "Pauper formerly Edge Tool Maker".

Given the size and location of the Fussell businesses, it is unlikely the workforces ever attempted to establish unions and strike for improved pay and conditions. But even if they did not engage in industrial action, some of their employees do seem to have been active supporters of the Chartist movement. In the late 1830s the Chartists began a national campaign for sweeping political reforms, including the demand that the vote be given to working men. A Chartist branch – the Frome Working Men's Association - was established in the area and 1,653 local people signed the movement's first national petition for reform of parliament in the spring of 1839. By April of that year Chartists were discussing what action to take if the petition was rejected, some arguing that working men should take up arms and gain their demands by force if necessary. On April 15th a troop of the 10th Lancers arrived in Frome "to take the Chartists of the neighbourhood in order".[12]

In the mid 1840s Mells had an active Chartist group, one its leading members being Richard Corp, a reaphook maker employed at the Lower Works. By that time the movement had set up the National Land Company, a scheme that aimed to establish 250 Chartists on self-supporting smallholdings on estates in Gloucestershire, Hertfordshire, Oxfordshire and Worcestershire. The Mells Chartists made regular contributions towards the company and some bought shares in it, qualifying them to have their names in the lottery that would decide the allocation of the smallholdings. Richard Corp was one of those who bought a share, although later he had a change of heart and offered it for sale in the Chartist newspaper, *Northern Star*. Another Mells Chartist, Thomas Ashman, held on to his share and was successful in the first ballot. He was initially allocated a cottage and two-acre smallholding on the company's estate at Snig's End in Gloucestershire in June 1848, but later took possession of a larger plot - describing himself in the 1851 census as "farmer of four acres". Following the collapse of the scheme, Ashman returned to Mells and by 1861 had resumed the life of a labourer.[13]

Others who could not find work locally, or who wished to improve their situation, emigrated to Australia and North America or moved to other parts of the United Kingdom. In the second half of the 19th century the single most common destination for migrants from the villages of the East Mendips was South Wales, the population of which grew by 320,000 in the period 1851 to 1881. Somerset coal miners, iron workers, labourers and even tradesmen moved to the Welsh valleys, attracted by the job opportunities and higher rates of pay.

The majority of workmen in Mells were tenants of the Horners who, always in debt, combined paternalism with neglect. Writing in the 1930s, Frances Horner recalled:

> The cottages at Mells were very old, very picturesque, and very unfit for modern standards of life. The roofs, generally of thatch and miserably bad,

The Methodist chapel in Mells, built by Thomas Fussell in 1835 to the rear of the 17th house called Holycroft.

> leaked everywhere . . . small windows, stone floors, damp walls and steep dark
> staircases . . . On the other hand, the rents were almost nil – 1s. 2d. and 1s. 8d.
> a week – and they had large gardens. There was constant competition for these
> cottages, and as the landlord did all the repairs the tenants put up with the
> drawbacks.[14]

Following Colonel Horner's death in 1844 his son John built a new school, repaired cottages, restored the parish church and founded a friendly society. The other side of the coin was that workers who lived in Mells were subject to the social control imposed by their landlord. Frances Horner remembered that "if anyone in the village 'went wrong', as the euphemism was, their parents were not allowed to stay as tenants unless they refused to take the erring children in".[15] Villagers were not allowed to keep dogs and it was said that at one time the Horners even went so far as to name their tenants' children.

As the Wadbury business expanded, there were fewer places in Mells for the growing workforce to live, with the result that an increasing number lived in Great Elm where new cottages were built to accommodate them. It is likely the more independent-minded workers may have moved to Great Elm to escape the paternalism of the Horners and the social control they imposed on their tenants. The

Primitive Methodist chapels at Chantry (left) and Great Elm.

Fussells themselves owned and built cottages in Chantry and Great Elm, which they rented to their workmen. Moreover, each of the Fussell edge-tool works included a row of cottages controlled by the business. These were often occupied by trusted workers such as foremen and provided additional security. There were a number of reported thefts of tools and iron from Fussell works in the 18th and 19th century and the high stone wall around the Stoney Lane works at Chantry shows the importance attached to making them secure.

The cottages of the Fussells' employees were scattered around the villages and their next-door neighbours might be agricultural labourers, estate workers or craftsmen. In Chantry, the workers were provided with allotments – described as gardens - close to their cottages, while in Mells it was said that every cottage had a "good garden attached to it, where potatoes were principally grown".[16] Despite the size and local importance of the Fussell businesses, the villages in which they operated were essentially traditional agricultural communities rather than industrial ones.

From the early 19th century Methodism played an increasingly important part in the lives of the Fussells' employees. Writing in the second half of the century, Edwin Long remembered how preachers "full of zeal, came to Mells holding meetings at Woodlands End. Soon many of the ironworkers were converted, and Mr. Thos. Fussell seeing their changed mode of life, became interested in the movement and joined it". That Thomas was indeed responsible for the building of the Mells chapel is borne out by a report in the *Wesleyan-Methodist Magazine* in 1835, which declared "we stand indebted to the kind and liberal exertions of Thomas Fussell" for building the chapel.[17] The Mells chapel, which was at the rear of a large 17th century house called Holycroft, continued in use until the lease expired in 1876, after which it was demolished.

In the year Thomas Fussell built his chapel in Mells, another was erected in the nearby village of Great Elm by the local Primitive Methodists. Established in the early 19th century, Primitive Methodism was created by working people for working people. Its founder was Hugh Bourne, a Staffordshire millwright and joiner, who later recalled how, in the early days, "our chapels were the coal-pit banks, or any other place, and in our conversation way, we preached the Gospel to all, good or bad, rough or smooth".[18] The sect grew rapidly in the 1830s, membership rising from 35,733 in 1830 to 73,990 in 1840, while the number of chapels rose from 421 to 1,149 in the same period.[19] The local Primitive Methodists established chapels or meeting rooms in Frome, Nunney and the future parish of Chantry. They had no success in Mells, however, putting their failure down to the fact that "all the land in and around the place belongs to the vicar of Mells, a Puseyite and an enemy of dissent".[20] John Horner was indeed High Church, introducing monthly communion and preaching in a surplice, both of which were regarded in some quarters as dangerous signs of leanings towards Roman Catholicism. It is also true that he gave no encouragement to Nonconformists, going so far as to only employ Anglicans on his estate.

The local Primitive Methodists relied heavily on part-time preachers, some of whom were edge-tool makers employed in the various Fussell businesses, including Joseph Biggs and Walter Izant of Great Elm. In 1863 the *Local Preachers' Magazine* reported the death of Hosea Frapwell, also a tool maker from the village, who was said to have been "in a desponding state of mind for some years, but he at length obtained the victory and died happily."[21] However, the best-known and most tireless local preacher among the Fussell workers was undoubtedly William Vickery of Nunney. When William and his wife Betty came to Nunney from Chew Magna in 1813 there was already a Wesleyan Methodist chapel in the village, founded in 1807, which the couple attended.

In 1837 William and Betty Vickery were converted to the cause of temperance following an open meeting in August held by Samuel Horton of Frome in Nunney market place. William's grandson later wrote that on that occasion the "whole village rose in arms against the Temperance advocates and treated them very badly; but Billy and Betty thought they were right and took them to their home away from the mob". The couple founded a family temperance society that night, and the Frome Temperance Society later reported that a "flourishing branch has been planted at Nunney. Brothers Vickery and Hird amongst the Primitives [sic] cultivate it with great care".[22] At that time Nunney had three public houses, but William had never bought beer in them "for Betty brewed her own which she and her husband drank at dinner time". Once converted to the cause of temperance, Betty turned the taps on her beer barrels and let the beer flow away.

The Vickerys had an uphill struggle, the accepted view being that "drink was a necessity" and particularly "that a man who did hard manual labour should drink intoxicants". Addressing the Whitsuntide meeting of the Bristol Total-Abstinence Society in 1846, William recalled that it had been said if he gave up alcohol he would be unable to do his job.

> He was told when he became a teetotaller that he should be unable to make pickaxes and the like, but if they would send to Nunney, to Mr Fussell, for whom he had worked more than 30 years, they would soon have an answer about that. He loved his master, and his master, he had reason to know loved him.[23]

William and Betty's advocacy of temperance led to their expulsion from the local Wesleyan chapel, after which they appear to have joined the Primitive Methodists. A number of the villagers in Nunney actively persecuted the couple for their beliefs, being particularly angry when William bought a trumpet and took to walking through the village at 6am on Sunday mornings blowing it - "calling sinners to repentance" and warning the villagers "to flee the wrath to come", after which he would go to a 7am prayer meeting at the chapel. On his return from this one Sunday, William heard a noise in the street and went outside to see what was going on. There he found eight men banging on saucepan lids, a common way of punishing unpopular members of a community and known as "rough music". Sunday was the one day of rest and William's wake-up call to the village is unlikely to have gone down well. Yet despite his lack of popularity in some quarters, William made a number of converts to the temperance cause and by 1843 had persuaded a number of his fellow workmen to sign the pledge to give up alcohol. These were William's son Lazarus, his son-in-law Uriah Trowbridge, Simon Joice, John Crees (all scythe grinders), Samuel Derry (the warehouseman), and Eno Turner (a spade steeler).[24]

William also took his religion to work with him, holding a prayer meeting in his workshop every day at noon. It was said that he was "usually joined by the Master who would put down his pen and hurry in when he heard that the meeting had begun". The master mentioned here was presumably John Fussell, who, if William is to be believed, seems to have encouraged, or at least tolerated, this interruption to the working day. Following John Fussell's death the new management forbade the holding of the meeting, an act that William's grandson saw as godless and that he linked to the subsequent decline of the business.

Gentlemen and Convicts

By the early 1850s the firms of James Fussell & Co. and Isaac Fussell & Co. both lacked younger family members to take over when the managing partners died, Thomas Fussell's elder sons both having entered the church and John Fussell having no male heir. The absence of obvious successors meant the Fussell brothers were forced to look beyond their immediate families to the sons of more distant relatives who had fallen on hard times.

The first of these to enter the businesses was James Fussell Payne, son of John and Elizabeth Payne (née Fussell) of Nunney. Born in 1804, he was named after his maternal grandfather James Fussell, with whom his father had been in partnership in the early 1820s. James Fussell Payne's father appears to have got into financial difficulties around 1830, after which he moved to Cricklade in Wiltshire to live with another son, John Robert. John Payne was not forgotten by the Fussells, his brother-in-law James Fussell of the Chantry leaving him an annuity of £25 in his will in 1845. Following the death of John Robert in July 1852, John Payne returned to Somerset, where he died two months later in Frome at the house of his son-in-law, William Brand, at the age of 73.[1] James Fussell Payne appears to have remained in Somerset when his father moved to Wiltshire, having been found a post at the Fussells' Nunney works, first as a commercial traveller and later as its manager.

Under the terms of John Fussell's will, the Nunney works passed into the hands of his trustees, John Kent and Frederick Dowding. They continued to operate the business for the benefit of his wife and daughters for six years after his death. The running of the works was entrusted to James Fussell Payne, who in 1859 was described as having been for "many years manager of this concern".[2] In that year the trustees took the decision to sell the works, along with Nunney Court and Vobster Colliery. It was later explained to the employees at the colliery that the decision to sell was taken because of a need to rationalise the estate in order better to determine its income, possibly as a result of Maria Mary Fussell's marriage a few months before and her demands that her fortune be settled on her new husband.

On 20 July 1859 an advertisement appeared on the front page of the *Frome Times* announcing that an "IMPORTANT SALE of HOUSES, LANDS, IRONWORKS, COLLIERIES and other PROPERTY, at NUNNEY and VOBSTER, near FROME", was to be held at the George Inn in Frome on 3 August. The sales particulars described the ironworks - lots three and four - as follows:

> 3. - Also an undivided Moiety of the freehold IRON WORKS and EDGE TOOL MANUFACTORY, adjoining the above Messuage and Premises, together with the Mill, Water Wheels and Water Courses, Sheds, Smiths' Shops, Carpenters' Shops, Grinding Houses, Workmen's Cottages, Gardens and other premises.

> 4. - Also the ENTIRETY OF THE GOODWILL of the very profitable Business carried on at the above Works for nearly a century past, by the late proprietor and his family and now in full work with a staff of 30 experienced workmen.[3]

At the auction James Fussell Payne bought Nunney Court and the above lots for £2,000.[4] Later in the month the *East Somerset Telegraph* reported on a dinner held to mark the change of ownership.

> The workmen employed at the extensive edge-tool manufactory, for many years carried on by Messrs. Fussell & Co., met at Nunney Court Mansion, to testify their gratification at the arrangements lately made, through the purchase of the property, by Mr James Fussell Payne, for many years manager of the concern. A substantial dinner was provided, and utmost good feeling pervaded throughout. The day was closed by a supper, after which the men sang the Evening hymn and separated.[5]

Payne and his wife Anne did not live in Nunney Court, which in March 1861 was described as unoccupied. In the census of that year Payne described himself as an edge-tool manufacturer employing 16 men and eight boys. After almost a century the Nunney works was no longer being run by a Fussell, although it was still in the hands of a direct descendant of the James Fussell who had acquired it for the family in the 1760s. As it turned out, Payne's time in control of the works was not to last long, for within three years the works was back in the hands of the Fussell family.

Over the years Thomas Fussell, like his brother John, found white-collar jobs for members of the wider Fussell family circle. Among them were William Thomas Jesse and Stephen John Charles Skurray, both of whom entered the business as recipients of Thomas Fussell's patronage following their fathers' bankruptcies. William Jesse became a member of the extended Fussell family when his sister Jane married Robert Moore of West Coker. The Moores were already connected with the Fussells by this time, Thomas Fussell's sister Mary having married Robert's brother, John. The

Rock House, Great Elm, bought by William Jesse from the Rev Jacob Fussell in 1847.

relationship was strengthened further when Thomas married their sister Susannah Chaffey Moore. In the years that followed Thomas was involved in a number of business dealings with his brother-in-law Robert Moore, who was a sailcloth maker. Jane and William Thomas's father, William Jesse senior, was a linen manufacturer and bleacher and may well have had an existing commercial relationship with his future son-in-law.[6] In 1837 William Jesse and his son were declared bankrupt and Thomas Fussell helped the family out by finding his son, William Thomas, a position in the Mells edge-tool business.[7] Thomas also took a hand in sorting out the Jesse family's affairs, becoming involved in a number of property transactions in 1840.[8]

William Jesse appears to have been working for Thomas Fussell by 1847, when he bought three dwellings in Great Elm from Jacob Fussell for £400 and was described in the sale document as "gentleman of Mells".[9] At the time of the 1851 census he was living in one of these properties - Rock Cottage, now called Rock House - and describing himself as "Commercial Traveller Edgetool Manufacture". In 1852 his father died, leaving all he possessed to William's half-sister and housekeeper, Keturah Jesse.[10] One can only speculate as to why he left nothing whatsoever to his son. It is possible that he had little to leave, or perhaps father and son were not on good terms.

Stephen Skurray, like William Jesse, entered the business through family connections, being a grandson of Thomas and John Fussell's sister Elizabeth.[11] Elizabeth Fussell had married John Payne of Nunney in 1798. One of the couple's daughters, Jane, married Charles Francis Skurray of Beckington in March 1828. The following year Stephen was born, by which time Charles and Jane were living at Wanborough near

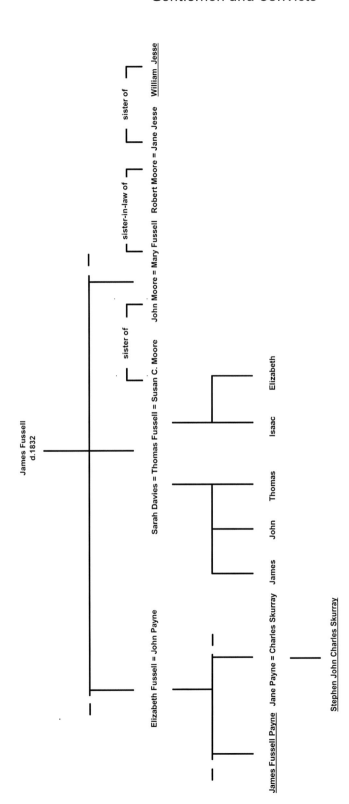

Partial family tree of the Fussells showing how they were related to James Fussell Payne, Stephen Skurray and William Jesse.

Swindon. Twelve years later the Skurrays were to be found in Cricklade, where they ran an ironmonger's shop in the High Street close to the chemist's shop where Jane's father and her brother John Robert lived.

Charles Skurray's business did not thrive and in April of that year he was declared bankrupt.[12] At the time of the 1841 census Stephen, then aged 12, was not living at home, probably because the Skurrays were finding it hard to make ends meet, and it may be that he had already been found a position working for his Fussell kinsmen in Mells. By 1851 Stephen was living at Elm Cottage in Great Elm and held the position of clerk at the ironworks. When the census of that year was taken on 30 March his mother and four of her children were also living in Great Elm, although on census night Jane was away from home visiting her dying sister Elizabeth Ann Brand in Frome.[13] By then her husband Charles was not living with his wife and children, the reason for his absence being provided by the Elm parish register entry for his son Arthur's christening in September 1851, which gave his occupation as "gentleman settler Australia". It seems likely that Charles's emigration was the result of his financial difficulties and it may be that John Fussell used his connections with the colony to assist him. In this period gentleman settlers were not popular with some people in New South Wales. A former governor, Lachlan Macquarie, complained it had become common "for persons who wish to get rid of some troublesome connections to obtain permission from the Secretary of State's office for their being allowed to come out here".[14] Jane Skurray and three of her children did eventually follow Charles out to Australia, but Stephen remained behind in Great Elm and continued to work for James Fussell & Co.

The death of Thomas Fussell created a career opportunity for Stephen Skurray because the new owner of the business, Thomas's son James, was an ordained priest of the Church of England and therefore barred from taking an active part in its management. For the first time in its history the company was no longer managed by one of its owners and was dependent on its salaried, white-collar staff. By 1857 Stephen's prospects were sufficiently good for him to marry Elizabeth Charlotte Russwarm and by 1861 the couple were living in a house called Mount Pleasant in Great Elm (although later directories give their residence as Rosemont Villa).[15] In the census of that year Stephen was described as "Manager of Iron Works", a post he would occupy for the next 15 years.

Crime and Punishment

Charles Skurray died in New South Wales on the 20 January1859. A fortnight later, two letters were sent from Mells to a former inhabitant of the village, Michael Long, who was also living in the colony. In one of these Michael was asked to pass the following piece of local scandal on to another Mells man, Joe Wise, who lived nearby.

> Tell him that trade at the Mills is rather slacker than when he left. James Fussell
> has had the management of it for nearly three years. They have been making
> an inspection of the books for the last few days and they have found Mr Jessie
> had defrauded them in that short time of £700. He is therefore forbid the works.
> What they will do with him I do not know, but they are now looking over old
> Thomas Fussell account to see what he has done there.[16]

The Mr Jessie in question was undoubtedly William Jesse and as a gentleman and family member, albeit a distant one, it is unlikely he would have faced prosecution. One can only speculate as to why William embezzled the money. It may simply be that his lifestyle required a greater income than that provided by his salary. To prevent a public scandal, he seems to have been quietly dismissed, and within two years was living in Dunsford Place, Bathwick, where he remained until his death in 1874.

The Fussells might have been prepared to cover up fraud perpetrated by a member of the family but they were not going to overlook theft by their own workmen. In July 1839 a young employee of James Fussell & Co., Joseph Beard, was sent to the company's bank in Frome with a cheque to get change. When Joseph had not returned by the time expected, the alarm was raised and it was found he had cashed the cheque and made off with the 80 sovereigns and 30s in silver. He was tracked down to Ilminster, where he was arrested and committed for trial.[17] On 14 August he was sent to the county gaol at Ilchester. On his release he left the area and in 1861 was working as an edge-tool maker in Bromley. This did not last and in 1871 he was working as timekeeper in the East End of London, in 1881 as a labourer in Broughton, Huntingdonshire, and in 1891 as a watchman back in the East End.

Beard was not the only local man to be punished for theft from the Fussells. In April 1827 Joseph Smith was sentenced to 14 years' transportation to Australia for "stealing iron at Mells".[18] Ten years later, the Michael Long who received the letter revealing William Jesse's crime suffered the same fate. Michael was the eldest of eight children of a Mells handloom weaver, Isaac Long. Isaac and another local man, William Cook, were tried at the Wells Lammas Assizes in August 1836 on the charge of stealing 18 pounds of leather. Having three previous convictions for poaching, he was sentenced to death, although this was commuted to 14 years' transportation. In October of the following year Michael, aged 19, appeared at the Wells Quarter Sessions. The first charge against him was that he had assisted John Ruddock to sell goods stolen from the factory of Mr Thomas Fussell of Mells - these comprising two large bearing brasses and a single lead pipe. The second charge was that he had stolen lead from the roof of the coach house of Thomas Strangeways Horner of Mells Park. Unfortunately for Michael, he had previous convictions for stealing a goose and poaching, and so he too was sentenced to be transported for 14 years.

Michael Long was sent to Tasmania, where he proved a far from model prisoner. In May 1838 he was reprimanded for insolence, in October 1839 he was given 36 lashes for disobedience, in April 1840 he served three months hard labour in chains for absence without leave, and in February 1841 he was given nine days solitary confinement for drunkenness. Despite his poor record, he was granted a ticket of leave in 1846 and a conditional pardon in 1849.[19] Once free, he moved to Victoria, joining the Australian Gold Rush of 1851 and working as a miner at Creswick, near Ballarat, where he died of dysentery in April 1866. He left behind a wife, Elizabeth, who bore him seven children, five of whom survived childhood.

Michael's mother Sarah continued to live in Mells, where she supported her family by working as a washerwoman. His father Isaac arrived in Australia in February 1837 and in August was transferred to Port Macquarie, where he worked as an assistant to the washermen until his death three years later, being remembered at his inquest as a quiet and well-behaved man. In the letter Sarah Long wrote to her son in 1859, she seems to have been unaware that her husband had been dead for nearly 20 years. By then she was living with her daughter Elizabeth Litman, also a washerwoman, and son-in-law Henry, an agricultural labourer.

The message for Joe Wise in the letter to Michael Long that "trade at the Mills is rather slacker than when he left" indicates that the firm was suffering from the effects of a decline in business as well as from the losses caused by William Jesse's embezzlement. The Joe Wise would appear to be Joseph Wise, a former Fussell employee, who is described in the 1851 census as a journeyman edge-tool maker. The fact that the letter also passes on the news that James Fussell "has had the management of it for nearly three years" suggests that Joseph left the village before the death of Thomas Fussell in 1855.

Vobster and Coal Barton Collieries

One of the most important collaborations between Thomas and John Fussell was the partnership they established to work collieries at Vobster and at Coal Barton in nearby Coleford. By the time the Fussell brothers became involved in the coal industry, the older southern coalfield - sometimes referred to as the Mendip Collieries - was already less important than a newer field to the north that had been developing around Radstock since the 1760s.

Writing in 1795, John Billingsley observed that "The southern district is on a more limited scale of working", employing 500-600 men and boys. By the first decade of the 19th century there were 10 pits in the area, four of which were at or near Vobster.[1] He estimated the output of pits at only 800-1,000 tons a week and reported that the profits for their operators were "very trifling, if any, owing to the consumption of timber and expense of drawing water".[2] Billingsley also stated that Vobster coal sold for less than coal from the pits to the north because it was softer and did not travel so well.

The expansion of the industry in the early 17th century had had a serious effect on the state of the roads in the area, the inhabitants of Stoke St Michael complaining in 1618 "that of late by reason of many 'colemines' which are set to work in the country there near adjoining, there is so much travelling that way that the highways there are much in decay and grown very founderous".[3] The building of turnpike roads in the second half of the 18th century improved the situation, although these were greatly resented by the local miners, who made a number of attacks on the gates and keepers' cottages. One of the last of these occurred on the road of the Buckland Trust between Vobster and Mells in July 1831, when a group of 40 miners tore down both the gate and wooden toll house. The proposed Dorset and Somerset Canal seemed to offer a solution to the coalfield's transport problems but hopes were dashed when the project was abandoned in 1803.[4]

The geology of the area was also against the local pits. Writing in 1858, George Greenwell noted the "remarkable contortions of the seams" in the area,[5] while in 1869 James McMurtrie observed there was an "amount of confusion and distortion that literally baffles description".[6] Moreover, the pits were prone to both flooding and firedamp, McMurtrie declaring that they were "as fiery as any in England". John

The collieries and coal seams of the Nettlebridge Valley.

Stoke Bottom

Stratton Moor

Barlake

Duck's Nest

Holcombe

Dorset & Somerset Canal

Edford

Whitehole

Ham

Coal Barton

Coleford

Moons

Ringing

MacIntosh

Goodeaves

Main ?

Perrink ?

Dungy Drift

Luckington Fault

Vobster Breach

Newbury

Old Newbury

Soho Toll Gates

New Vobster

Vobster

Catch Ground

Dungy Drift

Melcombe Wood

Old Vobster

Old Tor

Bilboa

Water Engine

Main

Perrink

Great Course

Mells

Mells Park

Key

⋯	Coal Seam
▶	Colliery for which there is documentary evidence
△	Colliery for which there is archaeological evidence

Anstie, writing in 1873, thought it was "marvellous that works can be carried on here under the united disadvantages of broken strata and dangerous firedamp".[7]

From the miners' point of view, firedamp was the greatest danger – suffocation, or death resulting from the ignition of gas, being the greatest causes of fatalities underground in the pits in the area. One of the worst disasters occurred at Vobster Colliery in September 1791, when an explosion led to the deaths of 11 men and boys.[8] Seven of the dead were buried in Mells churchyard, the parish register recording "Colliers burnt to death at Vobster Coalworks" against their names.[9] Eleven years later a similar tragedy involving a man and four boys occurred at nearby Coleford; the report on it stated, "No less than 17 persons have lost their lives there in this manner, within these few years".[10]

The largest and most costly problem for the mine owners, however, was that of keeping their workings free of water, particularly in pits in the valley bottoms. By the early 17th century waterwheel-powered pumps were used to drain collieries in the area, a document of 1610 recording that miners at Holmes in Stratton-on-the-Fosse had "latelie found meanes with much facilitie to exhaust the water…namelie with pumpes, whose wheeles are moved by fall of a stream conducted to the same".[11] Writing later in the century, James Twyford of Kilmersdon said a Mr Salmon had drained his coalworks on Vobster Marsh using four mills - "two at the east end and two at the west end".[12] Unfortunately, these proved inadequate to the task, Twyford reporting "the water being too great the mills could not discharge, and so Mr Sallmon that had a lease for lives, on it was forced to quit the works".[13] The Mr Salmon in question was John Salmon, who was still leasing Vobster coalworks in May 1656 when one of his colliers, Morgan Wilcox, was accused of stealing hay. Wilcox, whose miner's cap had been found in the hay, defended himself by saying that "working for John Salmon in the coal worke at Vobsters Marsh, he did weare a cap of his master's providing as other workmen did, and did leave the cap every night in the coalhouse as the manner is".[14]

In the 1760s the leat that had supplied the water to Salmon's mills was extended down the valley to drain a new "coalwork of Mr Horners" on Vobster Marsh. In the same period the Horners' neighbours, the Knatchbulls, constructed a leat on the north side of the stream to drain a new colliery on their land. Water power continued to be widely used in the Mells valley, even after steam pumps were introduced into pits to the north during the mid 18th century. The output of the collieries was insufficient to warrant the expense of installing and running steam-driven pumps.

In 1809 Colonel Thomas Horner commissioned Richard Perkins of Oakhill to prepare a report on the future prospects of the Vobster Collieries. Perkins was manager of, and a partner in, Old Rock Colliery near Benter. Although a surgeon by profession, he had more than 20 years' experience in the coal industry and provided information to John Billingsley for his *General View of the Agriculture of the County of Somerset* of 1797. Perkins was also a committee member of the Somersetshire Coal Canal and in the summer of 1794 had accompanied William 'Strata' Smith, the father of English geology, on a two-month fact-finding tour of England looking at how others were building canals. There is no evidence that Smith shared his theory of stratigraphy with Perkins and their companion Sambourne Palmer, possibly because he sensed they had no interest in his ideas. For he later recalled: "Though I was continually talking rocks and other strata, they seemed not desirous of knowing the guiding principles."[15]

The report Perkins submitted to Horner was cautious and seems to have been designed to dissuade him from embarking on future ventures.[16] Considering the possibility of resuming activity in Vobster Marsh, he pointed out the main problem was, as ever, that of removing water from abandoned and flooded workings. This was exacerbated, he argued, by the Horners' former workings on the south side of the stream being interconnected with those of the Knatchbulls to the north, which meant that any pumps would have to drain both workings before the coal could be worked. The depth of these old pits and quantity of water in them required, in his opinion, "an extent of capital exceeding all probability of future reimbursement". In Upper Vobster, Perkins saw the problems as the severe faulting of the coal and the exhaustion of workable reserves. He described the former Old Tor Work to the north of the Vobster Inn as badly faulted and worked out, concluding that "nothing remains but to observe that no future working can be resumed by Col. Horner or his successors without a total loss of the capital thus applied". He was equally pessimistic about the future of the existing works at Bilboa in Upper Vobster (sometimes referred to as Bilboa Ketch), which had been sunk following the granting of a lease in March 1803 to a partnership managed by Samuel Button of Vobster.

> In no coal land within my experience have the veins been found more irregular or difficult to work; yet notwithstanding, under the management of Samuel Button, they have been effectually tried, and the coal got in every probable direction, except in the instance of a very recent appearance of coal, which may occupy a few months in working, when the whole may be considered as radically exhausted, so that no attempt to renew working hereafter in this quarter can be made with the least prospect of success.[17]

The geologists Buckland and Conybeare later confirmed Perkins's view of the extreme irregularity of the seams at Bilboa, declaring that "the flexures are so great as to twist the strata like a letter Z, so that the same coal-seam is thrice cut through by the same perpendicular shaft".[18]

The only area where Perkins saw any serious opportunity for reward was in the land to the north of the existing workings. The Pagets' collieries in neighbouring Babington were then working the Great Course and Firestone seams, which he reported "prove well and must yield considerable profit, with every reasonable assurance of their supporting a permanent work".[19] He believed it possible these extended under Horner land and thought it might be worth making a trial excavation. Yet even here he was cautious, refusing to make any assessment of the likely cost of a trial, and declaring: "The great advances of wages, and every article of coal pit use being either doubled or trebled within the last twenty years, sets all calculation at defiance".[20] He also warned Colonel Horner against taking the advice of working colliers, whose "want of judgement and defect of memory" had, he claimed, resulted in £10,000 being sunk into the collieries in the area.

Five years after Perkins declared Bilboa Colliery to be worked out, Samuel Button and his partners were still operating it, although the end finally appeared to be in sight. In February 1814 the colliery's bailiff, Thomas Denning, resigned because he thought the pit was finished. Hearing of this, a young miner from Babington called Tradua Plummer presented himself to Button and asked for the chance to prove there was still coal to be won.[21] Button agreed, appointing him bailiff, and Tradua set about finding new coal.

> I well remember it was my study by night and by day were to seek and how to proceed. I had not long tried before I was favoured (though amidst the laughs and jeers of all by whom it was surrounded) by finding a small portion of coal. I still keep [sic] trying and shortly discovered another quantity which lasted for not only a fortnight but for several years I remember we landed on an average about 240 bushells per day [12 tons] for the space of seven years.[22]

The following month Samuel Button, ignoring Perkins's advice, began to sink a new pit - Vobster Marsh Colliery - to the south-west of the Vobster Inn. As Perkins predicted, the work of the sinkers was made difficult by water and the presence of abandoned workings, referred to by Tradua Plummer as "Old Men Broken". In 1815, shortly before the pit went into production, Tradua encountered the other major hazard - firedamp.

> I met with a very bad accident about 12 months after its commencement just as the pit was down and the pump put in I went down to examine the water having

no thought of any gass [sic] . . . I caught it a fire in the pit as I was riding down
and should have been burn to death had it not been for the clothing I had on.[23]

The pumps at the new pit were driven by a large waterwheel, which was supplied
with water by extending the 17th century leat that had formerly driven Downs
Mill, Everett's edge-tool works and the Horners' mid 18th century coalworks. The
watercourse, traces of which are still visible today, was now almost one mile long and
came to be known locally as the Nettle Canal.

The colliery continued in production for at least 25 years and in March 1834 Mells
Select Vestry resolved that "the rate charged on Samuel Button & Co as proprietors of
Vobster Marsh Colliery be increased from 2/6 to 5/-".[24] In 1837 Samuel Button died,
leaving his share in the colliery to his sons Isaac and James. For a few months the
concern was operated by the Buttons and Thomas Horler of Stoneash Farm, Mells,
but by March 1838 had passed into the hands of John and Thomas Fussell.

Soon after taking over Vobster colliery, the brothers began the expensive business of
sinking a new pit to the north-west of the existing one. This was conceived on a more
ambitious scale than its predecessors, the shaft being sunk to an initial depth of 360
feet, but then deepened to 600 feet and, ultimately, to 912 feet. The brothers are likely
to have invested in excess of £1,000 in the development of this pit before a significant
quantity of saleable coal was landed. Sinking the shaft to 360 feet alone would have
required an outlay of around £500, added to which were the costs of equipping the pit
with pumps and winding gear, and of driving headings to the south to reach workable
coal. Costs were kept down by using water rather than steam to power the pumps,
since a steam engine would have cost in excess of £1,000 to buy and install.[25]

The Fussells entrusted the running of the colliery to William Brice of Kilmersdon,
the manager of their colliery at Coal Barton. A new foreman was also appointed, the
post being given to Abraham Hamblin, who was also from Kilmersdon and may well
have been chosen by Brice.[26] Abraham had been working at Coal Barton for at least a
decade, for in 1829 the poor rate lists him as living in one of the company's cottages
close to the pit. By 1840 he had moved to Vobster, the tithe award listing him as living
in a cottage next to the pit. In his will, made in 1847, he was still described as foreman
of the coal works.[27]

The way in which Vobster Colliery was worked at this time was determined by two
factors. The first was that the coal on the north side of the Mells Stream was owned
by the Knatchbull family and could not be touched. The second was a knowledge, or
rather belief, that the Main and Perrink seams to the south were sloping at a steep
angle, having been thrust upwards when the Mendip Hills were formed. With these

Above: the site of Vobster Colliery, sunk in 1814 by Samuel Button and latter operated by John and Thomas Fussell.
Below: Vobster Colliery as shown on a map of Mells of c.1830 (reproduced by kind permission of the Earl of Oxford and Asquith).

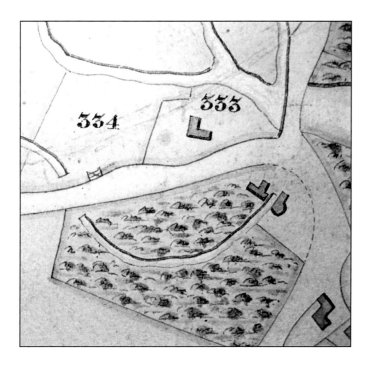

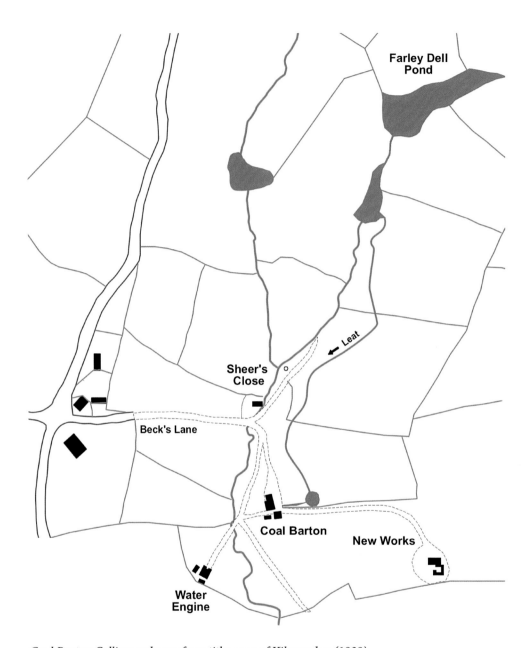

Coal Barton Colliery redrawn from tithe map of Kilmersdon (1839).

considerations in mind, the approach taken was to sink the shaft through the old workings to an initial depth of 360ft and then drive a level until the coal was reached. Tradua later described how at 120 feet they cut through the Main Coal, after which extraction began. The coal seams, or veins as they were locally known, were followed to the west for 1,080 feet - the furthest practical distance to work them. The shaft was then deepened and a new tunnel driven to the south to meet the same coal seam lower down and closer to the shaft. When Tradua wrote his memoirs in 1850 he said this process had been carried out three times and the shaft had reached 600ft. At the southern end of the lowest of these levels a cut was made down which found the Perrink seam. Some had been sceptical about the chances of finding coal at this depth and Tradua recalled "I remember being asked by John Fussell Esq. if I thought there was any coals there my reply was I have no doubt of it".[28] Tradua's confidence was justified and the pit would eventually be sunk to just over 900 feet, a depth that would have seemed inconceivable to local miners of earlier generations.

Around the same time that the Fussell brothers leased Vobster Colliery, they also took over Coal Barton Colliery in Coleford. John Fussell already had business interests in that village, owning a quarry near the colliery and sitting on the committee set up to oversee the building of Coleford church. In 1829 the committee noted, "Rough stone may be purchased from a quarry close to the aqueduct belonging to Mr Fussell, provided that sufficient stone cannot be found on the spot".[29]

Coal Barton Colliery was situated to the north-west of Coleford village, occupying an extensive area of land that included Sheer's Close and Bullocks Hill, both of which had long histories of coal mining. In 1489 the manor court of Kilmersdon commanded that the "colpitt called Bullocke-hill, which is deep and dangerous" should be filled in.[30] Almost a century later in 1571 the partnership of John Hobbs, Richard Spark, John Sheppard and Richard Purle were working "one Cole Mynd upon the hill called bullock hill" for which they paid a rent of 40s.[31] In the late 17th century James Twyford, then lord of the manor, reported the workings at nearby Sheer's Close were "all wrought out and dammed up" but a new works had been started at Bullock's Close.[32] By the early 19th century the land and mineral rights were owned by the Jolliffes of Ammerdown.

The survey drawings for the first Ordnance Survey map of the area, made around 1810, show it as an extensive colliery with three shafts. Around that time Charles Tucker, the local schoolmaster, resigned his post and went to Coal Barton Colliery as "manager and clerk". A local man, born in Kilmersdon in 1771, Tucker was remembered by one of his pupils, Benjamin Padfield, as "a good Christian man, of very even temper".[33] By this period coal mining was an important industry in the area, the Greenwoods noting that in 1821 65% of families in the parish were classified as being engaged in neither agriculture nor trade and that "a considerable proportion" of this group "is employed in the coal mines, which has occasioned a great increase in the population of the parish".[34] In 1829 the colliery was rated at £129, and by 1839 comprised four shafts: Coal Barton, Sheer's Close, Water Engine Barton, and Coal Barton New Work.[35]

Water was also a problem at Coal Barton, and by 1810 the colliery was drained by a water-powered pump, the leat and ponds for which are shown on the drawings for the first Ordnance Survey map. The tithe map of Kilmersdon of 1839 also shows them, the larger of the ponds being called Farley Dell Pond. The device used to raise the water was later described in *A Rudimentary Treatise on Coal and Coal Mining*, published in 1869.

> A singular pumping machine . . . was still, in 1857, to be seen at the little colliery at Coal Barton where 50 fathoms [300 feet] length of 8 inch pumps were worked by a fall of water passing 26 yards down a pit, and utilised upon a chain with buckets of sheet iron lapping over wheels above and below.[36]

This description closely matches that of the water-powered pump patented by John's father James in 1803 - raising the possibility that it was not simply a theoretical exercise. In his patent James declared that the fall of water should be at least 50 feet, and at Coal Barton it was 72 feet. It is not clear where the adit that carried away the water came out, since the valley in which the colliery was situated has insufficient depth to allow for a tunnel of this depth. One possibility is that it was driven through to the Mells valley to the south, the mouth of such an adit being visible on the stream side close to Hittite Bridge near Ham.

In working the colliery, it was necessary to contend with contorted coal seams, Anstie writing later that the shafts at Coal Barton provided the best illustration of the reversal of the coal measures that occurred in the area.

> The coals met with in the north pit [Sheer's Close] dip south at an angle of 35°; at the middle pit [Coal Barton], the dip has increased to 45°and from this point the increase was so rapid that before reaching the south pit the seams were actually vertical, and the author was informed that the coals were brought up by means of fifty nine-feet ladders, placed in the workings one below another.[37]

In April 1841 "Messrs Fussell and Co. Coal Barton and Vobster Collieries" were inspected by the Children's Employment Commission. The inspector's report noted that they employed 100 hands, half of whom were under 15. Giving evidence to the Commission, William Brice, described as "clerk and manager", testified that among the workforce "there are some at seven and under" and "many of the adult colliers state that they began work between six and seven".[38] Brice himself had worked at Coal Barton for 16 years, and had "succeeded his uncle as manager of these coalworks".[39] Brice was born in Kilmersdon in 1812 and so must have started work at the colliery around the age of 13.[40]

Brice said no girls were employed and the youngest boys were "employed in opening and shutting doors, which direct the current of air, and keep the passages free of firedamp". The older boys hauled the coal along the passageways, while the men hewed the coal. On the positive side, the inspector thought the miners were better paid than most working men in the area and most could read and write. The colliers went below at 6am and returned to the surface between 3 and 4pm, a relatively short working day for the period. On the negative side, working conditions were said to be cramped and dangerous, the inspector reporting that the presence of gas made them unhealthy pits to work in. Brice thought the men generally strong and healthy unless they worked in the presence of firedamp, in which case they tended "to get asthmatical, from the gas and foul air" and "commonly get broken in their health about 40 or 45 years of age, and then are not a long-lived race". The inspector also noted the high risk of explosions. "About six months ago there were seven persons burnt in one day at Vobster works, and one of them died from the effects of this accident. About the same time, at Coal Barton, there were five persons injured in the same way, and one of them died." Ten years later there was another explosion at the pit, as the *Bath Chronicle* reported on 31 October 1850.

> On Wednesday morning in last week, soon after the workmen had descended the shaft, at Coal Barton Colliery near Mells, one of the men foolishly carried a lighted candle, instead of a Davy Lamp, into a part of the workings where a quantity of gas had accumulated, and thereby caused an explosion. Four boys and two men were severely burnt. They were got up out of the mine with all despatch, and every attention paid to them by the bailiff and others, and it is thought they will recover.[41]

The use of candles in such circumstances was very dangerous, although even the Davy lamps in use in the Fussell pits were not as safe as they might have been. William Fairley, who managed Vobster Colliery in the early 1860s, recalled it being "as fiery a hole as a miner ever put his head into". Writing later in that decade, he said that when he came to Vobster as manager in 1861 he found that "not one of the lamps then in use was provided with a lock".[42] Fairley was, in fact, highly critical of the Davy lamp, recalling in a letter of 1886 how at Vobster he "had three men burnt owing to an explosion occurring with the Davy, and ever since that I have looked with suspicion on that miserable thing".[43]

In December 1847 John Fussell of Nunney took a 10-year lease from the Reverend John Horner to survey and work coal in the valley from Vobster towards Coleford.

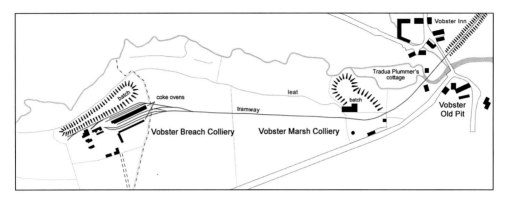

Vobster and Breach collieries in 1865.

By this time his partnership with his brother Thomas appears to have ended and it is significant that in 1850 Tradua Plummer referred to him as "my present respected master"[44]. Following John's death in 1853, his "leasehold coalworks" passed into the hands of the trustees of his will, who were empowered to run them and renew the leases at their discretion. Coal Barton Colliery appears to have closed in 1857, being included in the list of Somerset collieries working in 1856 but absent from that of the following year. The management of both pits remained in the hands of William Brice, who in 1851 was described as "Clerk of Coal Barton Colliery" and living on Kilmersdon Common close to the pit. Following its closure, he seems to have moved to Vobster, for in 1858 his son Seward, then at school, is listed as living at "Vobster Coal Works".[45] John Fussell's trustees continued to operate Vobster Colliery until the summer of 1859, when they put it up for sale by auction along with his house, Nunney Court and the Nunney works.[46]

The sale particulars reveal that the trustees had taken out a new 10-year lease on the colliery in July 1858, under the terms of which they were permitted to work the coal under 500 acres of land in Mells, Leigh-on-Mendip and Coleford in return for a rent of £100 and 30 tons of coal to the lessor, the Reverend John Horner. The lot included "all the Steam Engines, Whimseys, Machinery, Working Gear, Tram Roads, Tools, and Implements . . . and also, the Weighing Engine, Counting-House, Cottage, Garden, Stables, Sheds, Coke Pits, and other outbuildings, Wagons, Cart Horses, and Stores of all sorts". From this it can be seen that steam power was now being used and that coal was being coked on site. The sale particulars provide further indications of the scale on which the colliery was by then working, stating there were "upwards of 100 men in regular employ at the Works" - a significant increase on its size in 1841 when the combined workforces of Coal Barton and Vobster had been 120. Similarly, the output was said to be about 250 tons of coal a week compared to approximately 90 tons in the late 1830s. Interested parties were asked to contact the auctioneer, Charles

Harding & Son, or the office of Frederick Dowding in Bath.

The auction took place in August but no bids were made and it was not sold. The executors continued their efforts to dispose of the colliery and finally succeeded in 1860, when it was bought by a company headed by Stephen Steeds of Norton Down, Midsomer Norton. Born in Kilmersdon in 1817, Steeds was the son of a butcher, a trade he also followed for some years. In 1851 he was living in Frome and described as a butcher and farmer, but by 1854 he had moved to Norton Down and was variously described as "farmer" and "gentleman". In this period he became closely associated with local coal proprietor Charles Hollwey, becoming a partner in the firm of Hollwey & Co. In 1856 his widowed sister Martha married Thomas Lee Pilditch, a railway contractor from Plymouth who had come to Frome in 1847 when he was awarded a contract to work on that section of the Wiltshire, Somerset and Weymouth Railway. Pilditch also became a business associate of Steeds and it is possible that both men were partners in the Vobster venture.

The change of ownership from the Fussells to Steeds was marked by a dinner held for the colliers and their families at the beginning of February. The event, possibly the largest ever held in the village of Vobster, was attended by 820 men, women and children. The *East Somerset Telegraph* reported that the dinner took place in a room "upwards of 78 feet in length, used to store coke, but had been lately fitted up for the purpose, with temporary tables and forms".[47] The host for the evening was a Mr Vincent of the firm of Dowding & Burne, which had organised the event. Vincent explained that the reason the executors were selling the colliery and other properties and businesses "was not because they did not pay, but certain family affairs rendered it necessary that the property of the late John Fussell should be brought into a narrower compass, in order that the exact amount of income which the estate produced should be ascertained". He described the late John Fussell as "kind, liberal-hearted gentleman, and was happy to say that he knew some of the present proprietors, and believed them to be equally liberal, and kind".

The manager appointed by the new company, William Fairley, also addressed the guests, saying that "he stood there as the representative of Mr Steeds, who was the principal owner". He proposed the health of the outgoing manager, William Brice, which was given to the accompaniment of "musical honours". Brice had managed Vobster Colliery for more than two decades and been in the coal industry for more than 35 years. However he was not ready to retire and by 1861 was once more living on Kilmersdon Common and working as the managing partner of a new mining venture at nearby Edford. The Geological Survey's Mineral Statistics for 1860 record the partnership of Fussell, Walters and Brice was operating two collieries – Edford and Edford New Pit. The partnership ran the colliery until 1879 and in 1880 it passed into the hands of Howard Ritler, who operated it until the winding-up of that

Reconstruction of coke ovens at Breach Colliery, Vobster.

company in 1913.[48] By 1881 William Brice, now aged 69, had retired and was living at Newnham in Gloucestershire, describing himself in the census of that year as "Late Colliery Proprietor". Following his success in the Oxford examination, William's son Seward became an assistant at Shepton Mallet Grammar School before going on to study law in London. In the 1860s he wrote a book on the Somerset coalfield and in November 1871 was called to the bar.

The interest of Steeds and his partners in working coal in the Vobster area was kindled by two factors. One was the opening of the railway from Frome to Radstock in 1854 (which passed within two miles of Vobster Colliery), and the second was the discovery of large deposits of iron ore in nearby Wiltshire at Seend and Westbury. In 1856 around 10,000 tons of ore were raised at Seend, a local paper reporting that it had caused a stir in the mining world "and is creating among the proprietors of land there the pleasing excitement of finding the value of their property suddenly converted from hundreds to thousands of pounds". In 1857 the Great Western Iron Ore, Smelting and Coal Company was established to produce iron at Seend but this went into liquidation in 1859. Another firm took over the works and the first furnace went into blast in January 1860. At nearby Westbury an ironworks was erected next to the railway station, work commencing in 1857. The promoters of the Westbury venture included Charles Hollwey, Thomas Pilditch and Stephen Steeds - men who were well aware that Vobster was now a convenient source of the coke and limestone

Remains of coke ovens at site of Breach Colliery.

needed for operating their blast furnaces. In 1858 the Westbury company began sinking Newbury Colliery in Babington, the proprietors having also leased land from the Reverend John Horner on which to lay a broad-gauge mineral railway to link their new pit to the Frome to Radstock line.

There were high hopes for the new venture at Westbury, the 1857 report of the Geological Survey reporting that it was expected that Messrs. Greenwell & Co's furnaces at Westbury would soon be in blast. The following April William Henry Fox Talbot, the pioneer of photography and owner of Lacock Abbey, wrote enthusiastically, "They seem to be going on with spirit at Westbury so that the value of Wiltshire iron will soon be tested on a sufficient scale".[49] Fox Talbot, encouraged by the finds at Westbury and Seend, searched for and found iron ore on his property and hoped to exploit it. The optimism was short-lived, however. Fox Talbot's agent, West Audry, wrote to him in August:

> We regret to have to state that the tower furnaces erected for smelting the iron ore having cracked so much as to be rendered useless, they will have to be pulled down and re-built. The cracking has arisen from using the furnaces before they were sufficiently dried and seasoned to the heat. The delay in the operations of the company during the re-building, will be more serious than the cost of their re-erection.[50]

It was a serious blow and when the ironworks finally went into production in 1860 only one of the two furnaces was in blast.[51] The problems at Westbury may well have delayed the development of the company's pit at Newbury, since the work on the Newbury railway does not seem to have begun until 1861. An entry in the minutes of the Mells Vestry on 26 September 1861 records that "Messrs. Mogg, Holway [Hollwey], Greenwell, Pilditch attended the meeting on behalf of the Westbury Iron Company" to discuss how the parish roads "would be affected by the railroad now being made by the said company".[52]

Within weeks of buying Vobster Colliery Stephen Steeds set to work sinking a new colliery at Vobster Breach, 750 yards west of the old Fussell pit. It was sunk because the existing one had worked as much of the Main Coal and Perrink seams as possible, and a new shaft was needed to follow the coal westward and also to work coal on the north side of the Mells Stream under the lands of the Jolliffe family. Work on the shaft began on 23 April 1860 and on 27 May 1861 it made a connection at 600 feet with a branch driven from the old pit so that all coal could be raised at the new colliery. Breach Colliery was served by a narrow-gauge tramway, which ran across Vobster Marsh to Lower Vobster, up a rope-hauled incline to the abandoned Dorset and Somerset Canal, and then on the level to a coal depot on the site of the former Bilboa Colliery and to the Newbury railway.

In April 1862 the surveyor for the parish of Mells, William Fussell, son of John Fussell of the Upper Works at Mells, was asked to measure the recently completed Newbury railway and also "the tramway made by the Vobster Coal Company".[53] The tramway was clearly in operation in 1862 because Mells Vestry received complaints about level crossing gates being left open at both Upper and Lower Vobster in that year. The new tramway ran close to the front door of Tradua Plummer's cottage (now Willow Cottage). Tradua was by then retired and 75-years-old, a good age for a miner who had spent his life in a succession of unhealthy and dangerous pits.

Once Breach Colliery was completed and linked underground to the old pit, coal winding at the latter ceased. Breach was in the parish of Leigh-on-Mendip and so in March 1863 Fairley attended a meeting of Mells Vestry to ask "that the Vobster Colliery be struck out of the rate altogether as no coal was being drawn from the parish". Mells was not, however, going to let the company get away with paying no rates, resolving in March 1864 that "the Vobster Coal Company be rated on the tramway £37-10-0 p. ann. in addition to the sum heretofore charged".[54] By then coal was being raised by steam winders, although the pumps at the old pit continued to be water-powered. As late as February 1868 a new waterwheel was purchased from Paulton Foundry, making Vobster the last colliery in the coalfield to be drained by this means.

William Fairley did not stay long at Vobster Colliery. He resigned as manager in 1864 and went on to manage a number of other collieries, including ones in the Dortmund area of Germany. His successor at Vobster was William Beachim, the son of Stephen Steeds's late brother-in-law, Zebedee Beachim of Lower Vobster.[55] According to Richard White, who was also related by marriage to the Steeds family, William had begun his career in the coal industry when he became an engine driver at Newbury Colliery and ended it owning a number of collieries, changing his name along the way to William Beachim Beauchamp. His son, Colonel Sir Frank Beauchamp, Bart, CBE, JP, went on to take the family business into a dominant position within the Somerset coalfield in the decades before its nationalisation in 1947.

In 1864 Stephen Steeds, in partnership with W.B. Naish, began work on a new colliery to the north of the abandoned Bilboa pit. In October 1864 William Beachim invited tenders for sinking and walling a new pit,[56] and the following February the company advertised for 20 sinkers and a blacksmith to sharpen their tools.[57] Mells Colliery, as the new pit was known, was sunk to work the area Perkins had thought might repay exploration in his report of 1809. In the event, the amount of coal found was less than expected and in 1871 the pit was described as "unpromising".[58] With the opening of Mells Colliery the name of the business was changed to the Vobster and Mells Coal Company.

By 1865 coke making at Vobster had been transferred from the old pit to the Breach Colliery. Two batteries of coke ovens were built alongside the tramway and within a few years most of the coal raised was converted into coke on site. Turning the coal into coke at the colliery made good economic sense, since Vobster coal did not travel well and coke fetched a higher price. Between February 1869 and December 1874, coke accounted for no less than 68% of the output of the colliery and 77% of its sales. It is likely the ovens were built to supply coke to the Wiltshire blast furnaces. In November 1866 an agreement was reached with the Wiltshire Iron Company at Seend under the terms of which "Mr. Steeds, on behalf of Hollwey and Co. and the Vobster Coal Company, in Somersetshire (being a partner in both firms), agreed to supply as much coke as was needed for the maintenance of the furnaces at Seend".[59] Unfortunately, an order for the winding-up of the Seend concern was made in November 1866. However, this was not the end of Steeds's involvement with Seend, for at some point he took a half-share in the iron mines there. The Vobster Coal Company also seems to have continued supplying coke to Seend, for in 1874 it contributed 2s 6d to the village school.[60]

In the mid 1860s the prospects for the coal industry around Vobster seemed promising. The parliamentary session 1865-66 saw a proposal for an extension of the Bristol and North Somerset Railway, which included a line along the Nettlebridge Valley from Mells Station to Old Down. This would have passed close to Breach Colliery, thereby reducing the company's transport costs significantly. Moreover, in

February 1865 it was reported that workmen from the Westbury Ironworks were conducting trial excavations for iron ore in Ham Wood to the north of Shepton Mallet. The *Trowbridge Chronicle* was enthusiastic about the venture, claiming to have heard "there is a very rich deposit there, very pure in quality and rich in metal" and that around 100 tons were to be "sent off in the present week to Westbury Ironworks for the purpose of testing the quality".[61] In December the following year the *East Somerset Telegraph* announced that iron ore had been discovered on the land of the Reverend J G C Fussell at Wadbury. Haematite is visible in exposed rock faces around the village of Mells, though it is not clear what induced James Fussell to conduct trial excavations on his father's former estate and what the outcome was.[62] There is surviving evidence of exploratory mining on the south side of the Mells Stream at Wadbury in the form of an adit on the manganese haematite vein, although whether this was connected with James Fussell's activities is not known.

The combination of the proposed railway and an enlarged coal industry, together with the possibility of the existence of large quantities of iron ore, raised the possibility that the area might be industrialised. There was even talk of blast furnaces being erected at Coleford and Shepton Mallet. In the event, the railway was not built and the amount of iron ore found was insufficient to be worth working on a commercial scale. Other trial excavations in the area at Gurney Slade and near Emborough had also proved abortive, as did a new scheme to build a railway down the Nettlebridge valley in 1872. In his 1873 book on the coalfields of Gloucestershire and Somersetshire, John Anstie was cautious about the prospects of finding workable quantities of iron, noting that although red haematite was found in a number of places in the area "the mode of occurrence renders the return of mining uncertain".[63] A number of iron mines were established in east Somerset in the years that followed, including two in Nunney; one operated by the Furzeham Iron Company between 1874 and 1878, and another which opened in 1880 involving George Bolus, then manager of Isaac Fussell & Co.

The early 1870s saw the growth of trade unionism in the coalfield following the establishment of the Somerset Miners' Association in 1872. Two years later the miners of the area went on strike when the colliery owners announced their intention to impose a wage reduction. The Vobster collieries joined the action but resumed work in May 1874 when agreement was reached that their wages would be reduced by only 6%, rather than the 10-15% imposed in the pits to the north. The reasons given for the smaller reduction were the problems of working the seams and "the fiery nature of the pits".[64]

The exact date of the closure of the Vobster and Mells collieries is not known, and it may be that they were run down over a number of years. In 1876 Breach Colliery paid no rates in Mells, although it still appeared in the Geological Survey's list of Somerset coal mines in 1877. However, it had finally closed by September 1878, when an advertisement was placed in the *Bristol Mercury* by the Horners' agents, Messrs Hippisley & Sons, offering the lease of the collieries, which were said to be "fitted with all necessary appliances, having a connection with the Great Western Railway, and yielding a valuable Smith's and Coking Coal".[65] A month later an advertisement was placed in the same paper announcing the plant and machinery at "Breach Pit, Old Pit and Mells Pit" were to be sold by auction.[66] The sale was held on 14th, 15th and 16th of January 1879 and was conducted by Messrs. Tribe, Clarke & Co. The first lots to be sold were those at the Breach Colliery, including a 28in horizontal winding engine with two nine-foot winding drums, an eight-inch donkey pumping engine and a nine-inch portable engine. A day later the plant and machinery at Vobster Old Pit was sold. These included a pair of 20in horizontal winding engines with 10ft drum, an old horse gin and drum, and the collieries' 18ft waterwheel with 24ft iron beams for working pumps. The catalogue shows that the Old Pit had a brickworks, probably for making firebricks, as the lots included a crushing and pug mill, brick machine and firebricks. On the same day the Bilboa Wharf was sold, this comprising weighbridges for road and rail wagons, 50 tons of rail, horse harnesses, and even an eight-day clock from the office. On the final day of the sale, Mells Pit and sidings were sold, the main lots being the colliery's pair of 24in horizontal winding engines and their 10ft drum. Attention was also drawn to a pair of pneumatic rock drills and a compressor, very modern equipment for the period.[67]

By the time the Vobster and Mells pits closed, Stephen Steeds was in serious financial difficulties. In 1876 he disposed of his share in the Seend iron mines to Richard Berridge, who had bought the Seend Ironworks in 1873.[68] By the following year his coal business - the Somerset Coal Company – owed the West of England Bank £33,394 and when that bank failed on 10 December 1878 the writing was on the wall. On 27 December the coal company went into liquidation, although as late as 1881 Stephen Steeds was still describing himself as a "Coal and Iron Master". Following the collapse of the West of England Bank, six of its directors were prosecuted by the Treasury for conspiracy and fraud for having misrepresented the bank's financial position in its official reports. It emerged in their trial that the Somerset Coal Company had provided security for only £25,000 of its debt.

The dismantling of the Breach and Old Pit marked the end of the coal mining industry in Lower Vobster - but not in the Manor of Mells. Mells Colliery reopened in 1909 and struggled on until it was finally abandoned in October 1943.

John Fussell & Sons

By 1860 the only Fussell business owned and managed by a member of the family was the Upper Works in Mells, which was still in the hands of John Fussell of Mells - a great-grandson of its founder. The 1851 census describes him as an edge-tool maker employing 23 men and boys, and a farmer of 50 acres employing 19 men and boys. John was very different to his cousins John and Thomas Fussell in that he seems to have been less ambitious for himself and his children. All the indications are that John Fussell was content to continue renting the works from the Horners and to train his sons up to follow him into the family business. Unlike his cousin Thomas, John Fussell played an active roll in the life of his village, serving as a churchwarden and member of the vestry and socialising with his fellow farmers. He also superintended the restoration of Mells parish church and worked with the Reverend John Horner to establish the Mells Friendly Society. Following his death in 1868, his contribution to the local community was recognised in the following tribute.

> The Vestry is unwilling to separate without recording their sense of the great loss they have sustained in the late John Fussell, for 33 years a respected and valued member of the Vestry, having during that time filled the office of Parish Churchwarden 29 years, and under whose judicious superintendence the late restoration of the church and churchyard have been so effectively carried out.[1]

John's younger sons, William and Walter, were also actively involved in local affairs. In March 1857 William was appointed assistant overseer to the parish and appears to have acquitted himself well enough for the Vestry to resolve to provide a testimonial to him on the "satisfactory manner" in which he had discharged his duties as surveyor in support of his application for the job of District Surveyor to the Frome Union.[2] He also acted as an enumerator for Mells when the census of 1861 was taken, and later became treasurer of the friendly society his father had helped to establish. Walter's talents lay in a different sphere, the Vestry agreeing in April 1865 to pay him £10 a year to play the organ in church, lead the singing, attend choir practices and teach the choir boys for one hour a week.[3] All three of John Fussell's sons spent time in the family's edge-tool business but it was the eldest, John Hounsell,

Rock House, Mells, the home of John Fussell of the Upper Works.

who was to be the only one to stay in it for his entire working life.

At the time of the 1861 census John Hounsell, then aged 32, was still in the family home of Rock House in Mells, but by 1863 was living at Nunney Court and had taken over the management of the Nunney works from James Fussell Payne. In that year John married Elizabeth Rendle of Beaminster, the entry in the parish register describing him as "manufacturer of Nunney", while the announcement of the wedding in the *Gentleman's Magazine* gives his place of residence as Nunney Court.[4] It is not known why James Fussell Payne gave up the management of the works so soon after buying a half-share in it, and whether he retained that share and became a sleeping

Photograph taken of the Nunney Works shortly after its closure (reproduced by kind permission of Charles Daniel).

partner. John Hounsell Fussell, or his father, had somehow acquired a share in the business. The half-share bought by James Fussell Payne was that inherited by John Fussell from his older brother James in 1846. James Fussell, in his turn, had inherited a "third part or share" from his father in 1832 - indicating a new partnership in two equal parts had been created between 1832 and 1845. Robin Atthill in *Old Mendip* said John Hounsell had bought his share from his cousin James George Curry Fussell, which, if true, is surprising because it is not clear how the latter might have come into possession of it, as it does not seem to have formed part of the estate left him by his uncle James in 1846.

Once in charge of the Nunney Works, John Hounsell set about revitalizing it, Cuzner's *Hand-Book to Froome-Selwood* of 1866 declaring that "considerable skill and energy have been imported into the firm, since the accession of Mr. John H. Fussell, of Nunney Court".[5] The firm appears to have been prospering and its reputation for quality tools remained high, Cuzner reflecting the commonly held opinion "that if you see a tool doing its work well, you are sure to find that it bears the name of 'Fussell' ".[6] Following the death of his father John in that year he also took over the running of the Upper Works at Mells, the 1871 census describing him

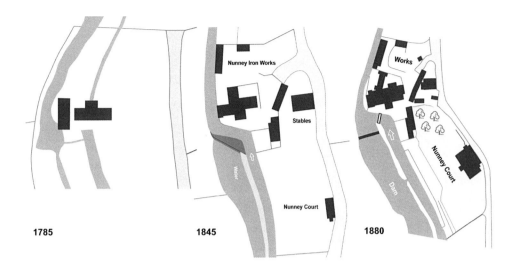

Phases in the development of the Nunney works.

as an employer of 50 Men and boys - the size of the combined workforce of the Upper Works and Nunney Works at the time of the 1861 census. It is also significant that *Morris's Directory* for 1872 uses identical descriptions for the products produced by the two works: "Spade, shovel & edge tool manufacturers". Nonetheless, business conditions for firms like Isaac Fussell & Co. were becoming more difficult, as they faced increased competition from the larger and better-resourced competitors of the industrial North and the West Midlands. John Hounsell Fussell seems to have invested in the Nunney business, a comparison of a plan of the works made in 1859 with the Ordnance Survey map of 1884 showing that at least one new range of workshops had been added in the intervening period. A photograph of the works taken around 1900 shows this building and also a tall brick chimney, suggesting that steam power had been introduced. Steam was also introduced at the Mells Upper Works in this period. In his article of 1934 Edward Tylee wrote "in the Upper Works were heavy hammers run by steam power", confirmed by the fact that the works had a chimney, which survives to this day. By the mid 1870s John Hounsell Fussell's businesses were seeking to keep up with their larger competitors by offering a range of cast steel tools, which would have required considerable investment in manufacturing equipment.

Following John Fussell's death, his second son, William Austin Fussell, continued to live in the family home at Rock House in Mells and took over the running of his father's farm. He also set up a small business making handles for spades and shovels,

Photographic self-portrait of William Austin Fussell (1830-1911).

which initially employed two men and one boy. In March 1873 he seems to have had ideas of expanding, placing an advertisement in the *Somerset & Wiltshire Journal* addressed to spade and shovel tree makers for "two or three good workmen, also a lad to learn the trade"[7] He must have been successful in recruiting the additional workers, for in 1881 he was described as an "edge tool handle maker" employing five men and two boys.

At this time the making of spade and shovel handles was a trade in its own right, the edge-tool manufacturers buying in the handles they needed. Handle making was one of a number of woodworking crafts practised in the area, others including the manufacture of hurdles, rakes, brooms, thatching spars and even hoops. Local woodland supplied the raw materials, the largest area being Asham Wood at Downhead. Asham was exploited in a systematic and sustainable way by local woodsmen who bid at auction to buy felled timber and for the right to work blocks of growing coppiced woodland, the auctions alternating between the Tadhill Inn at Downhead and the White Horse at Chantry. A surviving advertisement for one such auction in 1817 announced the sale of lots including "eleven acres of very Prime Wood, containing Hurdle Rods, Spar Gads & co. growing and standing in Asham Wood aforesaid, divided into seven lots and marked with red paint".[8]

The woodsmen lived in the surrounding villages of Chantry, Downhead and Leigh-on-Mendip. The Reverend William Michell of Chantry remembered them as independent-minded and self-reliant, "working on their own account, owing allegiance to no master". In matters of religion they were equally independent, described by Michell as "mostly Primitive Methodist with their own little chapel in existence years before the church was built".

The handles of many types of edge-tool were traditionally made from ash, its strength and elasticity making it the wood of choice. Other advantages of ash are that it is relatively fast growing for a hardwood tree and can be coppiced every few years to provide straight poles. Ash was also in demand for pit props, John Billingsley noting

A coppiced ash tree in Asham Wood. The wood was worked by local woodsmen who bid at auction for the right to work blocks of growing coppiced woodland.

the "more ash in these coppices the more valuable, as the poles are very saleable at the coalpits", and observing that the woods of Mells and Leigh "being near the coalworks are very valuable".[9] Evidence of the activities of the woodmen can still be seen in Asham Wood, grown-out ash stools showing where areas of managed coppice once existed.

By the 1870s the largest manufacturer of tool handles in the area were the Ashmans of Leigh, who are reputed to have made handles for the Fussells, and may also have supplied them to other shovel makers such as Coombs family at Doulting and the Steeds at Gurney Slade. A Fussell catalogue produced around 1890 includes a range of replacement tool handles, including ones for shovels at six shillings a dozen. These too are likely to have been bought in by the Fussells and sold on to the wholesalers at marked-up prices. The Fussells' businesses also benefited from the expansion of woodland crafts from the mid-18th century and met the increased demand for woodmen's tools by making a wide range of axes, billhooks and slashing hooks.

William Fussell may have set up his business with a view to supplying handles to the two works run by his older brother John, where spades and shovels were the main products. Demand would increase further in the 1880s when all the Fussell businesses came together in a single company and placed greater emphasis on the manufacture of spades and shovels. This latter development may, however, have worked against William, who now had to compete for orders with the Ashmans, whose Leigh timber

Photograph of the interior of William Austin Fussell's house at Weston-super-Mare. Enlargement and manipulation of these images has retrieved the only surviving portraits of what are almost certainly members of the Fussell family. Image 1 may be a photograph of his mother, while image 2 shows a lady in early 19th century costume who could be his grandmother. Among the photographic prints on the mantelpiece is a family group (3) which appears to include William (seated at the table).

yard had been expanded to include a steam-powered sawmill and was employing eight or nine men exclusively on the making of tool handles. William continued to make handles for a number of years but his business did not grow to meet increased demand. By 1881 he had diversified into selling garden furniture and equipment and in 1883 was described as "chemical manure and spade tree manufacturer".[10]

Following the death of his wife Tinal in 1888, William remarried and retired to Weston-super-Mare, his second wife, Annie, running a boarding house in Beaufort Road. William was a keen amateur photographer and at the turn of the century he sent a number of photographs to the Horners at Mells. These include an exterior view of his house in Weston, and two interiors that show pictures of what must be some of his Fussell ancestors. One of these, which is reflected in a mirror, may well be his mother Mary; another, which is a portrait in oils of a fashionably dressed lady in early 19th century costume, could be his grandmother. Although small and distorted by perspective and reflection, enlargement and manipulation of these images has retrieved the only surviving portraits of what are almost certainly members of the Fussell family. On the mantelpiece in one of the interior shots are a number of unframed pictures, one of which appears to be a view of the Upper Works at Mells; another shows a family group that includes an elderly man who is probably William himself. This is suggested by the similarity of his appearance to a self-portrait taken by William around this time, a reproduction of which is to be found in Robin Atthill's *Old Mendip*. William died in 1911 and the fate of the family portraits and his photograph collection is not known.

Two years after his father's death, the youngest of John Fussell's sons, Walter, also set up his own business. In 1870 he went into partnership with William Wise, a young edge-tool maker from Mells, and the two men leased the Stoke Lane Ironworks and traded under the name Fussell and Wise. It seems likely Walter provided the capital for the venture and William the technical skills. William Wise was himself the son of an edge-tool maker, also called William. Edge-tool making was in the family's blood: William Wise junior and his older brothers Joseph and Francis all followed their father into the works, while their sister Barbara married an edge-tool maker, Benjamin White.[11] William appears to have been intelligent and ambitious, his abilities coming to the attention of the Reverend James Fussell, who in 1866 enlisted his help in inventing an apparatus for teaching writing. The following year the two men were granted a patent for a scythe that was designed so that it could be adjusted "to suit the stature of the workman, the nature of the crop on which it is intended to operate, or other circumstances under which an alteration or temporary adjustment to the blade may be required".[12] It is not clear how successful the design was, although an adjustable scythe was still in the Fussell catalogue 20 years later.

In setting up the business, Walter Fussell had re-established the family's connection with Stoke Lane, a link that had been broken over a century before when his great-great-grandfather James moved his business to Mells. Interestingly, the partners set out not only to make edge-tools but also heavy agricultural equipment. In the

Photograph of the site of the Cook's Farm edge-tool works, Stoke St Michael, taken by Robin Atthill in the 1960s (archive of Downside School's archaeological society).

Somerset and Wiltshire Journal in October 1870 they advertised the products and services they were offering.

> New Scrap Iron made AXLE MOULDS and axles, Steeled Turned and Fitted to Boxes. PLOUGHS, HARROWS, and DRAGS, of the best Quality, made to order. TYRES and BONDS for WHEELS made from the best Scrap Iron. EDGE TOOLS of all descriptions supplied; and every description of Agricultural Implement Repaired in the best possible manner, and at the most moderate prices.[13]

For some reason they made great play of the fact that they used scrap iron in the manufacture of certain items, although why this was regarded as a selling point is not clear. It is known their predecessor at the works, John Giddings, had made use of scrap iron, for in 1862 he bought 13cwt of rails stolen from the recently completed Newbury railway at Upper Vobster.[14]

Walter, his wife Anna, and their children moved to Stoke Lane and in the 1871 census he is described as "Edge Tool Maker (Master) employing 11 hands". The business did not prosper, however, and almost exactly one year after the above advertisement appeared, the *Journal* carried another announcing the sale of the "GOOD WILL, and TENANTS FIXTURES" of "that old and well established and increasing iron works and edge tool business, for many years carried on by Mr Giddings, deceased, and recently by Messrs. Fussell & Wise".[15] The advert claimed the works were "well adapted for the Business, are most advantageously situated, have an excellent fall of water applied to Overshot Wheels, and are let at moderate rental". It would seem no one was interested in taking on the business, since the works were never again occupied and soon became dilapidated. All that remains today are traces of the dam and a few fragments of buildings hidden in trees and scrub.

Within days of the advertisement appearing, Walter left the country bound for the United States on the S.S. Aragon, an emigrant ship operated by the Great Western Steam Ship Line of Bristol. He arrived in New York on the 16 November 1871 but moved on to Morristown, New Jersey, where his family later joined him and his second son Rawlings was born in 1875. Walter's precipitate departure left his financial affairs in disarray and two months later, in January 1872, the *Journal* carried an advertisement asking "any creditors or persons having a claim on the estate of Walter Fussell" to contact the Frome solicitor Henry McCarthy.[16] Walter did not stay long in the United States, for he and his family had returned to England by 1878, when his son Richard was born in Salisbury. By the spring of 1881 he was living in Warminster and trying to earn a living as a "professor of music", using the skills that had led to his appointment as organist and teacher of the choir at Mells church. Ten years later Walter was an inmate of the Wiltshire County Lunatic Asylum in Devizes, where he died in 1906. With the benefit of hindsight, the failure of the business, his sudden departure to the United States and subsequent return to England can be read as manifestations of the mental illness that would finally lead to his being committed.

Cricket for Girls

A Church of England national school was built in the middle of Chantry following the creation of the parish in 1846. By the time of the 1851 census, the school was run by Mary Biggs, the widow of one of James Fussell's workmen, Joshua Biggs. Mary was assisted by her daughters Mary and Ann, both of whom were listed as teachers. The original school, now a pair of houses, did not last long in its original form, for in July 1857 James Fussell opened a new one on a more ambitious scale at the east end of the village.[1] This school was in fact four schools in one - a national school (for boys and girls), an infants' school, an industrial school to prepare girls from poor families for domestic service, and a girls' boarding school.

The first headmistress of Chantry School was Miss Susan Kyberd, described by *Cuzners Hand Book to Froome-Selwood* as "a lady eminently qualified for her work" and by the Reverend William Michell as "a proved teacher and disciplinarian". She came well qualified for the post, having attended Whitelands Institution for the Training of School Mistresses, where in 1848 she "passed the most satisfactory examination of all the candidates" and went on to be awarded a first class certificate of merit.[2] It is possible that she first came to James Fussell's attention in June 1854 when he inspected the Rochester Diocesan Training School, near Bishop's Stortford, of which she was principal governess. Susan Kyberd was a strong believer in female education, and in 1864 signed a petition asking the University of London to open its examinations to women. She also put forward candidates from Chantry School when Cambridge University allowed girls to sit its local examination for a trial period.[3]

The purpose of the girls' boarding school was described by *Kelly's Directory* as being "to bring within reach of persons of limited income the benefits of good education, including French, German, music, drawing and such other accomplishments as are usually imparted in Schools of superior character". *Cuzner* reported that the school was chiefly for the daughters of clergymen",[4] while William Michell, curate of Chantry in the early 1870s, described its pupils as "farmers' daughters".[5] Giving evidence before the School Enquiry Commission in 1867, James Fussell said the school did not confine itself "to the children of any particular class, provided they are respectable and can pay the terms".[6] When the chairman, Lord Taunton, asked Miss Kyberd about the social rank of the pupils, she replied: "We have daughters of an architect, a bookseller, and a clergyman; five, whose fathers farm their own land; two, the daughters of tenant-farmers, two of ironmasters, two of mechanics, one of a portrait painter, five of solicitors, two daughters of surgeons and two of surveyors."[7] Lord Lyttelton enquired if the children of clergymen and solicitors were unwilling to mix with those of farmers and mechanics. She replied they were not in the habit of divulging the positions of parents: "The parents know that we do not confine ourselves to the children of any particular class, provided they are respectable and can pay the terms."[8] Lyttelton asked if they took girls from all classes, to which James Fussell replied that they did, "providing they are well-behaved and well-conditioned".

The fees for the boarding school were 30 guineas a year but extras included laundry, music, dancing and German lessons, making the average cost of sending a girl to Chantry £46 per year. The lower age limit for admission was nine but it was preferred that they came at around 13. There was no fixed requirement of knowledge for admission, the majority of the pupils having been previously home taught rather than coming from other schools. The girls arose between 6.30 and 7.15am, attended divine service at Chantry church daily at 8.30am, and went to bed between 9 and 10pm. They were provided with four meals a day, one of which included meat. Subjects offered included French, arithmetic, reading and writing, drawing, history, geography, needlework, music, Latin, German, singing and dancing. For outdoor recreation the school possessed a lawn of a quarter of an acre, although James Fussell also allowed the girls to use some of the surrounding fields. Only the older girls were allowed to walk out unaccompanied by a teacher, and only then with special leave.

When asked by the commissioners if the school was on a considerable scale, James replied: "It is on a smaller scale than originally proposed. We are interested in the manufacturing population of an adjoining parish, and we intended to take their children into our National School."[9] The inference here is that the Reverend John Horner of Mells had objected to the children of his village going to school in Chantry. This is not surprising, given that there were national schools for both boys and girls in his village.[10]

Horner had built the boys' national school only 15 years before and took a close interest in it. Richard White remembered how he had "raised the tone" of the school by employing "a young man of the name of Pettit to teach the boys and a more educated teacher for the girls".[11] A report on church education for the poor in the diocese of Bath and Wells in 1846 commented favourably on innovations John Horner had introduced in recent years. Among these was the provision of a hot dinner every day that was prepared, served and cooked by the girls. Vegetables were grown in a one-acre garden tended by the school's 20 boys and pigs were kept to supply meat. Horner reported with pride: "We have at present a very good show of vegetables. We had a piece of Mangold Wurzel, as fine as I ever saw. We have just killed two pigs, ten

Scholars of St Andrew's College, Mells walking in procession past the parish church (Michael McGarvie Collection).

score each, and have three in the sty." When asked to describe the school, he wrote that it was "of a mixed sort, uniting instruction with industrial employment – boys and girls – the boys are in School during the mornings, and during the afternoons on the land, except one small class: the girls are employed in turns, two each week, in the household work."[12]

If James Fussell's primary interest was in girls' education, John Horner's was that of the further education of young men. In 1848 he founded St Andrew's College in the Manor House at Mells to cater for "those who could not reasonably expect to be members of the Houses of our Universities". Students were admitted on the understanding that the purpose of their training was to "make them useful members of Christ's Holy Catholic Church" and it was hoped that "within these walls youths go forth to undertake duties of Schoolmasters at home or Missionaries abroad".[13] John Horner recognised there was a growing demand for teachers to educate "an immensely increased population" and meet the needs of "an intelligent middle class loudly calling for instruction". There were striking similarities between the institutions founded by Horner and Fussell, both of which sought to provide a good education to the children of middle-class parents of limited means and to fit them for careers appropriate to their social status – whether as governesses, teachers, or missionaries. St Andrew's College closed in 1858, the same year that James Fussell opened his school in neighbouring Chantry.

James Fussell's co-worker in the founding of the school was his legal advisor Joshua Julian Allen, whom William Michell described as being "connected in the iron factory and business of Mells with Mr Fussell, and more closely in Educational work, and in the foundation and maintenance of Chantry School for Girls". Allen was one of the earliest leaders in the movement for the higher education of women and played an active part in the planning, establishment and running of the school.

The school was not self-supporting, the additional expenses being defrayed by Fussell and Allen, who acted as guarantors for the payment of salaries and other running expenses. The government had given a grant towards the building of the school, although as James Fussell later testified "the funds were chiefly provided by Mr. Allen and myself".[14] The management of the school was firmly in the hands of the founders, who appointed the headmistress, exercised "general superintendence", made suggestions and occasionally gave directions.

Having their own school gave James Fussell and Joshua Allen an opportunity to try out their ideas on the education of girls. In this field they were undoubtedly innovators, the school having a number of unusual features. One of these was the practice of using older girls, known as "blues", to help maintain school discipline.

The story of the origin of the blues was recounted to the Schools Commission by James Fussell. He explained that before the school first opened they partitioned off the south end of the dormitory from the rest of the room and plastered over the doorway "so that the pupils when they came had no idea that there was any room beyond". This aroused the curiosity of the girls, who . . .

> . . . found out there were more windows than could be accounted for, and they came to the conclusion that there was some mystery about the room; in short they said we had a Bluebeard's chamber there. When our numbers increased sufficiently we opened the door way of this room, furnished it with blue curtains, and put six of the head girls into it.[15]

The girls who occupied this room had a "distinct position", being "the police of the school".[16] In its report, the School Enquiry Commission said the practice of giving the older children a role in maintaining discipline was rare in girls' schools, but it had "been introduced with excellent effect by Mr Fussell and Miss Kyberd in the Chantry School at Frome, and it appears to us highly deserving of consideration".

An even more unusual innovation, and one also commented on by the commission, was the introduction of cricket for girls, the commissioners noting "the pupils are allowed to play cricket, and the best cricketers are said to be the best scholars". It is also mentioned in the memoirs of William Michell, who wrote "the girls played cricket Mr F with them so did I, rarely, and my children". Cricket features prominently

The west elevation of Chantry School as it looks today.

in two accounts of the school written by former pupils, Helen Mather and Isobel Fortey. Helen Mather attended the school in the 1860s and based the description of the school days of the heroine of her novel, *Comin thru' the Rye,* on Chantry School.[17] This includes a scene in which the character based on James Fussell – called Mr Russell – arrives unexpectedly and immediately decrees a cricket match be held. In her day the girls played in bloomers rather than dresses, an innovation of which she wholeheartedly approved: "To Mr Russell…be our eternal thanks due, in that he has, for a time at least, emancipated us from the slavish thraldom of petticoats, and enabled us to stretch our limbs and use them." Cricket was still on the curriculum when Isobel Fortey attended the school a decade later, as she later recalled.

> In Helen Mather's time the girls would take off their crinolines and play cricket in little bloomer costumes; in ours, mercifully uncrinolined, we still played cricket in our ordinary clothes, something very unusual for girls.[18]

Helen Mather and Isobel Fortey also provide some clues as to James Fussell's appearance and character, the former describing him as "tall, erect, a little grey, his

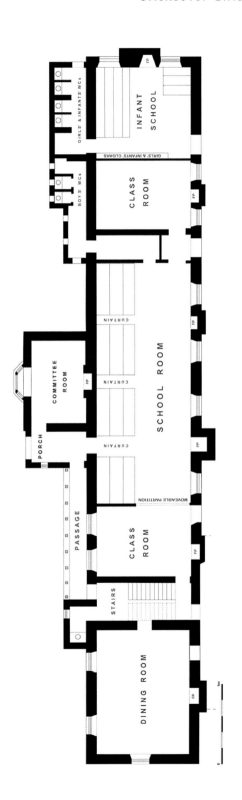

Ground floor plan of Chantry School as originally designed.

The subject of this portrait taken by the fashionable photographers Maull and Polybank may be the Reverend J.G.C. Fussell. It is in the archive of the Royal Geographical Society - of which he became a fellow in 1860 – and is catalogued as being an image of the Reverend Jacob G. C. Fussell (reproduced by permission of the Royal Geographical Society).

dress showing but little of the clergyman about it",[19] while the latter thought him "highly original and interesting".[20] William Michell was more guarded when writing of his former employer, merely stating "we got on together well enough. He held himself responsible for the payment of the Organist and Choir, and with his wife and daughters looked well after the needs of the people, land and houses, being almost if not altogether his property".

It is clear that while James may have had advanced views on the education of girls, his approach to religion was very traditional. In advertising for a new curate in 1858, he required "a clergyman of moderate views",[21] by which he meant a traditionalist. William Michell remembered him as "jealous of ritual observance, or novelty" and recalled that he gave communion only once a month and "persisted in preaching in his gown after I had introduced the surplice".

In mid-19th century England the wearing of the gown was a symbol of Protestantism, while the surplice was associated with Roman Catholicism.[22] It is interesting to note that James Fussell, a member of a recently risen family, kept to the Protestant tradition, while his neighbour John Horner at Mells, who was from an established landed family, was a reformer - adopting the surplice, introducing regular holy communions, stripping the church of some of its large monuments, and cutting down the sides of the family pew to make its occupants visible to the rest of the congregation. James was also a traditionalist in his politics, being an active supporter of the Conservative Party, while John Horner was a Liberal.

James Fussell's resistance to change was to bring him into open conflict with Michell's successor George Collins (1872-77), one of their arguments being on the unlikely issue of whether the key of F or G should be given out to the church choir. This seemingly trivial dispute reached such intensity that the churchwardens attempted to mediate, passing notes between the two men and seeking to find a compromise. At a parish meeting on the 10 June 1875, James's son read a letter from his father stating that "he had distinctly arranged with the vicar before he presented him that he (Mr Fussell) was to retain the entire control of the musical arrangements, and that unless this arrangement could be carried out in entirety Mr Fussell would feel compelled to relinquish the conduct of the music to Mr Collins with its attendant expenses".[23]

Quite why the church music was of such importance to James is not clear, although it may have been because the choir was made up of girls from the school and the choirmistress was his youngest daughter, Sarah Julian, who was later remembered by Isobel Fortey for "her beautiful voice and face". George Collins only lasted a further four years as curate of Chantry, leaving in 1879. From his obituary in 1895 it is surprising that he was ever appointed, this indicating that he was High Church - being for some years Dr. Pusey's deputy lecturer at Oxford.

The recollections of former pupils suggest that the school was a happy institution run in a humane way. According to Isobel Fortey, punishments tended to lean on "mercy's side". One was being sent to bed, as happened to her sister Emily ("Mil") on at least one occasion.

> One afternoon I remember the word going round, 'Where's Emily Fortey?' 'She's been sent to bed.' 'Then she'll have to be got up; Mr. Fussell's just come, and he's sure to ask for her.' And so it turned out. How did he have that insight?[24]

Isobel was impressed that James Fussell "saw what there was" in her sister, when most adults thought her "a naughty girl who gave trouble." On one occasion she was rebuked by a mistress, "whose sense of humour was inferior to Mr. Fussell's", for writing the following verse on the set subject of A Stormy Night.

> The night indeed was very rough,
> The day was full of sorrow,
> I cannot do this stupid stuff,
> I'll leave it till tomorrow.[25]

Like all establishments of its kind, Chantry School was not without its strains. When Helen Mather came to the school at the age of 13 she was put in a class with girls several years older than herself and, being ambitious, worked so hard to keep up that her health broke down and she became partially deaf. Her condition, it was later claimed, had the effect of focusing her mind on literature. She began to write incessantly and before she was 16 had completed her poem *The Token of the Silver Lily*. Through a friend of the family, it was shown to Dante Gabriel Rosetti, who sent her a "kindly message" that encouraged her to pursue her literary ambitions.[26]

A far more tragic incident occurred in 1862, only five years after the opening of the school, when the school governess committed suicide. Mary Jane Bullock was 20 years old and had been a pupil at the school for three years before joining the teaching staff. Six months before her death she become low-spirited and began to accuse herself of "past wickedness", fretting that "she did not fulfill the duties of her position".[27]

A doctor was brought in from London to examine her, shortly after which she went to Miss Kyberd claiming to have swallowed a bottle of embrocation and asking for an emetic. After this incident she was watched closely, but on the morning of her suicide she went out - saying she was going to church - and drowned herself in a water tank in the school grounds. An inquest was held and the coroner's jury returned a verdict of "Temporary Insanity". Her death, which was widely reported, brought the school unwelcome publicity just as it was beginning to establish itself.

The diary of William Michell provides an insight into the relationships between those who had a role in the running of the school in this period. It was inevitable that in such a small world these relationships would extend beyond work into the social lives of those involved. By the early 1870s Joshua Allen was spending a great deal of time in the area, having rented a house in Mells. In July 1870 Michell took a steamer from Bristol to Milford Haven to visit Allen on his Pembrokeshire estate, where Susan Kyberd was also staying as a guest.

While in Wales the three of them visited the Reverend John Fussell, James's brother, at his seat at Amroth Castle. Unfortunately, the visit was marred by an accident resulting from John Fussell's bad driving, attributed by Michell to his nearsightedness.

Michell later recounted how his host had cut the corner of a village green, causing the wagonette in which the party was travelling to overturn. He and his wife were unhurt but Joshua Allen broke a bone in his wrist and Miss Kyberd suffered damage to her spine. For a few days she attended to Mr Allen, but was forced to give in and did not recover her strength for more than twelve months.[28] She resigned the headship of the school shortly afterwards and by 1881 was living with Joshua Allen at Bathwick as his adopted daughter. Her replacement, Caroline Senior, was not a career teacher but the former governess of James Fussell's children.

By this time James was in financial difficulties and the school was an additional burden. In May 1867 he borrowed £1,500 from Mary Steel Hodgson of Croydon, Surrey, on the security of land and properties not tied up in the marriage settlement.[29] In the same period he also contracted other loans, including one for £12,000 from the Reverend Thomas Astley Maberly, nephew of one of the trustees of his wife's marriage settlement, Joseph Maberly. Having failed to attract enough of the type of pupils originally intended, the school now sought "the daughters of the Clergy and professional men who would be glad to obtain a sound and thorough education at a moderate payment".

As James's money problems increased in the 1870s, pressure mounted for the school to become self-sufficient by admitting more paying pupils. It was built to house about 30 paying boarders but by 1881 the number had risen to 66, The Chantry itself having been converted into a boarding department lodging 35 pupils. The conversion of his country seat into a boarding house was clearly a desperate measure and gives a clear indication that his financial situation had become precarious.

13

The Chantry Riot

The most bizarre event in the story of the Fussell family must surely be the Chantry riot of March 1875, the story of which has been reconstructed from contemporary descriptions and reports of the legal proceedings that arose from it. On the 31 March 1875 the *Frome Times* announced: "A serious disturbance took place on Thursday at Little Elm by a large body of colliers, who assisted to obtain for one of their fraternity forcible possession of a cottage and land, the title of which was in dispute."

The property in question comprised a cottage, two fields and a close opposite the George Inn. It had been bought in 1806 by a farmer called Thomas Bryant from Kilmersdon and was the only part of the Stoney Lane estate not sold to James Fussell. The 1851 census described Bryant as a farmer of seven acres, a tiny holding even by the standards of the period. William Michell later described him as the "most quaint and interesting of my people", recalling how he "used to speak of the hard times of his youth, back into the last century, when he was sent into the fields at daybreak, bird scaring 'with a leetle bit o' barleybree-ad as big as my two fingers, an' that was all I had till I comed home for supper' ". From these humble beginnings Bryant "got some education, and a little property, land, cows and pigs, on which he and his old wife lived". In fact, he married twice. Sarah, his first wife, died in 1852 and a year later, at the age of 64, he married Mary Ann Wilcox from Leigh-on-Mendip.

Mary died in 1870 and the childless Thomas, an octogenarian living alone, became of considerable interest to his nephews and nieces. He was aware his death might lead to family conflict and yet made no will and only one specific bequest, entrusting its execution to the Reverend William Michell.

> When nearing his end, he desired me to take charge of £50 for a niece, which I did, stipulating that there must be no change in his disposal of his money, and had his determination in writing. Very soon this matter leaked out, and attempts were made to alter this disposition. But I had banked the money in my own name, and stuck to his instructions. There was discontent and grumbling, suggestions that he had altered his mind. But the money was paid over by me to his nominee, and I heard no more of the matter. It would have been safer for

me to have declined the trust. But the money was in gold, in his house. And if I
had not removed it, someone else might have done so.

Following Thomas's death a nephew from Stoke Lane, also called Thomas, claimed
his uncle had bequeathed the cottages to him on his deathbed, although the fact
that Michell had received no written instructions in the matter casts doubt on this
assertion. Other members of the family did not accept the story, arguing the property
belonged to them all. In the meantime, another relation seems to have taken it on
himself to sell the property to the Reverend James Fussell. Unaware of the transaction,
Thomas Bryant took possession of the cottages, only to be told they were the property
of James Fussell and that he must vacate them within six months.

Two weeks before the riot, Bryant paid one of his occasional visits to Chantry and
found that James Fussell's bailiff, William Gough, together with his coachman had
entered the premises and removed his furniture, stopped up many of the windows,
put new locks on the doors and moved some of Gough's furniture into one of them.
Returning a few days later, the Bryants and some friends forced an entry, only to be
ejected by a body of grinders called out from the nearby edge-tool works. Thomas
Bryant then openly declared his intention to bring "a body of men to take forcible
possession of the premises" at the expiry of the notice to quit. The *East Somerset
Telegraph* reported that "to meet any emergency" James Fussell's grinders had been

Thomas Bryant's cottage in Chantry as it looks today.

provided with "substantial truncheons" and thought it likely that "a scrimmage will result".[1] Thomas Bryant was a coal haulier from Stoke St Michael and his son Francis a coal miner. The Somerset miners had recently become unionised and the Bryants seem to have tapped into this network to drum up support from a number of pits in the coalfield.

On the day of the riot Thomas and Francis appeared in the village at the head of a large crowd of miners, who had converged on Chantry from Leigh-on-Mendip, Mells, Stoke Lane, Coleford, Radstock, Clandown, and Holcombe. The size of the mob was later estimated at between 200 and 300, although among these were hangers-on and local residents who had either come to support Bryant or simply to watch. Sometime after 9am Richard Cox - watchman at the ironworks - and a party of grinders occupied the cottages and made ready to defend them. Sergeant Edmunds later described how "Mr Fussell sent for me and told me he had sixty men on the premises and that they would fight desperately". The "substantial truncheons" the Fussells' men were armed with were wooden staves made at the works – presumably turned on the handle makers' lathes. One of these weapons was later produced in court and was described as "rather shorter and stouter than a policeman's truncheon…a formidable looking bludgeon". Because trouble was expected there was a police presence in the village that morning. PC Abel Chandler arrived at 10am to find a large number of people, men and women, moving towards the cottages "in groups of twelve or twenty". PC Chandler went to the cottages and advised one of the grinders to lock the front door and let them break it, as that would "constitute a damage".

By late morning police reinforcements were on their way to Chantry from Frome under the command of Sergeant Gerrity. On approaching the village at 11.55am, Sgt Gerrity heard a loud cheer and on arrival saw a crowd "in a very excited state". He later described how he witnessed "men with crowbars battering down what appeared to be newly-erected masonry, and smashing out the frame-work and glass of the windows of two cottages". Shortly afterwards, PC John Best saw some of the Fussell grinders pulled out of the cottages "by main force", while William Gough would later testify that he had been standing in the doorway of one of the cottages and had been dragged out and thrown into the garden. Richard Cox corroborated Gough's story, testifying that he saw eight or ten of the attackers pulling Gough out of one of the cottages. Cox also claimed to have seen Stephen Russell of Finger Farm, Mells, incite the mob by calling out to them "go in my lads". One of the coal miners, John Hiscox, then began throwing furniture out of a window until PC Best called on him to stop because he was breaking the law. Hiscox desisted for a while but then resumed at the urging of the crowd outside.

The police constables, being greatly outnumbered, wisely decided not to charge "so large and excited a mob". Instead, Sgt Gerrity went to Mells and returned with the

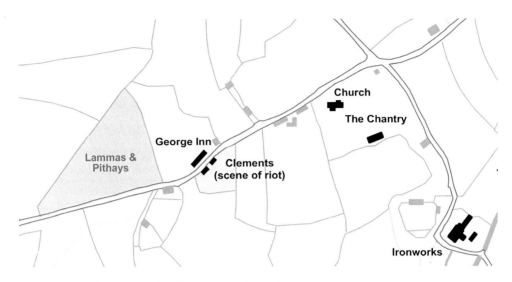

Map showing the scene of the Chantry riot of March 1875.

Reverend John Horner, who in his capacity as local magistrate addressed the colliers "in a kind and conciliatory manner, and advised them to go home".[2] Meanwhile, a telegraph message had been sent asking for reinforcements, but by the time Superintendent Morgan arrived from police headquarters with 20 constables it was evening and the village was quiet. Bryant's supporters expected Fussell to make an attempt to regain possession of the cottages the next day, and so established a chain of "stations" from Chantry to Radstock in order to be able to bring a still larger force of colliers to the village at short notice if the need arose. When no move was made to repossess them, the colliers were stood down and Bryant and a few friends held a party amidst the wreckage to celebrate their victory.

The last act of the drama was played out in Frome Magistrates Court. Thomas and Francis Bryant, along with 20 of their supporters, were summonsed to appear before the petty sessions to answer a charge that "they did with divers other evilly disposed persons to the number of 200 or more unlawfully and riotously assemble to disturb the public peace, and did then and there make a riot and disturbance to the terror and alarm of Her Majesty's subjects".[3] The prosecution was brought by the Reverend James Fussell - the Frome Bench having declined to advise a prosecution on the part of the police, while the chief constable refused to institute proceedings on the grounds of expense and the fact that a question of title was involved.

The magistrates decided a riot had indeed been committed and proceeded against 11 of the defendants, including Stephen Russell. The case was then adjourned until 11 May. In the intervening period Henry McCarthy, solicitor for the defendants, took out summonses for riot, wilful damage, and forcible possession against the Reverend

James Fussell, his son James and a number of their company's employees. It was decided that both cases should be heard together and the court was crowded with spectators hoping for a good show. The outcome was an anticlimax, the magistrates deciding not to proceed with either case on the grounds that a question of title was involved and that it should, therefore, be heard in the Court of Chancery. The *Frome Times* reported that "considerable disappointment was expressed at the sudden termination of what was expected to be a 'big affair' ".[4]

There are a number of aspects to the episode that are hard to explain. The first is that James Fussell must have bought the cottages and land without receiving any clear proof of title from the vendor. The second is that throughout the period in question the Poor Rate books for the parish list Thomas Bryant rather than James Fussell as owner of the property. In the event, James Fussell did not bring a Chancery case to establish his title and Thomas Bryant remained in possession of the property, which later passed to his son Francis. Francis married Jane Toop of Chantry in 1880 and emigrated to the United States, settling in Pennsylvania, where his son Henry was born in 1883. However life in America does not appear to have suited the Bryants, for by 1889 they returned to England and were living in Bedminster, from where they then moved back to Chantry. Today the Bryants' house is called Sunny Nook, a quaint name for a building with such a turbulent history.

Stephen Skurray Steps Down

In December 1873 Stephen Skurray's wife Elizabeth died at the age of 37. Two years later Stephen married Mary Jane Fussell, daughter of the late John Fussell of the Upper Works, and sister of John Hounsell, William, and Walter Fussell.[1] Following her father's death in 1868, Mary had lived with William at the family home of Rock House in Mells and was described in the 1871 census as of independent means. Stephen and Mary were distant cousins, both being great-great-grandchildren of the James Fussell who had moved the business to Mells in 1744. Following their marriage the couple lived at Stephen's house in Great Elm; but by 1877 he had resigned as manager of James Fussell & Co and they had moved to Chippenham in Wiltshire.[2] There Stephen established his own edge-tool making business, working in partnership with his cousin Francis Skurray, a corn factor, and Edward John Howeld.

It is not certain when Stephen Skurray resigned or what his reasons were for doing so. He was still in post in 1872, when *Morris's Directory* described him as "Manager of Mells Iron Works", but may have left by 1873 when an article in the *Bristol Mercury* named the manager as William Morgan.

It is possible that he was, in fact, William Morgans, a civil engineer born in the iron-making town of Risca, Monmouthshire. In the 1860s William worked with his father, Morgan Morgans, the engineer in charge of the Brendon Hills Iron Mine in West Somerset, and in 1865 was awarded a patent for "Improvements in coke and charcoal ovens and in the manufacture of coke".[3]

Interestingly, William Morgan(s) was not the first engineer of that name to work for the Fussells, for in 1870 the *Proceedings of the Institution of Mechanical Engineers* listed among its members Thomas Morgans of "Mells ironworks near Frome". In the Great Elm census of 1871 he was described as a "mechanical engineer" from Mynyddyslwyn in Monmouthshire, a village close to Risca. It is not known what work Thomas Morgans was engaged in, or how long he remained with James Fussell & Co, although by 1878 he had moved to Bristol and in the 1881 census was described as the manager of a factory employing six hands.

By then there was yet another Morgans working for the Fussells - Geoffrey Morgans, a young civil engineer who at the time of the 1881 census was living on site at Lower Ironworks Cottages. Geoffrey, who was 28 at the time of the census, also came from

Risca. It has not been possible to establish a family connection between the three men, but the coincidences of names, profession, and places of birth are very striking.

One can only speculate on the circumstances that led to Stephen leaving his job at James Fussell & Co. An important factor may have been the increasing involvement in the business of his employer's son, James Thomas Richardson Fussell. James Fussell junior had been called to the bar in 1872 but does not seem to have gone into practice and by 1875, if not before, was living in Chantry. It is possible that he was making his presence felt - voicing views on the conduct of the business and pushing for expansion in order to generate the increasing profits needed to clear his father's growing debts and provide a suitable income. The timing of Stephen's departure from the Fussells' employment to set up his own business shortly after his marriage raises the question of whether the venture might have been funded, in part at least, out of Mary's inheritance.

In September 1877 Stephen and his partners leased the Railway Works in Chippenham from Frederick Hastings Goldney. The works comprised two smith's shops, a hammer shop, stores, packing room, and an office over the yard. It also included use of a siding to the Great Western Railway. Two years later Stephen took out a patent for "Improvements in the Manufacture of Scythes, Reaping Hooks, Hay Knives, and such like Cutting Instruments".[4] In this he describes himself as being of the firm of "John Skurray and Company, of Chippenham, in the County of Wilts, Edge Tool Manufacturers". His stated object was "simplicity and economy of manufacture, as well as superiority of the article produced". He argued the traditional means of making tools required the welding together of "four separate pieces of metal, three of which are of iron, and one of them for the cutting edge is of steel", a process which involved the exercise of "considerable skill, cost, and labour". Skurray's invention consisted in "forming all the metal parts of the instrument out of one piece of steel". An advertisement in Kelly's Directory for Wiltshire of 1880[5] describes the patent steel tools in glowing terms: "These Solid Steel Tools for Toughness, Strength, Lightness, and Elasticity are unsurpassed, and will be found by all workmen using them to keep their edge longer, and to require less grinding than any welded tools."

Stephen Skurray had come to believe the future of edge-tool making lay in steel, and made his case with all the fervour of an evangelist.[6] The 1870s saw a revolution in the iron trade, steel output in Great Britain increasing fivefold between 1870 and 1890 as railways converted from rolled iron to steel and steel plates and girders became the basic units of the shipbuilding industry.[7] Steel was now available in large quantities and was relatively cheap compared to bar iron. As a result edge-tool manufacturers now began to make products of cast steel rather than from a combination of forge welded iron and steel. In 1871 *Griffiths Guide to the Iron Trade* included a chapter on the "new trade in steel casting", noting the "rapid progress" of the trade and observing "it is really surprising to learn how many and varied uses these castings are applied to . . . . In fact, crucible steel castings are fast replacing metal work and wrought iron forgings, their superior qualities, viz., greater tenacity, strength and lightness, giving special advantages over other metals".[8] Stephen's belief that the future lay in steel tools raises the possibility that he had argued the case for a switch to the new method of making tools but had the proposal vetoed by his employer. There is no evidence that James Fussell & Co had begun making cast steel tools by this time, although Isaac Fussell & Co were already doing so. A report on the Annual Exhibition of the Frome and District Agricultural Society in September 1876 mentions that "Messrs. Isaac Fussell & Co. of Nunney Iron Works, had an interesting collection of steel faced and other spades, shovels and draining tools; cast steel spades; also bill hooks; axes and hoes of various patterns".[9]

Within months of his arrival in Chippenham, Stephen and his partners decided to seek additional finance by floating the company with a nominal capital of £10,000. The new limited company was incorporated on 10 June 1880 – Stephen receiving 400 shares, Francis Skurray 200, and Howeld 300 shares. Of the shares that remained, the majority were taken up by business and professional men in the Chippenham area. The census of 1881 describes Stephen as "Managing Director Of Skurrays Edge Tools Limited", employing 21 men and one boy. In September the company put an advertisement in the *Frome Times* : "Wanted, one or two good grinders. Apply to Skurray's Edge Tool Company (Limited), Chippenham, Wilts".[10] By then Stephen had already poached six of Fussell's employees: Henry Ashman (grinder), Joseph George (grinder), Arthur Rossiter (journeyman), Lewis Rossiter (edge-tool maker), Frank Montague (edge-tool maker), and Silas Hobbs (edge-tool smith).[11] A number of these men may have gone to Chippenham when the business was first established. Henry Ashman, for example, moved there between the birth of his daughter Frances in Nunney in 1877 and of his daughter Flora in Chippenham in 1878.

Arthur Rossiter was a third-generation edge-tool worker. His grandfather John Rossiter was born in 1802 in Great Elm, where he married in 1824. At some time in the next five years he moved to take up a position at the new Stoney Lane works. It was in Whatley that Lewis was born in 1829. By 1841 John and his family had returned to Great Elm and by 1851 were living in Mells, where Lewis too was now working for the Fussells. By 1871 Lewis, now married, had in his turn moved to Chantry to work at Stoney Lane. It seems likely, therefore, that Lewis and Arthur moved to Wiltshire soon after Stephen Skurray set up in business there.

Skurray's Edge Tool Company (Limited) continued in business for three years but did not thrive, and at an extraordinary general meeting on 28 February 1883 it was resolved to wind it up, with Edward Howeld acting as liquidator.[12] The stock-in-trade was sold by auction in October 1884, comprising more than 12,000 patent steel and other edge-tools, together with two tons of bar steel and a quantity of iron. In the advertisement for the auction, it was stated the plant and machinery would be disposed of in a separate sale at a later date.[13]

The reasons for the failure of Stephen Skurray's venture are not known. One possibility is that Skurray's was not a known brand and the company may have found it difficult to get established in what was by now a very competitive market. Moreover, hardware dealers and their customers may well have been suspicious of the newfangled tools, which may or may not have lived up to the claims made for them by their inventor. Stephen retired when the business ceased trading and at the time of the 1901 census he and Mary were living in Bath. He was now 72 and described as "Late Tool Manufacturer" living on own means. Soon after, the Skurrays moved to Weston-super-Mare, where Stephen died in 1906 at the age of 77.

A New Partnership

Following the departure of Stephen Skurray, the management of James Fussell & Co was placed in the hands of James Thomas Richardson Fussell. In March 1878 the Reverend James Fussell and his son signed a partnership agreement for the running of the business, and on the same day James junior leased the works from the trustees of his mother's marriage settlement, Messrs Wyatt and Mabberly.[1] The deed of partnership "recited the fact that the father being in holy orders was unable to trade, and appointed his son as manager of the firm. It gave the details as to how the business was to be carried on, and the mode in which payments were to be made".[2] The problem was that James Fussell junior had not been brought up to the

business and lacked the experience and knowledge of his predecessor. What is clear, though, is that young James had big ideas, for in the years that followed steps were taken to open up new markets and increase the productive capacity of the business. In 1873 the company exhibited at the Vienna Exhibition, at which the Reverend James Fussell was present as a juror in the educational section and on which he wrote a report on the various educational appliances on display.[3] Three years later it had a presence

Photograph of William Wise demonstrating the correct way of holding a scythe. Note the pegs supporting the blade to keep it steady during a long exposure and the white background (reproduced by kind permission of the Earl of Oxford and Asquith).

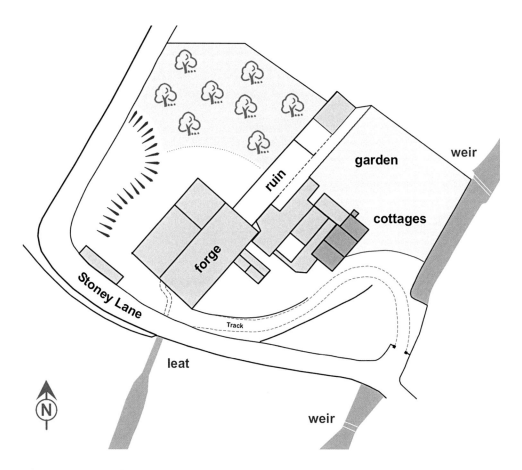

The Stoney Lane Edge-Tool Works as they looked after major alterations in the 1870s.

at the American Centennial Exhibition in Philadelphia of 1876, sending "two cases of sickles of various sizes, suitable for cutting grain and for trimming trees etc." and "a small assortment of scythes".[4] In 1878 it exhibited at the Paris Exposition, the name of the company appearing in the catalogue of the British Section.[5]

Another means by which the company publicised itself in this period was by producing a pamphlet entitled "A Short Treatise on scythes and mowing". Described by one reviewer as "a most interesting little book and well illustrated", it was said to be available from Mells Ironworks, priced 6d.[6] No copy of this pamphlet has been found, but a photograph that may well have been taken as an illustration for it does survive in the Oxford Archive, Mells. This image shows William Wise demonstrating the correct way of holding a scythe. Close inspection of the photograph reveals that William has been photographed against a white cloth or painted background and the scythe blade is supported on iron pegs to prevent movement during the long

The Lower Works from the south-east with the rolling mills in the foreground.

exposure (the hammer used to drive the pegs in is visible in the foreground). It is not known who wrote the pamphlet, the author using the pen-name "Whetstone".

The Fussells were still able to trade on their reputation for quality tools, especially the manufacture of scythes, as the following piece from the *Bromley Record* illustrates.

> Science however has long since come to the mower's aid he can now get a good
> scythe for less money than a bad one formerly cost. Fussell was the first who
> brought out a thorough good and light scythe, and I believe there are no better
> now.[7]

Little is known about the business in the 1870s, although there are indications that James Fussell was investing in new buildings and plant even before the resignation of Stephen Skurray. There is evidence to suggest a considerable amount of work may have been done at the Stoney Lane works in the middle of the decade, for it does not appear in the Whatley Poor Rate book for 1875, and when it re-appears in the following year its assessment had doubled. This would seem to indicate it was closed for major alterations for much of that year, changes the assessors believed had greatly increased its value. By the time the large-scale Ordnance Survey map was surveyed in the early 1880s, the appearance of the works had indeed altered – a number of new buildings having appeared. Tylee mentions that, in addition to grinding and plating, the works had "a blast furnace for casting iron tools for their own use, where the

Perspective reconstruction of the appearance of the rolling mills.

iron bars were baked in a reverberatory furnace for three weeks; and a steel furnace for making steel". The claim that there was a reverberatory furnace is backed up by archaeological evidence - pieces of slag-covered furnace linings made from refractory bricks having been found on the site of the new buildings mentioned above.[8]

The pace of development increased in the late 1870s, with more than £12,000 being invested in the business. The bulk of the money was spent on projects at the Lower Works in Wadbury, these including a new gas plant with a cylindrical holder and a "portable engine" housed in a brick shed with galvanised roof.[9] The biggest investment, though, was the building of a steam-powered rolling mill to the east of the existing buildings. A photograph of the works taken around 1890 by James Long of Mells shows the mill in the foreground. The building was a stone-built structure, so large that it straddled the stream. It housed two rolling mills - a "Merchant Mill" capable of rolling bars of up to 12 inches in thickness and a 10in one for rolling sections. The purpose of rolling mills was to squeeze and flatten out heated pieces of wrought iron by passing them between a pair of rotating rollers (known as rolls). The merchant

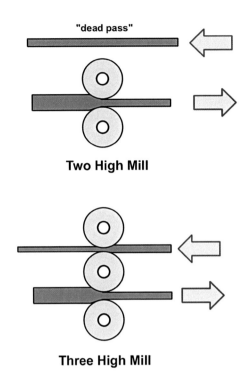

Two High Mill

Three High Mill

Schematic drawing showing the differences between "two high" and "three high mills".

mill at Mells was of a type known as a "three high mill", so named because it had three rotating rolls in a vertical column. In the traditional two high mill the heated iron was fed through the rolls, in what was called a "live pass", and then manhandled back over the top (a "dead pass") before being fed through again. This method of working was inefficient and meant that the iron cooled significantly between live passes. The advantage of the three high mill was that there were no dead passes, the heated iron being fed between the lower and middle rolls on the first pass and then straight back again between the middle and upper ones, thereby reducing both the amount of labour involved and the degree of cooling between passes.

The Fussells' merchant mill had a number of spare rolls with profiles for producing iron plates in what were termed "Flats, Rounds, Half Rounds, and Squares".[10] The two mills were powered by a 20in horizontal steam engine with two 14ft flywheels positioned between them and driving by direct action. Merchant mills could also be used to improve the quality of wrought iron by repeated heating and rolling. Bars of poor-quality iron were piled up and tied together with wire, then heated and rolled, a process that might be repeated several times until the quality of iron desired was obtained. The iron would have been heated in furnaces within the building and it is probable these were sited at its north end. The building of the mills gave the business the ability to convert bar iron into plates suitable for tool making and to produce sections and "merchant" bar iron for its own use and for sale to other firms.

The rolling mills may have been completed by 1878, for in that year the gross annual rental value of the works for the Poor Rate more than doubled, rising from £120 to £300. Evidence provided by the census of 1881 points to the mill being in existence by 1880. This lists among the inhabitants of Great Elm an "Iron roller", Lewis Roberts, and a "bar iron and wire roller", James Newton. Lewis Roberts was born in the iron-making community of Dowlais, but had been working in the Yorkshire steel-making town of Middlesbrough prior to his moving to Somerset to work for Fussells.[11] Roberts came to Great Elm between 1877, in which year his son Thomas was born in Middlesbrough, and 1880, when his daughter Lucy was born in Great Elm. James Newton, like Roberts, was brought in from outside the area, coming from the iron-making area of Staffordshire. Another recruit from the Midlands in this period was Charles Smith, who moved from Oldbury in Worcestershire to take up a position as a works foreman. Smith moved to Great Elm between 1876, when his daughter Amelia was born in Oldbury, and 1880, when his son Walter was born in Great Elm.[12]

The cost of building and equipping the rolling mill must have been considerable and must have put a great strain on the Fussells' already stretched resources. Unfortunately, the mill seems to have proved a hindrance rather than a help and was in Edward Tylee's opinion a contributory factor in the decline of the company.

> Unfortunately for the business, as it turned out, a change was made, with the object of improving on the old system by rolling instead of hand forging . . . So rolling mills were built at great cost . . . For a long time the new system was not successful, though eventually it was perfected, but too late, for things had gone wrong, and the business was declining.[13]

The yard of the Lower Works, Wadbury, c1880 with carts loaded tools ready for dispatch. The brick building on the right was a portable engine house. In the background one of the chimneys of the rolling mills is visible.

It is important to remember that Tylee was relying for much of his evidence on memories of former employees of the company, and it may be that their views of the rolling mill were coloured by an understandable resistance to change and the threat that it posed to the traditional craft of hand forging. That said, subsequent events provide evidence that the mill did give trouble and may indeed have been the straw that broke the camel's back.

Bankruptcy

In the late 1870s James Fussell's financial position was deteriorating rapidly, the result of his expensive lifestyle, the cost of running Chantry School and the problems faced by the edge-tool business. In January 1879 the situation had become so bad that he resorted to borrowing £1,000 from his daughters Mary and Sarah on the security of the Parsonage in Chantry (now Chantry Grange). By then he also owed large sums of money to his brother John and to his old friend and colleague Joshua Allen. Later in the year the edge-tool business attempted to reduce its costs by appealing against its poor rate assessment for the Lower Iron Works and succeeded in getting a reduction of the rateable value from £240 to £208.[1]

Matters came to a head in April 1881 when James and his son made separate applications to the London Bankruptcy Court for the appointment of receivers.[2] James Thomas Richardson Fussell was described as being of Mells Ironworks, of Chantry, and of Victoria Street, London. It was reported the Reverend James Fussell had debts of £63,000, which were said to be "for the most part due to creditors in Bristol, Birmingham, and Sheffield", presumably to iron merchants or manufacturers. Stuckeys Bank in Frome was the largest local creditor, being owed £7,000. The two petitions for bankruptcy were opposed by another creditor, James's brother John Thomas Richardson Fussell, who was owed £8,000, having "borrowed money on a life policy to lend to his brother".[3] He declared "the petition ought to have been a joint petition of the father and son, as there was a partnership", an argument that was rejected by the court.

On the 27 April the *Frome Times* reported that William Morgans of Bristol had been appointed as receiver of the estate and in May a committee of inspection was formed, comprising George Walters JP of Wadbury House, Hugh McMurtrie of Stuckeys Bank, Frome, and Joshua Allen.[4] Morgans was practising as a "civil and mining engineer" in Bristol, and can be identified as the William Morgans who started his career in the Brendon Iron Mines. So if the identification of the William Morgan who was working for the Fussells in the early 1870s is correct, then the receiver of the business had once been its employee. In addition to being appointed receiver, Morgans was also given the power to manage the estate, the argument being:

It was essential that he should possess the power of manager, because there was a large amount of stock in the process of manufacture which, in its present unfinished state would be nearly valueless. In order to finish off such stock it would be absolutely necessary that the workmen should be kept employed, that the manufacturing process might be continued uninterrupted. The value of the manufactured stock would not amount to less than £4,000, and there were orders on the books of the firm which had been accepted, but which cannot be executed unless the stock is finished up.[5]

The works buildings and the land on which they stood were held by the trustees of James's marriage settlement, meaning that the actual assets of the business were confined to its plant, stock-in-trade, raw materials, goodwill and trademarks. The receiver had two options: sell these off and get what he could for them, or keep business running and seek to maximise the return by converting the raw materials into finished tools. The problem of estimating the value of the business's assets was made more difficult by the fact that these were changing from day to day, it being reported that "the price of iron had gone down, as was evidenced by the fact that a sale of 50 tons of Mells bar iron recently at Radstock brought only about £4 net on the works, whereas the same iron had been valued in the assets at £7".[6]

If the creditors were to keep the works going they would also need to invest money in it, since the rolling mill was still not working properly. An "eminent civil engineer" was asked to report on the problem and duly advised that they should "cease operations until everything had been thoroughly repaired". The works manager estimated these repairs would cost some £400 or £500 but said "he did not agree with the engineer as to the necessity for all of them".[7] The representative of one creditor was concerned about the safety of the machinery, warning that working it in its present state would involve "most serious risks under the Employees' Liability Act", which all agreed could not be taken.

There was a general recognition that even a temporary closure of the works would have serious repercussions, since it would lead to the cancelling of orders. Moreover, all tools finished too late for the year's harvest would have to be sold "at great sacrifice". The future of the works was in the balance and much was believed to hinge on what settlement the creditors would accept. An offer of 3s 6d in the pound was acceptable to most but rejected by the three major creditors - Joshua Allen, Reverend J.T.R. Fussell and Stuckeys Bank - all of whom withheld their agreement and held out for at least 5s in the pound. Reporting on this decision, the *Somerset & Wiltshire Journal* regretted their action "as it is to be feared it may cause the temporary closing of the works, and the consequent discharging of old and deserving workmen".[8] A deputation from the Fussell employees met with representatives of Stuckeys on 23 June, at which the men were told "they had the sympathy of the Bank, and that they had no ill-feeling against Mr. Fussell or any of his family". However it offered no assurances on the amount of settlement the bank would accept. The men returned to the works, where a meeting was held and, following the advice of the manager, agreed to resume work until the decision of a meeting of the bank directors in London on Saturday 27 June was known. One correspondent voiced the hope that "the interests of the men and their families as well as the prosperity of the neighbourhood will not be forgotten by those gentlemen".[9]

There is evidence the creditors were pursuing contradictory policies. On 27 July 1881 the *Frome Times* carried an advertisement for an auction of "a miscellaneous collection of bar iron, scythes, scythe handles, alder poles, straw, oil, nails and other general stores" at Mells Iron Works. This would clearly have affected the ability of the business to continue. Fortunately, another advertisement appeared the following week announcing notice of the auction had been countermanded and it would not take place. The business had won a reprieve; the question now was whether it had a long-term future.

Unable to recover money from the business in the short term, the creditors concentrated on James's other assets. On 16 September there was an auction in Chantry to sell off his heifers, calves, horses, fowl, a "capital brougham", a four-wheel wagonette, and a four-wheel pony carriage.[10] On 22 October 1881 the *Somerset & Wiltshire Journal* carried an advertisement for an auction of feed and corn at The Chantry, and on 19 November one for the sale of James's wine cellar, which included "carefully selected clarets, rare old ports, the finest brown and dry sherries . . . and other choice wines".[11]

Distressing as this publicity was, it was nothing like as humiliating as what happened next. In November an application was made to the registrar that James Fussell should set aside a proportion of his salary as a school inspector for the benefit of his creditors. These proceedings were reported in the local papers and his income now became public knowledge.[12] It was reported he was received a salary of £800 and about £250 in expenses, while his wife was entitled to £100 "pin money" chargeable on the Chantry Estate under the terms of the marriage settlement. For his part, James denied he was in receipt of an allowance for expenses, declaring he received only actual expenses. The case was heard at London Bankruptcy Court in Febuary 1882, the trustees asking for £400 of his salary, which would leave him between £500 and £600 to keep himself and his wife. James's counsel pointed out the £800 was a salary for work done and should not be touched. He further argued his client was 68 "and had been in enjoyment of an income of £3,000 a year, and it was not possible that he could to any great extent curtail his expenses".[13] This suggests James was earning about £2,000 from the business and rents on land and property. In giving his decision, the judge pointed out the bulk of the debts were in connection with the liquidation of the ironworks rather than from "extravagant living". He thought £400 too much and after further negotiation it was agreed £250 should be paid in monthly instalments.

The family did its best to limit the damage caused by the bankruptcies; the trustees of the marriage settlement disclaimed the rent owed for the works on the grounds of onerous burdens, while Mary and Sarah took possession of the Parsonage in lieu of settlement of the debt owed to them. The creditors were particularly sympathetic to James Fussell junior, one observing that he "had put £12,000 into the business at Mells within the last few years and had worked hard to make it a success. Their opinion was that he had taken the business over with an exaggerated idea of its value and was thus handicapped from the beginning".[14] The question was, could the business be salvaged and, if so, in what form and in whose ownership?

The Limited Company

Over the next six months the members of the Fussell family, together with their legal advisors and potential investors, entered into discussions with a view to merging the two existing businesses and creating a limited company. John Hounsell Fussell, now 53 and with no son to succeed him in his business, agreed to sell his "whole plant and good will", and to assign to the company his half-share in the Nunney Works.[1] For some years he had been less directly involved in the running of the business, having hired a manager - George Bolus, a Londoner who had been working at an edge-tool factory in Wolverhampton prior to coming to Nunney.[2]

The prime movers in the company seem to have been Mary and Sarah Fussell, their solicitor Edward Vaughan Thompson, a barrister called Trehawke Kekewich, Kekewich's son Lewis, who was a London metal broker, and Joseph Wright, an accountant. It is possible the involvement of Mary and Sarah was motivated, in part, by a sense of moral responsibility towards the workmen and their families who depended on the businesses. On New Year's Day 1882 the promoters of the new company signed an agreement with James Thomas Richardson Fussell, who was offered a certain number of B shares in the new company on two conditions. The first was that he would:

> Use his best endeavours to promote the interests of the Company and shall from time to time whether an officer of the company or not give such advice and information in reference to the working of the company's business as shall be reasonably required by the company.

The second was a non-competition clause, requiring that he should not "carry on or be engaged or interested in the business of an edge-tool maker nor permit or suffer his name to be used or employed in carrying on or in connection with the said business".

One month later on 1 February 1882 the public limited company of James, Isaac and John Fussell Limited was formed to run all the works as a single concern.[3] On the same day James began to fulfil his part in the agreement by writing to customers, informing them:

Arrangements had been concluded with Messrs Isaac Fussell & Co. of Nunney Ironworks, and Messrs John Fussell & Co. of Upper Ironworks, Mells, for the carrying on of our respective businesses from this date, as one concern , under the style of 'James, Isaac, & John Fussell Limited' for which purpose a private limited company has been incorporated amongst ourselves.[4]

The letter, a copy of which is preserved in Frome Museum, reassured customers that "each department will continue under the same management as heretofore and you may therefore confidently rely upon the same attention being paid to both quality and pattern as has been usual with us for more than a century". The new company described itself as "bar iron steel – edge tool manufacturer", while its letterhead described the business as being carried out from the "Mells & Nunney Steel & Ironworks". This change of emphasis reinforces the argument that the manufacture of bar iron and steel had become a more important part of the business since the building of the rolling mill. Interestingly, as late as 1883 the company was buying large quantities of charcoal, possibly for making special steels by the crucible method, placing an advertisement in January for "300 bushels of Clamp Burned Oak Wood".[5]

The first manager of the new company was Geoffrey Morgans, the young Welsh civil engineer who had arrived before the bankruptcies and stayed with the business through the difficult months that followed. The company's memorandum of association stated its objects to be to "acquire the goodwill of James Fussell, Sons, and Company . . . and all or any of the stock in trade, plant, machinery, book debts, trademarks, and other property" and to "carry on the business of manufacturers of edge-tools, and in particular of scythes, sickles, and reaping hooks, spades, and shovels". The capital of the company was to be £12,000, divided into 120 shares of £100 each. Of these 105 were to be A shares, and the remaining 15 the B shares created to pay off James Fussell. Mary Fussell took 12 shares and her sister Sarah 13. John Fussell subscribed for a token single share and the following year sold Nunney Court to the Daniel family of Frome and retired to his wife's home town of Beaminster, where he died in 1910. Mary and Sarah raised part of the £2,500 they needed to pay for their shares by mortgaging the Parsonage to the Reverend Charles John Vaughan, Dean of Llandaff and Master of the Temple. The largest single shareholder at the outset was Trehawke Kekewich, who took 49 shares. A number of single shares were held by London metal brokers Drew Thomas, Tom Drew Bear, Carl Svedborg, Reinhold Abretz, and Lewis Kekewich. The first list of shareholders shows control of the business had already passed from the hands of Fussell family members.

The creation of the company and retirement of John Hounsell Fussell put the future of the Upper Works at Mells in question. The buildings were still owned by the Horners, whose agents, Hippisleys, offered to let it to the new company, but this

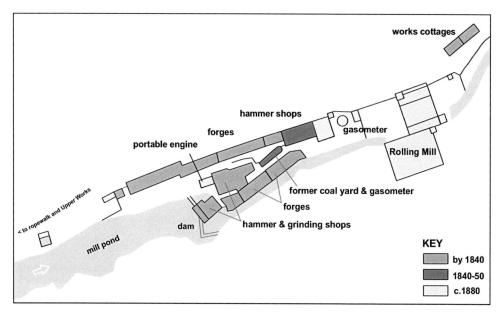

The Lower Works, Wadbury, c.1885 showing the principal phases in its development.

was declined in a letter of 1 September 1882 on the grounds that the rent was too high.[6] Two weeks later John Hounsell Fussell wrote to Hippisleys giving notice of his intention to quit the works, its cottage, and four other cottages he was leasing.[7] Negotiations on the future of the Upper Works dragged on for months, the company arguing considerable investment would be needed to make it usable. On 27 July 1883 a meeting was held on site to discuss the matter, and a few days later the company submitted an itemised list of work required, the total coming to £121 8s.[8] This included the removal of the old hammers, frames, and anvils, making concrete foundations for a new hammer, the purchase of the hammer, and the cost of its erection. It was argued a new 15ft cast-iron waterwheel was also needed, costing £45. In a letter of 25 August the company stated that £120 was far more than it was prepared to spend and it would not, therefore, be prepared to use the works as a factory but would consider taking it on as a warehouse at a lower rent.[9] Acting on the advice of the Hippisleys that they would not find another tenant, the Horners gave way and offered a 14-year lease of the mill and its cottages at a rent of £50 and agreed to allow £60 towards the work required, the lease being signed in November 1883.[10]

By this time it was becoming apparent to the company that more capital was needed, and at an extraordinary general meeting in London on 2 April 1883 it was resolved "that the Capital of the Company be increased by the issue of sixty £100 'A' shares, and the borrowing powers be increased to the extent of £3,000", making the nominal capital now £18,000. Ten of the new shares were taken up by Joseph

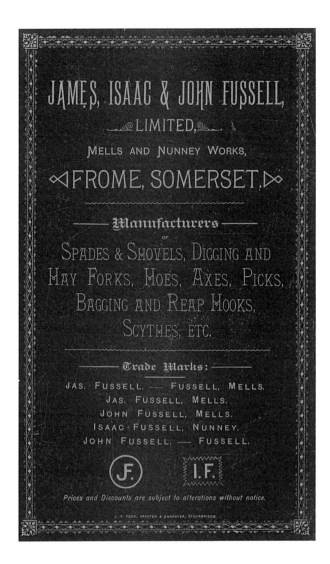

Catalogue of J. I & J. Fussell Ltd., printed in Stourbridge around 1890.

James Mabberly, the solicitor and trustee of Janet Fussell's settlement, and 30 more by George Nugel of Farlington, Hampshire.

Two months later, the Reverend James Fussell died aged 69 at his home in London. In his lifetime he had gained and lost a fortune, living to see his family's business empire reach the point of collapse and then be rescued at the eleventh hour by outsiders. He had been fortunate that he had been able to choose his own path in life, opting to make his mark in the field of education, rather than that of commerce. Following his death, his daughters Mary and Sarah continued to live in the Chantry, where they played an active part in their father's school. In 1886 Sarah Fussell married William Morgans, who she must have met with many times when he was acting as receiver and manager of the business during the bankruptcy proceedings. Sadly, she

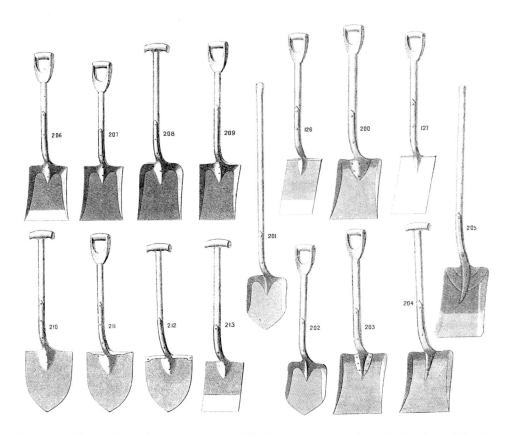

Pages from the catalogue showing just some of the large range of spades and shovels made by the company.

died in childbirth in April the following year. She and her stillborn son Hamish were buried in a grave close to the south-east corner of Chantry church. Following Sarah's death, the two sisters' shares in the company, together with the B shares allocated to their brother, were transferred to their cousin, John Dalrymple Maclean of Lazonby Hall, Penrith, possibly in part or full settlement of debts. By 1893 the only Fussell with any financial interest in the business was John Hounsell, who had retained his single share.

The creation of the limited company came at a time when the iron and steel industry was facing difficult business conditions. The slowdown in railway building and increased competition from American and European manufacturers made the industry one of the worst casualties of a recession that lasted from the 1870s to the mid-1890s. Many iron businesses closed in this period, including Frome's Butts Hill Ironworks, which was sold at auction in June 1886.[11] The edge-tool industry was also affected by the severe and prolonged depression into which British agriculture was plunged in 1870. In the two decades that followed, the acreage of wheat under cultivation more than halved and its price fell sharply.[12] This period also saw the increased use of horse-drawn mechanical reapers in place of traditional methods of harvesting.[13] These changes were bound to have an effect on a business whose products were agricultural and whose core products had been scythes and reap hooks. The limited company was aware of the need to be less dependent on these, placing greater emphasis instead on the making of spades and shovels. A catalogue produced by the new company around 1890 lists more than 50 different types of spades and shovels, including locomotive shovels, coal shovels, gravel shovels and American shovels. It is telling that the cover of the catalogue describes the company as "Manufacturers of spades & shovels, digging and hayforks, hoes, axes, picks, bagging and reap hooks, scythes, etc". Spades came first in the list, while scythes, so long the pride of the firm, were now placed last.

The change from agricultural tools to spades, shovels and forks required not only investment in new plant but also the hiring of men with the requisite skills to make them - including fork drawers, shovel and spade makers, finishers, grinders, and polishers. These workers were recruited in the West Midlands, mainly from the Stourbridge area, where spade and shovel making was an established trade. In the 1880s 30 or more men arrived from that area with their families – increasing the local population by more than 100. The majority of these moved to Great Elm and Mells, a major social upheaval for two such small villages. By 1891 almost half the edge-tool workers living in Mells and Great Elm were not born in the area. The influx of so many incomers into the area had its effects on the local community. The most notorious of these was the suicide of the Mells postman, Samuel Martin, in 1894 and the inquest gives a rare glimpse into the lives of Fussell employees in the period. What was revealed took the lid off a simmering village scandal involving the wife of a grinder recently arrived from the West Midlands. The unfolding story of the postman's infatuation with the young woman and her unwise friendship with him includes intimate details about Mells society in the 1890s and is told in Appendix A.

At the outset the limited company continued to operate all six of its works, but there is evidence that by the late 1880s a process of rationalisation and closure had already begun. One of the first works to stop production appears to have been Stoney Lane, the 1891 census listing only six Fussells' employees in Chantry, all but one of them grinders. Grinding seems to have continued at Chantry for a few more years, William Lapham of Stoney Lane still being described as a grinder when his son Alfred was baptised in November 1893. By the end of 1894 Nunney, Stoney Lane and Railford Works had all closed, production being concentrated at the two Mells sites.

The last share list for the company is dated November 1893, at which time it was dominated by two large shareholders - Trehawke Kekewich, who held 49 shares, and John Dalrymple Maclean, who held 44. By then the company was in decline and at an extraordinary general meeting on 20 October 1894 it was resolved:

> That it has been proved to the satisfaction of this meeting that the Company cannot, by reason of its liabilities continue in business, and that it is advisable to wind up the same and accordingly that the company be wound up voluntarily.[14]

The company's accountant, Joseph Wright, was appointed liquidator and set about winding up the company. On 31 October 1894 Wright wrote to Hippisleys informing them that the company was in liquidation and in the following month asked if the Horner Estate had any claims on the company. In November Hippisleys wrote back, asking if there was any prospect of another company taking over the works to carry on the business.[15] The reply to this letter has not survived but it is clear from subsequent events that a new company did indeed agree to take over the works and the agreement was made before February 1895. On the 12 February 1895 Hippisleys wrote acknowledging that "Mr Horner has received the lease of the Iron Mills from the late firm of Fussell and Co". They also seem to have enquired if the new company might be interested in the Upper Works, because four days later Wright wrote back: "Referring to your favour of 12th respecting the Upper Works we have to inform you that this company will not require these premises".[16]

The new company, which is not mentioned by name in any of the above correspondence, was Isaac Nash of Belbroughton, Worcestershire. Nash had begun making edge-tools in the 1830s and gradually acquired control of a number of forges in and around Belbroughton. Following his death in 1877, the company continued to expand, his son leasing an iron works in Stourbridge in 1881. By then the Nash business was a similar size to that of the Fussells and also had a reputation for making high-quality scythes.

By July the Lower Works was once more in production, for on 12 July Hippisleys wrote to the manager again asking if his company might be interested in leasing the Upper Works.

> The late firm of J. I. & J. Fussell & Co. having surrendered the lease of the Upper Mills at Mells Mr Horner desires us to ask if the new Co. desires to rent these premises . . . we have an application to rent them but Mr Horner thought that your Co. should first have the offer.[17]

The answer to this letter has not survived, but it seems that it was negative and the buildings were subsequently converted into a sawmill. The manager of the Lower

Works at this time was George Jordan, a native of Worcestershire who in the 1881 census was described as "Iron Works Manager" living in Lower Hagley, a village close to Belbroughton, indicating he was brought in by Isaac Nash & Co to run the Mells part of its empire.[18]

Five days before Hippisleys wrote the above letter, Janet Jemima Fussell was buried in Chantry. Her death at the age of 76 brought to an end the marriage settlement that had played a key role in preserving the business and precipitated the last act in the story of the Fussells of Mells. A number of major creditors, including the Mabberlys and John Dalrymple Maclean, were now in a position to insist that the estate, including the ironworks, be sold off to pay them what they were owed. Accordingly, it was offered for sale by auction in October 1895.[19] On the 19 October the *Somerset Standard* carried a report on the sale of what was described as "The Chantry and other estates in the parishes of Whatley, Mells, Nunney and Elm."[20] The auction was held at the George Hotel in Frome and the lots included the freeholds of "Mells Iron Works", "Nunney Steel and Iron Works", "Elm Iron and Steel Works", "Railford Iron Works", Chantry "Edge Tool Works", and the Fussell family mansions of The Chantry and Wadbury House.

The report of the auction provides further evidence that by this date the company had concentrated production at the Lower Works, this being the only one still in use at that time of the sale.[21] It is clear from the article there were hopes of a buyer coming forward who would be prepared to buy the works as a going concern. It may have been hoped that Isaac Nash, who had been renting the works from the trustees of the marriage serttlement, would now agree to buy the freehold. The auctioneer described the works as having been carried on by members of the Fussell family for more than 150 years, during which it had "seen times of great success and, of course, fluctuations". These "fluctuations" notwithstanding, he could "confidently recommend the property as a thorough investment, and if the works fall into the hands of capable men, he felt sure it would turn out a profitable undertaking". In the event the Lower Works did not find a buyer willing to take it on. Indeed, the whole sale proved very disappointing, many of the lots being withdrawn because they did not make the reserve price, or because there was no bid at all.

Two weeks after the auction on 1 November 1895 Isaac Nash & Co sent out a circular to customers informing them that from that date it was "removing the business of J. I. & J. Fussell, Mells Works, near Frome, and uniting it with our own trade". It had clearly acquired the goodwill of the company, since it was able to reassure customers that it would continue to "use the Fussell Trade Marks and shall also transfer all patterns for guidance in execution of orders". Isaac Nash also informed customers that it would be continuing "the services of such workmen as are required for the production of special Tools or patterns". A number of Fussell employees did indeed move to Belbroughton, including Sidney and William Rossiter and William Pickford, all from Great Elm.[22] In the 1930s two of the Fussell pattern books acquired by Isaac Nash were bound and presented to the Curtis Museum at Alton in Hampshire, along with one of the firm's own books.

The end of the limited company came on 29 August 1900, when the winding-up meeting of the firm of J. I. & J. Fussell was held in London, the receiver, Joseph Wright, laying before the shareholders the final accounts of the business. The end of the company was not, however, the end of the Fussell brand, for in August 1896 Isaac Nash & Co, trading as James, Isaac and John Fussell, acquired the four Fussell trade marks from the receiver and continued to use them for another half century.[23] By that time Nash had been taken over by Brades and Co. of Sheffield, which now traded as Brades Nash & Co. In 1962 this company was itself acquired by another Sheffield-based rival, Spear & Jackson.

Epilogue

"I end as I began, searching for something that is lost"

Robin Atthill, *Old Mendip*

Following the liquidation of the limited company, attempts were made to sell off or rent the various Fussell edge-tool works. The Lower Works at Mells stood empty for a number of years but proved too large to be of interest to prospective buyers. In 1899 the decision was taken to dismantle the machinery, the contract being awarded to the firm of Thomas W. Ward of Sheffield, by then the biggest scrap dealer in the country. In April Wards placed advertisements under the headline "Dismantling Mells Ironworks" to try to sell the rolling mills and their engine either as a single lot or three separate ones.[1] Once the machinery had been removed, the buildings were stripped of their roofing materials and left to decay - a sad end to what had been an impressive monument to the Fussell family's drive and

Photograph of the ruins of the Lower Works taken after the removal of the machinery in 1900.

Members of the Daniel family pose on a bridge above the weir of the Nunney works around 1900 (photograph courtesy of Charles Daniel).

ambition. The only part of the building to remain in use was the office building, one of the newest structures on the site, which was converted into a house and lived in until the 1950s.

The Upper Works at Mells, to which James Fussell had moved his business more than 150 years before, did find a tenant and was run as a sawmill for a number of years and then abandoned. The cottages at the works were pulled down at the beginning of the 20th century and the stone used for walling when Mells churchyard was enlarged. The Railford Works also became a sawmill, but is now a private house. At Stoney Lane, the site of the works was advertised for sale in 1905 as a "Pretty Cottage". By then the majority of the buildings were derelict and roofless, the one exception being the grinding shop, which housed a large waterwheel that pumped water up the hill to The Chantry and Parsonage (now Chantry Grange). In Nunney, the Daniel family, which had bought Nunney Court from John Hounsell Fussell in the 1880s, purchased the works and allowed the buildings gently to decay.

The only former Fussell works that appears to have continued to be used for edge-tool making was that at Great Elm. In 1901 it was occupied by Francis White, who was described in the census of that year as an edge-tool maker "working on his own account". Francis, who was born in the United States, was the son of Mells edge-tool maker Benjamin White and a nephew of William Wise junior. This business does not appear to have lasted long and by 1911 the works had became a private house.

The Fussell family's connection with the area they had done so much to shape continued for a number of years. Mary Fussell devoted her life to her father's school, working with her former governess Caroline Senior until its closure around 1908. Edward Tylee, who moved to Chantry in 1904, recalled in his article on the Fussells in 1934:

> Miss Mary Fussell, and Miss Senior were for many years joint head-mistresses of Chantry School, and well do I remember them in those days, but it has been closed for more than twenty years, though part of the building is still used for the village school, as it was formerly.[2]

When the school closed, Mary Fussell, together with Caroline Senior and their former French mistress, Mlle. Martin, retired to Elham in Kent, where they lived in a house they named The Chantry. After Caroline Senior's death in February 1912, Mary Fussell returned to Frome, where she died in 1921. Mary's older brother, James, moved back to London following his bankruptcy and in 1911 was living above a shop in Pimlico. Even here there was a local connection, for his landlady's mother, Rebecca Cook, was listed in the census of that year as having been born in Nunney. James lived on until 1927, having returned to the bar and developed an interest in amateur dramatics.

It is important to point out that the closure of the Fussells' business did not mark the end of edge-tool making in the East Mendips. In Doulting, the Coombs family had run a small business making shovels from the early 19th century until its abandonment in the first decade of the 20th century, while Arthur Steeds continued to run

Arthur Steeds photographed at the Gurney Slade Edge Tool Works.

his family's business making shovels at Gurney Slade until around 1930. It is a feature of the edge-tool industry that small manufacturers managed to co-exist alongside large ones without being driven out of business. Arthur Steeds, for example, made perhaps a dozen shovels a day at his water-powered forge, while a major manufacturer such as Brades produced several hundred. He survived because he supplied local quarrymen, miners and farmers with tools of known quality at competitive prices. However, such small family businesses had a finite life if their owner-operators had no heir or successor willing and able to take them on. This seems to have been the case with Robert Coombs and Arthur Steeds, both of whom closed their businesses when they were in their 60s when they became unable to continue running them. By then the Fussells and their contemporaries had become the subject of history and folklore.

The processes of celebrating the Fussell family and their tools began shortly after the removal of the machinery from the Lower Works. In 1903 the *Bristol Times & Mirror* carried an article which recalled with pride James Fussell's offer of a century before to supply 1,000 pikes to resist the expected French invasion, and paid tribute to the quality of the company's edge-tools, declaring:

> Good old patriotic James Fussell! When I was a lad, your name was still a household word in the district for bill-hooks, reaping-hooks etc., and my grandfather had tools of your make he set great score by.[3]

Writing in the early 1930s, Edward Tylee was able to draw on conversations with villagers who had worked for the Fussells. Moving forward another 30 years to the time of Robin Atthill, the Fussell businesses were now beyond living memory and could only be understood through historical research and fieldwork. Exploring among the ruins of the Stoney Lane works, Atthill saw large pits that the residents of the cottages were filling up with rubbish. Today those pits are no longer visible, but I have spoken to local men in their eighties who tell of having pushed motorbikes and even a Bull-nosed Morris car into them. Similarly, Tylee remembered Chantry School when it was still in existence and knew Mary Fussell; yet by Robin Atthill's time the school was used as a furniture store, its playground weed-grown and deserted. Since then the building has been converted into houses, its former purpose commemorated in the name The Old School House.

The Fussells have gone, their edge-tool works are ruins, but the impact they have had on the landscape remains tangible. Time moves on and perspectives change, each generation making its own observations, asking its own questions, drawing its own conclusions and making its own contributions to the unfolding story of the Iron Valleys.

Appendix A:
The Postman and the Grinder's Wife

On 10 July 1892 at 5pm, local policeman Samuel Redman pulled the body of Samuel Martin out of the lake in Mells Park. A post mortem examination subsequently found he had drowned. Samuel Martin, the village postman, was 47 and lived in Mells Post Office with his wife Mary - who was the postmistress - and five of their six children. An inquest into his death began sitting at the Talbot Inn the following Wednesday, William Austin Fussell serving as foreman of the jury. From the outset the proceedings focused on the relationship between Martin and the wife of one of the grinders from the Midlands, Harriet Walters.

Harriet and her husband Joseph had moved to Mells the previous year. Joseph was a spade grinder from Stourbridge, although he had lately been living and working in Aston, Birmingham. He was also a deaf mute, a disability that might well have prevented him from learning a trade had not his father, Henry, been a spade maker himself. Joseph's older brother, George, was also in the trade, and by 1891 was working as a spade finisher at Mells Iron Works. George Walters lived in Great Elm with his second wife Ann and his sons Walter, Charles and David, the first being a spade grinder and the other two spade finishers like their father. George came to work for the Fussells before Joseph and it is probable that he obtained a position at the works for his younger brother. At the time of Samuel Martin's death Joseph was 38, ten years older than Harriet. The couple would appear to have met in Aston and it was there they married in 1889.

When Joseph and Harriet first arrived in Mells they lived in the centre of the village, close to the post office. It was then that Samuel Martin made the acquaintance of Harriet. He soon paid regular visits to the Walters' house, a practice that continued after they moved out of the village to one of the ironworks cottages at Wadbury. He would also take her with him on trips to Frome in the trap he used for carrying letters and parcels.

The attention Samuel paid to Harriet soon became a subject of local gossip, and seems to have caused her to become greatly disliked in the neighbourhood. As the inquest progressed, attention focused increasingly on the relationship between Samuel and Harriet. On the night before he died, Samuel had taken letters to Frome, where he was seen at 9pm outside the Ship Inn in the company of Harriet and Mrs

The Upper Works at Wadbury around 1890. The building on the left is the row of cottages in which Harriet and Joseph Walters lived at the time of Samuel Martin's suicide (reproduced by kind permission of the Earl of Oxford and Asquith).

Lucy Brown, a widow. Under questioning, Harriet said Samuel had taken her into Frome that evening and then brought her home, leaving the house between 11pm and midnight, but returning again between midnight and 1am and staying for a late supper with her and her husband. Harriet explained the reason for the second visit was that her neighbour, Mary Vincent, had asked her to buy some laudanum for her in Frome, but she had forgotten and Samuel had volunteered to go home and fetch some.[1]

When the inquest resumed two weeks later, Harriet, who had been "molested" by some of the villagers, looked haggard and miserable. In answer to a question from the coroner, she explained she was expecting a child but denied that she and Samuel had discussed this on the way home from Frome. She had not told Samuel of her condition and did not know whether he knew anything about it. She maintained throughout the proceedings that she had not encouraged Samuel to visit the house and had told him it was making her unpopular in the village.

In summing up, the coroner addressed the question of the nature of the relationship between Samuel and Harriet. It was his belief the two were on terms of very great friendship and he would almost say of intimacy, although she denied that anything of an improper nature ever took place between them. He went on to observe that the jury, "as men of the world, though living in a country village, before absolutely believing the woman's statement, would weigh the surrounding circumstances". He then went on to summarize the evidence that seemed to support the contention that Harriet was "improperly intimate" with the deceased.

The jury retired to consider its verdict and when the court reconvened announced that it found the deceased met his death by drowning, and that he deliberately and "feloniously" killed himself "in a great measure in consequence of the improper conduct between himself and Harriet Walters". The coroner, jury and local opinion were clear that in their view Harriet was the guilty party, in that she had failed in her duty as both a woman and a wife by not rejecting Martin's overtures of friendship. Tellingly, no blame was attached to Martin for putting Harriet in a difficult position by paying attention to her in a public way. In the moral climate of the time, it did not strike them that another interpretation could be placed on events. Samuel Martin, who was old enough to be her father, had clearly become very attached to her, and she had been glad of his friendship - living as she did a lonely existence with a husband with whom she could not converse, in an isolated cottage far from her home town. His relationship with Harriet can also be seen as a symptom of his state of mind, rather than the cause. The truth behind what one local paper called "The Tragedy at Mells" may well lie somewhere in between.

Within four years of Samuel Martin's suicide most of the families from the West Midlands had left the area, only a few of the older men and women remaining. Between 1891 and 1901 the population of Great Elm dropped from 289 to 180 – a fall of 60%. One of those who stayed was Harriet's neighbour, Mary Vincent, who was widowed in 1893 and subsequently moved into Mells village and became caretaker at the Boys' National School in New Street. Samuel Martin's widow, Mary, continued to run the post office. In time, the sensation of the invasion of the iron workers from the West Midlands and the tragedy that followed were forgotten, forming no part of Mells folklore. It is not known when Joseph and Harriet left Mells but by 1901 they had returned to their home area. Harriet lost the baby she was carrying, but went on to have two more.

Appendix B: Sites

1. Gurney Slade Ironworks
2. Edge-tool works, Harridge Wood, Stoke StMichael
3. "Stangrist" site, Wulwell, Leigh-upon-Mendip
4. Topliffe's edge-tool mill (16th century), Stoke StMichael
5. Ironworks, Cook's Farm, Stoke StMichael (19th century)
6. Everett's edge-tool mill, Vobster, Mells
7. Bilboa Mill (stangrist, later corn mill), Mells
8. Bridge Cottage, Mells (Richard Hoddinott)
9. Upper Works, Wadbury, Mells
10. Lower Works, Wadbury, Mells
11. Great Elm Edge-tool Works
12. Kirty's Mill, Orchardleigh
13. Witham Forge, Trudoxhill
14. Nunney Edge-tool Works
15. Stoney Lane Edge-tool Works, Chantry
16. Railford Works, Chantry
17. Huntleys, Mells
18. Coombs' edge-tool works, Doulting
19. Downhead Mill (Corn)
20. Factory, Dead Woman's Bottom, Chantry
21. Nunney Mill (Woollen)
22. Fussell's conduit, Downhead
23. Dorset & Somerset Canal
24. Trial balance lock, Barrow Hill, Mells
25. Bilboa Colliery, Mells
26. Vobster Colliery, Mells
27. Vobster New Colliery, Mells
28. Breach Colliery, Leigh-upon-Mendip
29. Coal Barton Colliery, Coleford
30. Newbury Colliery, Babington
31. Mells Park
32. The Chantry
33. Holy Trinity Church, Chantry
34. Chantry School
35. Nunney Court
36. Rock House, Mells
37. Wadbury House, Mells
38. Egford House, Whatley

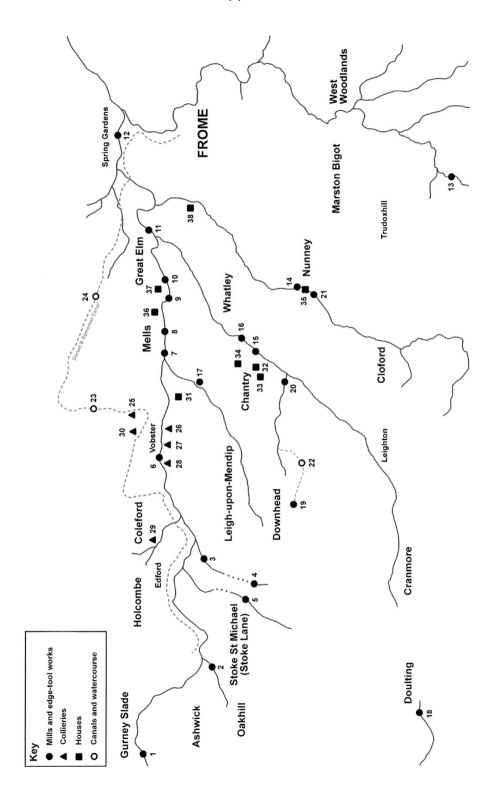

Notes

Introduction

1   Dr R.D. Reid, *Somerset Year Book* (1935) pp. 43-44

2   Ethelbert Horne, *Somerset Folk* (London, 1938) p.14.

3   Edward Tylee's article in the Somerset Year Book has been criticised for inaccuracies, but is important none the less for preserving information gleaned from talks with former Fussell employees which would otherwise have been lost.

4   R. Atthill, *Old Mendip* (Newton Abbot, 1971) p.184.

Chapter 1
The Iron Industry of the East Mendips before the Fussells

1   Places paying iron rents included Lexworthy in Enmore, Cricket St Thomas, and Whitestaunton, all of which are in the south and west of the county.

2   J. W. Gough, *The Mines of Mendip* (Newton Abbot, 1967) p.239.

3   M. McGarvie, *The Book of Marston Bigot* (Buckingham, 1987) p.22.

4   P. Stokes, *Downhead Landscape of Distinction* (Mendip District Council, Shepton Mallet, 2000).

5   The Feet of Fines in 1233/4 mentions "an old fulling mill on the water of Melnecumbe above Fobbestor which Henry Faber [Smith] once held with lands adjacent". (Rentalia et Custumaria, 1235-61 (Somerset Record Society, 1891) p.224. The entry reads: "Henricus Faber pro j stanegrist, xiid. Per. Annum".

6   Bilboa Mill is situated immediately beneath a tall cliff-like rock face. Daunt's stangrist was described as being "near the Cliff", while 18th century leases of Bilboa Mill describe it as "under the Rock".

7   A Lucas, *Wind, water, work: ancient and medieval milling technology* (Brill, 2006) p. 255.

8   Tool grinding mills existed in northern Italy by the early 15th century, five tool sharpening mills being recorded in the area around Florence. See G. Grenville and J. Astill, *Medieval Farming and Technology – The Impact of Agricultural Change in Northwest Europe* (Brill, 1997) p.284.

9   Robert and Adam were occupying the stangrist at Wulwell by 1301, in which year they are recorded as paying 6d. rent. It seems likely their surname was Hilberd, since two men of that name are recorded in the Mells accounts of the period (Mells Hallmotes of John of Kent, 1303 and 1305 in Mells Muniments, Oxford Archive).

10 Sir R.C. Hoare, *Monastic Remains at Witham, Bruton and Stavordale*, 1824, p. 127.

11 M. McGarvie, "Iron Smelting at Witham Friary, Trudoxhill and Nunney", *Somerset & Dorset Notes and Queries*, Vol. 31, 1984, p.354.

12 Ibid. It has been suggested that Blooms Mill Bridge on the stretch of the Mells stream that ran between Leigh-on-Mendip and Coleford (then Kilmersdon) may indicate the former presence of a water-powered forge in that vicinity. However, the fact that there was a family of the name of Blome, who were prominent in neighbouring Kilmersdon in the 16th century, provides an alternative origin of the name. No documentary evidence for a water-powered forge has yet been discovered in the valley of the Mells stream and

it is quite possible iron production in the area had ceased before the introduction of the technology into Somerset.

13 Both men were to die when the Black Death struck Mells in the summer of 1348.

14 Terrier of the Manor of Mells of 1515 (Mells Muniments).

15 *A Compleat History of Somersetshire* (1742) p.74.

16 J. Billingsley, *General View of the Agriculture of the County of Somerset* (Bath,1798) p.28.

17 Letter written 12th September 1840, cited in Report Relating to the Coal Field of India, Parliamentary Papers (London,1863) p.73.

18 L. Toulmin Smith (ed.), *The Itinerary of John Leland* (Southern Illinois University Press, 1954) p.294.

19 Ferris, J. P. "The Iron Lady of Somerset", *Somerset & Dorset Notes & Queries*, Vol. XXXI, 1984, p. 354. Cappoquin is on the River Blackwater and formed part of an extensive estate acquired by Lord Boyle from Sir Walter Raleigh in 1602. Boyle, seeing the potential for developing a local iron industry, imported English iron workers to build and run a furnace. The Yoghall mentioned in the letter is the port of Youghal, downstream of Cappoquin, and it is likely the iron produced at the Cappoquin furnace was brought down the Blackwater by boat and then loaded into sea-going vessels.

20 Ibid., p. 352.

21 Ibid.

22 Ferris Op. Cit., p.352.

23 A. Windrum, *The History of Nunney* (Frome Society for Local Study, Frome, 1998) p.97.

24 "Witham Friary: The First English Carthusian Monastery", in *Proceedings of the Somerset Archaeology and Natural History Society*, vol. 134, 1990, pp. 144-182.

25 Information provided by Mr M.D. Montague of Katoomba, NSW, Australia.

26 Inquisition on James Pewe, 1583. Somerset Record Office: DD/BR/Ich 7.

27 J. Jefferson (ed.), *History of Stoke St Michael* (Stoke History Group, 2006) p.39.

28 S & M.Morris (ed.), *Leases of the manors of Mells & Leigh on Mendip*, G10, 20th October 1663.

29 Undated memorandum relating to water rights on the Mells Stream (Mells Muniments).

30 S & M.Morris (ed.), *The Rent Book of George Horner*, 7 October 1693, No. 136. This lease refers to an earlier one of 8th January 1651.

31 J. A. Bulley, "To Mendip for Coal", Part 2. Somerset Archaeological & Natural History Society, vol. 97, p.18.

32 Robert Clarke, coal miner of Babington, is named in lease of 1671 (*Leases of the Manor of Mells*, R7).

33 The mention of Sir John having received no share of the coal is a reference to the fact that it was usual for the lord of the manor to receive a "free share", usually one-eighth, of all coal landed on his property.

34 *Leases of the manors of Mells & Leigh on Mendip* Op. Cit.

35 Ibid.

36 M. McGarvie (ed.), *The King's Peace: The Justice's Notebooks of Thomas Horner, of Mells,*

1770-1777 (Frome Society for Local Study, 1997) p.81. Thomas Horner dismissed the complaint on the grounds that it appeared "to be a contrivance of the complainant to induce Austin to stop a prosecution commenced against him for a debt of about six pounds. It seems Snook succeeded in such an attempt formerly on Robert Parsons an Alehousekeeper in Mells".

37 *Leases of the manors of Mells & Leigh on Mendip*, C68, 20 July 1769.

38 The lease is dated 8th September 1688 and is recorded in The Rent Book of George Horner.

39 M. McGarvie, "The Iron Industry in Mells and Nunney", *Somerset & Dorset Notes and Queries*, vol. 32, 1991, p.5. The lease was for 99 years, determinable on the lives of Richard Hoddinott, his wife Mary, and Richard's brother Joseph.

40 Ibid.

41 Document No. 422 (Mells Muniments).

42 S & M.Morris (ed.), *Mells & Leigh Court Rolls* (Kenilworth, 1992) p.290.

43 Windrum, Op. Cit., p.77.

44 Richard Hoddinott's will also includes a bequest of £3 to Joseph Cayford of Nunney, Edgetool maker.

Chapter 2
The Fussells Come to Mells

1   McGarvie, *Somerset and Dorset Notes and Queries*, Op. Cit., p.6.

2   McGarvie, *Somerset and Dorset Notes and Queries*, vol. 32, 1991

3   *Leases of the manors of Mells & Leigh on Mendip*, J-18, 20 August 1712.

4   Ibid. A-34, 20 December 1734.

5   Indenture of 1744 (Mells Muniments).

6   In January 1631 the Somerset Quarter Sessions ordered Naylor to take back an apprentice by name of Simon Wheller, whom he had assigned to one Philip Bradford, and to keep him for the residue of his term and pay Wheller five pounds "unless his said master Nayler shall make him perfect in his trade of a Cloathworker." *Somerset Quarter Sessions Records*, Somerset Record Society, Vol. 24, p.170.

7   Indenture of 1744 (Mells Muniments).

8   Rent Roll for the Several Manors of Mells, Samuels & Made the 28th day of September 1738 (Leases of the manors of Mells & Leigh on Mendip, M41). The same roll has entries for three other mills in the manor - Wragges Mill at the Duckery in Mells Park (corn), Burges Mill in Vobster (corn), and Gunnings Mill at Wadbury (fulling).

9   M. Morris (ed.) *Survey of Mells, Doulting, Cloford and Puddimore, 1762*.

10 McGarvie, *The King's Peace*, Op. Cit. p.113.

11 Robin Atthill wrote in *Old Mendip* that the occupation of shear grinder or shear maker is not found in the Nunney Parish Register until 1815. Atthill, *Old Mendip*, p.90.

12 Bowen to the Duke of Portland, PRO/HO/42/41.

13 Will of Robert Gunning, 29 September 1659 (PRO PROB 11/295).

14 *Somerset Quarter Session Records*, Vol 3, Somerset Record Society, 1912, p.367.

15 *Mells & Leigh Court Rolls*, Op. Cit., p.28.

16 Ibid, p.49.

17 Mells Terrier of 1673, reproduced in Leases of the manors of Mells & Leigh on Mendip, Rent Roll for the Manor of Mells.

18 Rent Roll for the Manor of Mells, 1742, reproduced in *Leases of the Manors of Mells & Leigh on Mendip*, Rent Roll for the Manor of Mells.

19 *Leases of the Manors of Mells & Leigh on Mendip,* D-14, 17 August 1769.

20 Edmund Rack's Topographical notes on the County of Somerset (SRO A/AQP a/1968).

21 *Iron: An Illustrated Weekly Journal for Iron & Steel* (1847) p.260.

22 *A Repartory of Patent Inventions*, 1799, p.288.

23 J. Collinson, *The History and Antiquities of Somerset*, 1791 vol. 2, p.461.

24 Abraham Crocker for Collinson (SRO A.AQP19).

25 Atthill, *Old Mendip*, Op. Cit., pp.104-119.

26 A large blubber knife with a cross handle and wrought-iron blade stamped Isaac Fussell Nunney was sold at auction in New York by Christies in January 2003.

27 McGarvie, *The King's Peace*, Op. Cit., p.138.

28 Great Elm Parish Register. 14 May 1786.

29 Tylee, Op. Cit. p.64.

30 The two properties owned by Bradley in Bristol were in Lewins Mead and Whitefriars Lane, respectively.

31 BRO 16164/2/r, 1829.

32 BRO 16164/2/s

33 BRO 16164/2/p, 1829.

Chapter 3
Canals and Inventions

1 *Bath Chronicle*, 17 January 1793, quoted in K. Clew, *The Dorset & Somerset Canal* (David & Charles, Newton Abbot, 1971) p.16.

2   Clew, *The Dorset & Somerset Canal*, Op. Cit., p.36.

3 The miller at this time was William Brown.

4 *Leases of the Manors of Mells & Leigh on Mendip*, T-3, 31 December 1781.

5 In addition, he secured a concessionary toll rate on the branch of not more than two pence per ton per mile on any coal, culm, or coke raised or made on his land. The usual toll for carriage of these loads on the branch was a flat rate one shilling and sixpence.

6 To put this in perspective, the Kennet and Avon uses 29 locks to raise the canal 237 feet in 2.25 miles at Caen Hill at Devizes.

7 Journal of Thomas Horner (Mells Muniments).

8 Burns, Robert. "Impromptu on Carron Ironworks", 1787.

9 "An Improved Apparatus Composed of Chains, Wheels, Rollers, and Conductors, for the Purpose of Lessening Friction in Raising, Lowering, Driving, and Conducting Heavy Bodies and Applicable to other Useful Purposes", Patent Number No. 2359.

10 J. Philips, *A general history of inland navigation* (1803) p.593.

11 K. Clew, *The Somersetshire Coal Canal and Railway* (David & Charles, Newton Abbot, 1970) p.46.

12 *Bath Chronicle*, 17 March 1803.

13 45 Geo. III, c.108.

14 Clew, *The Somersetshire Coal Canal and Railway*, Op. Cit., p.57.

15 Document giving distances between the Mendip collieries and "intended canal" (Mells Muniments).

16 A means of preventing water wheels from being flooded, Patent No. 2710.

17 An improved method of making and working forge and other bellows, Patent No. 3326.

18 *Trewman's Exeter Flying Post*, 16 January 1812.

19 *Trewman's Exeter Flying Post*, 25 April 1816.

20 *Monthly Magazine*, November 1808.

Chapter 4
War and Peace

1 Founded originally in 1797 as Frome Selwood Volunteers, in 1814 it was again reformed as the North Somerset Yeomanry.

2 Reverend F.W. Cleverdon, *A History of Mells* (Frome Society for Local Study, Frome, 1974) p.45.

3 L. S. Pressnell, *Country Banking in the Industrial Revolution* (Clarendon Press 1956) p.28.

4 Inventory of Lower Works, 1804. SRO DD/SAS/6795.

5 Inventory of Upper Works, 1804. SRO DD.SAS /6797.

6 In the lease Montague is described as "yeoman". In the lease the mill is described as having been "formerly in the tenure of . . . Halliday and late of Messrs. Griffith & Allen" (Orchardleigh Estate Muniments, transcribed by Frome Society for Local Study).

7 Dorset Record Office, Arundel of Wardour, 2667/1/13/79.

8 The banns had been published in Mells on 31 May, 7 and 14 June 1789. The couple were married in Whatley Church, the witnesses being Samuel Fussell and John Long.

9 Orchardleigh Estate Muniments. Map of 1818-1819 by Robert Burton, 8/111. Transcribed by Frome Society for Local Study and lodged in the Local Studies section of Frome Library.

10 The will of John Cayford was proved on 21 June 1809.

11 S. Montague, Montague Family History (MS, no date).

12 SRO DD/BR/nw/13.

13 G. Elwick, *The Bankrupt Directory* (London, 1843) p.209.

14 *The London Journal of Arts and Sciences*, 1831, p.281.

15 *Mechanics Magazine*, 23 February, 1828.

16 N. Barrington and W. Stanton, *Mendip: The Complete Caves and a View of the Hills* (Barton Productions with the Cheddar Valley Press) p.142.

17 The annual rent was set at £1 1s. On 1 September 1829 Edward Berkeley Portman

granted James Fussell the younger of Chantry House, Whatley, and Thomas Harris the younger of Frome, lace manufacturer (1793 directory has Thomas Harris, cardmaker of Frome), a 21-year lease of watercourse made by James Fussell the elder for a rent of £4 4s.

18 What James did not know was that the water that went down the slocker reappeared in his valley at the Seven Springs in Asham Wood, except in dry summers when it reappears in the valley beyond at Holwell Rising.

19 In April 1817, George Rossiter, son of James and Martha Rossiter of Stoney Lane, was baptised in Great Elm (Elm Parish Register).

20 Will of James Fussell, 1845, PRO/PROB/11/1797.

Chapter 5
Diversification and Litigation

1 The name Chantry appears to have been taken from the fields on which the house was built - Upper Chantry Field and Lower Chantry Field.

2 The house built by Henry A. Fussell in Corsley was, and still is, called Sturford Mead.

3 At an exhibition of the Bristol Botanical and Horticultural Society in July 1833 he won first prize for his pineapple (*Bristol Mercury*, 27 July 1833). In May 1834 he was forced to settle for third prize for his pineapple, but won first prize for his black grapes (*Bristol Mercury*, 17 May 1833).

4 D. J. Gill (ed) *Experiences of a 19th Century Gentleman: The Diary of Thomas Bunn of Frome* (Frome Society for Local Study, 2003) p.53.

5 E. Green, Bibliotheca Somersetensis: A Catalogue of Books, Pamphlets, Single Sheets (1902) p.422.

6 Atthill, *Old Mendip*, Op. Cit., p.74.

7 *A Treatise on the Progressive Improvement & Present State of the Manufactures in Metal* (London, 1831, revised 1853) p.53.

8 H. Coombs and R. N. Bax (ed) *Journal of a Somerset Rector* (London, 1930) p.179.

9 The Perforator was invented by a Bristol nurseryman called Munro and made at Isaac Fussell's Nunney Works (*Gardeners Magazine*, 1828 p.215).

10 *Outlines of British Geology* (SPCK, London,1850) p.202.

11 Dr R.D. Reid, *Somerset Year Book*, 1935, p.44.

12 *Aberdeen Journal*, 11 August 1830.

13 Coombs and Bax, Op. Cit., p.179.

14 K. Rogers, *Wiltshire and Somerset Woollen Mills* (Edington, 1976) p.207.

15 R.P. Beckinsale, *The Trowbridge Woollen Industry as Illustrated by the Stock Books of John and Thomas Clark, 1804-24* (Wiltshire Archaeological & Natural History Society, 1951) p.234.

16 Patent for "an improved method of heating woollen cloth, for the purpose of giving it a lustre in dressing" (No. 4999, 1824).

17 W. Carpmael, *Law Reports of Patent Cases* (London, 1843) p.449.

18 Patent for "improvements in pumps" (No. 6968, 1835).

19 J.B. Moore, *Reports of Cases Argued and Determined in the Courts of Common Pleas and Exchequer Chamber.* (London, 1831) p.458.

20 A. Smith, *An Inquiry into the Nature and Causes of the Wealth of Nations* (London, 1770) p.59.

21 Billingsley, Op. Cit., p.35.

22 Ibid, p.36.

23 Ibid. p.36.

24 Gill, Op. Cit., p.135.

25 C. & J. Greenwood, *Somersetshire Delineated* (London, 1822) p.91.

26 Moore, Op. Cit., p.461.

27 Ibid, p.461.

28 Ibid, p.470.

29 Ibid, p.470.

30 *Sherborne Mercury*, 17 October 1825.

31 K. Clew, *The Dorset and Somerset Canal Navigation,* Op. Cit., pp.68-69.

Chapter 6
The Struggle for the Lower Works

1 M. McGarvie (ed.), *Memoirs of a Victorian Farmer: Richard White of Mells, Norridge and Zeals (1828-1905),* (Frome Society for Local Study, 1990) p.55.

2 Cleverdon, Op. Cit., p.45.

3 M. McGarvie (ed.), *Memoirs of a Victorian Farmer,* Op. Cit., pp.54-55.

4 Atthill, Op. Cit., p.80.

5 *The Champion and Weekly Herald,* 5 May 1839.

6 *Bristol Mercury,* 7 September 1839.

7 *Bristol Mercury,* 23 November 1839.

8 Atthill, Op. Cit., p.78.

9 Henry Austin Fussell lived in Corsley in Wiltshire and was variously described in this period as merchant and dyer. His wife Margaret was daughter of James Carpenter, an "eminent dyer'", who died in 1812. Henry took over the business on his father-in-law's death and went on to build Sturford Mead at Corsley. In 1826 he entered into a partnership to establish an iron works at Maesteg in South Wales. The works and the township that grew up around it took its name from Maesteg Uchaf farm, part of the mineral estate leased by the iron company. The coal and iron ore were brought from mines in the vicinity, and the works was connected to the Porthcawl tramway via a spur that joined the tram road at Garnlwyd. It was the building of this spur, opened in 1827, which marked the beginning of the settlement of Maesteg. By 1831 the partnership had been expanded and by then included Joseph Stancomb (a Trowbridge mill owner), Thomas Motley (a Leeds wool-stapler), and Henry Cooper (a London cloth factor). The business also took over the Margam Tin Plate Works and by 1840 was trading as Motley, Fussell & Co. In 1838 three of the partners in the iron works opened the Vale of Neath Brewery, the largest in South Wales at that time. Within five years, however, the brewery was in fi-

nancial difficulties and large loans were transferred from the Maesteg company to prop it up, although without success. In 1841 Motley & Fussell went into liquidation and in 1844 the partners sold their interest in the venture. Henry Austin Fussell died in June 1845.

10 Atthill, Op. Cit., 79.

11 One of James Fussell's more unusual speculations was his investement in the East Crinnis mine. This had been producing copper ores as early as 1809. Between 1815 and 1833 the mine produced 38,330 tons of 5.25% copper ore, making it one of the most productive and profitable mines in Cornwall. In 1817 one writer described Wheal Crinnis as the mine "which of late years has proved so lucrative to the present Lord Mayor of London, and the other proprietors". In 1821 the mine was rated one of the six highest-producing copper mines in Cornwall out of a list of 74.

12 In the 1835 list of electors in the Frome Hundred, the vote for the works – described as "leasehold house and mill" – was held by Thomas Fussell's eldest son, James George Curry Fussell.

13 Until the 1970s the engine house chimney at Railford bore a plaque with Thomas Fussell's initials on it and the date 1840. The fact that they were his initials underlines the central role played by Thomas in the second quarter of the century.

14 Atthill, Op. Cit., p.78.

15 M. McGarvie (ed.), *Memoirs of a Victorian Farmer*, Op. Cit., p.55. White lived at Holwell Farm, on the other side of Mells Park from Huntleys.

16 Fortescue Horner to Col. Thomas Horner, 11th June 1838 (Mells Muniments).

17 Fortecue Horner to Col. Thomas Horner, 22 September 1838 (Mells Muniments).

18 Reverend J. Horner to John Fussell of Nunney, 27 July 1839 (Mells Muniments).

19 Henry Austin Fussell to John Horner, 24 December 1839 (Mells Muniments).

20 Atthill, Op. Cit., P.72.

21 M. McGarvie (ed.), *Memoirs of a Victorian Farmer*, Op. Cit., p.55.

Chapter 7
The Best Laid Plans

1 Wilson would go on to design St Stephen's Church in Bath, the Grand Pump Room Hotel, and Wincanton and Swindon town halls.

2 Gill, Op. Cit., p.53.

3 Ibid., p.53.

4 Maria Mary Fussell to John Prideaux, 1 May 1837 (Bristol Record Office: 20535/56).

5 *The West Briton*, 19 May 1837.

6 Will of James Fussell, 1845. PRO PROB/11/2029.

7 *Bankers' Magazine*, 1850, p.506.

8 *Morning Chronicle*, 23 June 1845.

9 *Bristol Mercury*, 10 September 1836.

10 *Railway Magazine*, 1836, p.83.

11 *Bristol Mercury*, 4 February 1854. See also H. Glynn, Reference book to the incorporated

railway companies of England and Wales (London, 1847).

12 *Liverpool Mercury*, 26 November 1850.

13 *Railway Subscription Contracts deposited in the Private Bill Office of the House of Commons*, Bath and Weymouth Great Western Union Railway (London, 1837).

14 The ages of the couple are both given as 20, which, if their identification is correct, must be a mistake, because John would have been 23 at the time.

15 *Bristol Mercury*, 29 December 1838.

16 *Gentleman's Magazine*, September 1854, p.314.

17 James won the Members' Prize in 1844 for a dissertation entitled: "Quaenam beneficia a legibus prascriptis diligenter observatis Academie alumni percipicat?", *Gentleman's Magazine* August 1844, p.182. See also *Alumni Cantabriensis*, p.592.

18 *The Ecclesiologist*, p.192.

19 R. Atthill, Op.Cit. p.76.

20 *British Farmer's Magazine*, 1848, p254.

21 Luigi Bianchi told his story in his memoirs written in 1859 : *Passages in the Life of an Italian: Priest-Soldier-Refugee* (London, 1859).

22 Ibid., p.303-4.

23 Ibid., p.304.

24 Ibid., p.307.

25 Ibid., p.310.

26 Ibid.

27 Reverend J.G.C. Fussell (ed), *Divine Songs Attempted in Easy Language for the Use of Children* (London, 1851).

28 *Gentleman's Magazine*, November 1852.

29 Caroline Fussell died in April 1854 and the following May John married Elizabeth Hall Dare, daughter of the the late Robert Westley Hall Dare, MP. Three years later John resigned the curacy and the couple moved to Mells, where they rented the Manor House from John Horner. They remained in Mells for a few years but by 1868 had moved to Amroth Castle in Pembrokeshire.

30 Connell, W. F., *The Educational Thought and Influence of Matthew Arnold*, Routledge, 1999, p.233.

31 *Bristol Mercury*, 13 January 1853.

32 *Bristol Mercury*, 12 March 1853.

33 *Gentleman's Magazine*, May 1853.

34 *Bristol Mercury*, 15 May 1858.

35 *Glasgow Herald*, 9 February 1871.

36 *New York Times*, 5 February 1882.

37 *Monthly Notices of the Royal Astronomical Society*, 1898, p.132.

38 *Monthly Notices of the Royal Astronomical Society*, 1898, p.132.

39 *Bristol Mercury*, 10 March 1860.

Chapter 8
Life and Work

1 The 1851 census of Mells described Thomas Fussell as "Scythe and Edge Tool Maker employing about 200 hands".

2 The 1851 census of Mells described John Fussell as "Farmer of 50 acres and Edge Tool Maker employing 23 men and boys".

3 The details of the sale of Nunney Ironworks in 1859 claimed that the works has a "staff of 30 experienced workmen".

4 Tylee, Op. Cit., pp.63-64.

5 *Edinburgh Review*, January 1860.

6 Tylee, Op. Cit., pp.63-64.

7 M. McGarvie (ed.), *Memoirs of a Victorian Farmer*, Op. Cit., p.59.

8 J. Stringfield, *Statement of the case of Ezekiel Baynton, jun., of Mells* (Wells, 1846).

9 Cleverdon, Op. Cit., p.76.

10 *Bristol Mercury*, 24 March 1830.

11 Minutes of Mells Vestry, 9 June 1829.

12 This is how Thomas Bunn described the lancers' reason for being in Frome (Gill, Op. Cit., p.34).

13 *Northern Star*, 27 May 1848.

14 F. Horner, *Time Remembered* (London, 1933) p.75.

15 Ibid., p.73.

16 M. McGarvie (ed.), *Memoirs of a Victorian Farmer*, Op. Cit., p.27.

17 *The Wesleyan-Methodist Magazine*, p.774.

18 E.P. Thompson, *The Making of the English Working Class* (Harmondsworth,1964), p.436.

19 J. Petty, *The History of the Primitive Methodist Connexion from its origin to the Conference of 1860*, London, 1864.

20 *The Primitive Methodist Magazine*, 1862. Vol. XX, p.628. John Horner was a supporter of Tractarianism - an affiliation of High Church Anglicans, most of whom were members of the University of Oxford.

21 *The Local Preachers' Magazine, and Christian Family Record*, 14 July 1859.

22 J. Chapman, *Formation of a Temperance Organisation in Frome*, c.1882. The Mr Hird mentioned seems to have been William Hurd, a local wood turner.

23 *Bristol Mercury*, 6 June 1846.

24 R.B. Grindrod, *Bacchus, an essay on intemperance*, 1843, p.342.

Chapter 9
Gentlemen and Convicts

1 *Gentleman's Magazine*, October 1852, p.438.

2 *East Somerset Telegraph*, 20 August 1859.

3 Details of the sale by auction of the estate of John Fussell (SRO DD\BR\1s/17).

4   *East Somerset Telegraph*, 6 August 1859.

5   *East Somerset Telegraph*, 20 August 1859.

6   *Pigot's Directory* for Dorset (1835) describes William Jesse as a "Tick and Dowlas Manufacturer and Bleacher".

7   William Jesse was declared bankrupt on 30 June 1837.

8   SRO DD/S/BT/27.

9   SRO DD/BR/hck/17.

10 Will of William Jesse of Bourton, Dorset, PRO PROB 11/2157.

11 In *Old Mendip*, Robin Atthill mentions in passing that John Fussell "took into the Nunney Works a young cousin, with the intention of his having a share in the business" but that nothing came of it. Unfortunately, he does not provide a source for this information.

12 *Northern Star*, 8 May 1841.

13 Elizabeth Payne was married to William Brand a chemist and druggist with premises in the Market Place, Frome. She made her will on March 25 and died before the census was taken on the evening of March 30. In her will it transpired that Isaac Fussell had been involved in the arrangement of her marriage settlement, money having been invested on her behalf in government securities in the names of Henry Elliot Esq. and Isaac Fussell, Edge Tool Maker of Nunney. Moreover, one of her sons was named Isaac Fussell Brand.

14 N.D. McLachlan, "Macquarie, Lachlan (1762-1824), *Australian Dictionary of Biography*, vol 2 (Melbourne University Press, 1967) pp.187-195.

15 Charlotte was the daughter of Alexander Russwarm, formerly a lieutenant of the West India Regiment and a veteran of the battle of New Orleans in 1816.

16 Letter from Sarah Long to Michael Long (Clevedon MS).

17 *Bristol Mercury*, 20 July 1839. Joseph Beard was from Maiden Bradley in Wiltshire and was 24 at the time of the theft.

18 *Bristol Mercury*, 16 April 1827.

19 A ticket of leave was a document issued to convicts who had served a period of probation and had shown by their good behaviour that they could be allowed certain freedoms. Once granted a ticket of leave, a convict was permitted to find work within a specified district but could not leave it without the permission of the government or resident magistrate. Ticket of leave men were allowed to marry or to bring their families from Britain. They were also allowed to buy property. A convict who observed the conditions of his ticket of leave until the completion of one half of his sentence was entitled to a conditional pardon, which removed all restrictions except the right to leave the colony.

Chapter 10
Vobster and Coal Barton Collieries

1   In the early 19th century there were four coal works at or near Vobster: Marsh, Breach, Tor and Bilboa Collieries.

2   Billingsley, Op. Cit., p.28.

3   *Quarter Sessions Records for the County of Somerset, Vol. I, James I, 1607-25*, Somerset Record Society, Vol.23, p.227.

4   *Bristol Mercury,* 19 July 1831.

5   G.C. Greenwell, "On the Southern Portion of the Somerset Coalfield", *Transactions of the South Wales Institute of Engineers,* (1858) pp.105-111.

6   J. McMurtrie, "Faults and Contortions in the Somersetshire Coalfield", *Proceedings of the Bath Natural History and Antiquarians Field Club* (1867-1870) pp.127-149.

7   C. G. Down and A. J. Warrington *The History of the Somerset Coalfield* (Newton Abbot, 1971) p.237.

8   *Felix Farley's Bristol Journal,* 3 September 1791.

9   The names of those buried in Mells were John Button senior, John Button junior, James Richardson, Joshua Moore, John Moore, Benjamin Bryant and Charles Button.

10 *Annual Register,* p.124.

11 Bulley, Op. Cit., p.70

12 Memorandum and Account Book of James Twyford (SRO DD/HY/16/2/3).

13 Twyford. A diary of the sinking of Vobster Breach Colliery in the same location in 1860 records that it was necessary to pump 150-175 gallons of water an hour to keep the shaft dry (Fairley,W.)

14 *Somerset Quarter Sessions,* 26 May 1656. Somerset Record Society, Vol. 28, p.285.

15 John Phillips, Memoirs of William Smith, author of the *Map of the Strata of England and Wales,* (London, 1844) p.11

16 R. Perkins report on coal in manor of Mells (Mells Muniments).

17 Ibid.

18 "Messrs. Buckland's and Conybeare's Observations on the South-western Coal District of England", *Transactions of the Geological Society of London,* 1824, p.256. Bilboa Colliery is incorrectly called Bilborough Colliery in this article.

19 Ibid.

20 Ibid.

21 Tradua Plummer was born around 1785 in Babington, a parish that had produced many miners over the centuries. In the 1851 and 1861 censuses he gives Babington as his place of birth, but there is no entry in the parish register for his baptism. His duties as bailiff were to inspect and supervise the workings and "carry out the plans of the owner or manager in the most economical way" (W. Fairley, *Glossary of the terms used in the coal mining districts of South Wales and Bristol and Somersetshire* (London, 1868), part 2).

22 Letter written by Tradua Plummer to the Reverend J. Horner, December 1850 (Mells Muniments).

23 Tradua Plummer to Reverend J. Horner, Op. Cit.

24 Minutes of Mells Select Vestry, 31 March 1834.

25 Tradua Plummer estimated output at the old pit at 15 tons per day, which gives an annual output of around 4,000 tons. In that period coal sold at around 9d a bushel at the pithead (15s a ton), which would realise £3,000 per annum gross if all coal raised was sold.

26 Hamblin's name was also spelled Hambleton and Hamilton on occasion.

27 Will of Abraham Hamblin (SRO D277 267/994).

28 Tradua Plummer to Reverend J. Horner, Op. Cit.

29 Lord Hylton, *Notes on the History of the Parish of Kilmersdon* (Taunton, 1910) p.96.

30 Ibid., p.128.

31 Ibid, p.254

32 Ibid, p.104.

33 Padfield, MS. Charles Tucker's parents were John and Mary Tucker. In 1800 he married Sarah Turner, also of Kilmersdon.

34 Greenwood, Op. Cit., p.21.

35 Kilmersdon Tithe Award, 1839.

36 W. W. Smyth, *A Rudimentary Treatise on Coal and Coal Mining* (Strahan, 1869) p.178.

37 J. Anstie, *The Coalfields of Gloucestershire and Somersetshire and their Resources* (London, 1873) p.60.

38 *Reports from Commissioners, Children's Employment (Mines)*, vol. 1 (1842) p.23.

39 Ibid.

40 William Brice's parents were Joseph and Hester, who married in 1789.

41 *Bath Chronicle,* 31 October 1850.

42 W. Fairley, Op. Cit., p.11.

43 *Birmingham Daily Post*, 21 October 1886.

44 Tradua Plummer to the Reverend J. Horner.

45 *Literary and Educational Yearbook*, 1859, p.144.

46 *East Somerset Telegraph*, 20 July 1859.

47 *East Somerset Telegraph*, 11 February 1860.

48 The Edford Colliery Co. (limited company 132104) was wound up in 1913 (PRO BT 31/21826/132104).

49 Fox Talbot to George Cotterell, 10 April 1858 (Fox Talbot Archive).

50 West Audry to Fox Talbot, 27 August 1858 (Fox Talbot Archive).

51 R. Hunt, *Mineral Statistics for the United Kingdom and Ireland* (1860), Geological Survey (1861) p.76.

52 Minutes of Mells Vestry, 26 September 1861.

53 Ibid, 21 April 1862.

54 Ibid, 28 March 1864.

55 Zebedee Beachim married Betsy Steeds, one of Stephen Steeds's older sisters.

56 *Bristol Mercury*, 22 October 1864.

57 *Bristol Mercury*, 4 February 1864.

58 Down & Warrington, Op. Cit., p.229.

59 *Law Times,* 14 January 1872, p.668.

60 E Bradby, *Seend: A Wiltshire Village Past and Present (Alan Sutton, 1981) p.100.*

61 *Trowbridge Chronicle*, 4 February 1865.

62 *East Somerset Telegraph*, 29 December 1866.

63 Anstie, Op. Cit., pp.99-100.

64 *Bristol Mercury*, 6 May 1874.

65 *Bristol Mercury*, 24 September 1878.

66 *Bristol Mercury,* 29 October 1878.

67 *Bristol Mercury*, 31 January 1879.

68 Stephen Steeds to Richard Berridge of a moiety of the Seend Iron Mines in chapelry of Seend and parish of Melksham (WRO ACC/1406/120).

Chapter 11
John Fussell & Sons

1 Mells Vestry Minutes, 17 April 1868.

2 Mells Vestry Minutes, 16 April 1863.

3 Mells Vestry Minutes, 17 April 1865.

4 *Gentleman's Magazine*, October 1863, p.501.

5 S. Cuzner, *Cuzner's Hand-Book to Froome-Selwood* (Frome, 1866) p.130.

6 Ibid, p.130.

7 *Somerset & Wiltshire Journal*, 8 March 1873.

8 O. Rackham, "Woods, Hedges and Forests", in M. Ashton (ed.), *Aspects of the Medieval Landscape of Somerset* (Somerset County Council, 1988) p.28.

9 Billingsley, Op. Cit. p.128.

10 *Harvey's Frome Almanack* (1881), and *Kellys Directory, Somerset* (1883).

11 In the 1850s Barbara and Benjamin emigrated to the United States, returning on the eve of the outbreak of the American Civil War and settling at Stoney Lane, Chantry, where they were living by March 1861. The couple's son James was born in Montgomery, Alabama, in 1857.

12 "Improvement in the Construction of Scythes", Patent No. 2439.

13 *Somerset and Wiltshire Journal*, 15 October 1870.

14 *Frome Times*, 20 August 1862.

15 *Somerset and Wiltshire Journal*, 14 October 1871.

16 *Somerset and Wiltshire Journal*, 24 January 1872.

Chapter 12
Cricket for Girls

1 With the building of the new school, the services of the untrained Mary Biggs were no longer required and she ended her working days as a servant in the school.

2 Reverend F. Watkins, "Report on the Institution at Whitelands for the Training of School Mistresses", *Committee of Council of Education* (1848).

3 Both these initiatives were the work of Emily Davies, one of the foremost pioneers of female education.

4 *Cuzners Hand Book to Froome Selwood*, Op. Cit., pp.142-3.

5 *The Diary of Reverend W. Michell,* (private MS).

6 *Schools Enquiry Commission: Minutes of Evidence* (London, 1868) p.710.

7 Ibid., p.709.

8 Ibid., p.710.

9 *Schools Enquiry Commission*, p.709. In April 1866 Chantry School had 73 pupils. Thirty-eight of these were boarders, 14 of whom were girls training as "domestics", while the village school had 35 children.

10 A National School (the current Mells First School) was established in 1813. In 1842 a separate boys' school was established in New Street, Mells, after which the original school became a girls' school.

11 M. McGarvie (ed.), *The King's Peace*, Op. Cit., p.56.

12 J. B. B. Clarke, *An Account of the Church Education Among the Poor in the Diocese of Bath and Wells in the Year 1846* (Taunton, 1847) p.105.

13 Cleverdon, Op. Cit., p.81.

14 *Schools Enquiry Commission*, Op. Cit., p.709.

15 Ibid., p.712.

16 Ibid.

17 Helen Mather was the pen name of Ellen Mathews.

18 P. Armitage (ed.), *A Torchbearer: Memoirs of Emily C. Fortey* (Oxford, 1947). p.9

19 H. Mather, *Comin thru' the Rye* (1875) p.94.

20 Armitage, Op. Cit., p.9.

21 *Ecclesiastical Gazette*, 14 September 1858.

22 Horton Davies, *Worship and Theology in England*, 1962 pp.116-117.

23 Chantry Parish Minutes, 10 June 1875, SRO/D/P/Chantry/9/3/2.

24 Armitage, Op. Cit., p.10.

25 Ibid.

26 *Bristol Mercury*, 14 September 1895.

27 *Birmingham Daily Post*, 9 March 1863.

28 Michell , p.7.

29 Fussell – Maberly deeds (SRO DD/BR/la/2).

Chapter 13
The Chantry Riot

1 *East Somerset Telegraph*, 27 March 1875.

2 *Somerset and Wiltshire Journal*, 1 May 1875.

3 *Somerset and Wiltshire Journal*, 1 May 1875.

4 *Frome Times*, 12 May1875.

Chapter 14
Stephen Skurray Steps Down

1 Elm Parish Register, 1875.

2   The Skurrays' house was in a part of the town that was in the neighbouring parish of Langley Burrell.

3   *Chronological index of patents applied for and patents granted* (London, 1865) p.168.

4   Patent for "Improvements in the Manufacture of Scythes, Reaping Hooks, Hay Knives, and such like Cutting Instruments", No. 2485.

5   *Kelly's Directory*, Wiltshire, 1880, p.61.

6   He preferred steel produced from Swedish iron and mentions the "Warranted Cast Steel for Scythes" produced by the Carlisle Works of the Sheffield firm of Wilson, Hawksworth, Ellison & Co. Rigidity was obtained by dressing the blades into an angular section, and hardness by immersion of the heated blade in fish oil (by preference whale oil).

7   The introduction of the Bessemer converter in 1856, followed by the Siemens-Martin open-hearth furnace in 1866 made possible a massive increase in steel output and a resultant lowering of prices.

8   *Griffiths Guide to the Iron Trade of Great Britain*, 1873 (Newton Abbot, 1967) p.201.

9   *Somerset & Wiltshire Journal*, 30 September 1876.

10 *Frome Times*, 29 September 1881.

11 1881 Census for Chippenham.

12 The final meeting was held on 2 March 1885.

13 *Bristol Mercury*, 11 October 1884.

Chapter 15
A New Partnership

1   *Somerset and Wiltshire Journal,* 18 February 1882.

2   Ibid.

3   Reverend J.G.C. Fussell, *Extract from report on Educational Appliances* [exhibited at the Vienna Exhibition 1873 by G. W. Leitner], Brighton 1875.

4   *Somerset and Wiltshire Journal*, 2 September 1876.

5   *Official Catalogue of the British Section, Paris Exposition, 1878* (London,1878).

6   *English Mechanic*, vol. 31, 1880, p.3. It was also advertised in the *Journal of Horticulture, Cottage Gardener and Home Farmer* (vol. 34, 1878, p.167), and *Bristol Mercury* of 18 March 1878.

7   *Bromley Record*, 1 June 1860.

8   The refractory bricks found at Stoney Lane include one made by Griffiths of Stourbridge.

9   The portable engine house is clearly visible in a photograph of the works taken around 1880.

10 *Glasgow Herald*, April 25 1899.

11 At the end of the 1850s the Dowlais company built the innovative Goat Mill, a rolling mill which incorporated the mechanisms and capacity of three working mills. It was said to be capable of producing a thousand tons of rail per week. Seventeen furnaces served each of the three-storey high mill's sections and the main engine was noted as providing "double the power of any engine yet built in Britain".

12   Not all the new workers hired by Fussells in this period were recruited from outside
     the area. Nearby Frome had a pool of skilled ironworkers and engineers which could be
     drawn upon. By the 1870s the town had a number of engineering works and foundries,
     among which were Cockey & Sons (the oldest foundry in the town), Abraham Haley
     & Co (steam engines, mill gearing, textile machinery, lathes and planing machines),
     and Rogers & Son (millwrights work, including steam engines and iron waterwheels).
     One Frome ironworker to be recruited by the Fussells at this time was Henry Cray, who
     moved from Frome to Mells between 1878 - when his daughter Margaret was born in
     Frome - and 1879, when his daughter Emily was born in Great Elm.

13   Tylee, Op. Cit., p.64.

Chapter 16
Bankruptcy

1   *Somerset & Wiltshire Journal*, 8 November 2008.

2   Ibid, 13 April 1881.

3   Ibid, 14 May 1881.

4   *Somerset & Wiltshire Journal*, 14 May 1881.

5   Ibid, 23 April 1881.

6   Ibid, 2 July 1881.

7   Ibid.

8   *Somerset & Wiltshire Journal*, 29 June 1881.

9   Ibid., 25 June 1881.

10 *Frome Times*, 14 September 1881.

11 *Somerset & Wiltshire Journal*, 19 November 1881.

12 Ibid, 25 November 1881.

13 Ibid, 25 November 1882.

14 Ibid . 2 July 1881.

Chapter 17
The Limited Company

1   Atthill, Op. Cit., p. 84.

2   On 18 December 1880 the *Somerset & Wiltshire Journal* reported that first sod of a new
    iron mine had been turned at Nunney, the proprietor being a Mr E.L.Owen and George
    Bolus being one of those mentioned as present.

3   Registered Company No. 16359 (PRO BT31/2932/16359).

4   Letter from James Fussell preserved in Frome Museum.

5   *Bristol Mercury*, 8 January 1883.

6   Hippisley & Co., to J. I & J. Fussell, 12 September 1882 (Mells Muniments).

7   J.I &J Fussell to Hippisley & Co, 28 September 1882 (Mells Muniments). The cottages
    were occupied by Ann Budgett, Thomas Stock, George Reed, James Clark.

8   J.I &J Fussell to Hippisley & Co, Letter of 8 August1883 (Mells Muniments).

9   J I & J Fussell to Hippisley & Co, Letter of 25 August 1883 (Mells Muniments).

10 Hippisley & Co., to J I & J Fussell, 10 November 1883 (Mells Muniments).

11 *Bristol Mercury*, 23 June 1886.

12 P. Mathias, *The First Industrial Nation: An Economic History of Britain, 1700-1914* (London, 1969) p.474.

13 The mechanical reaper was invented by Cyrus McCormick in 1831, and by the second half of the century a number of companies were manufacturing such machines.

14 *Bristol Mercury*, 23 June 1886.

15 At time of liquidation the company was behind with the rent of Upper Works. On 22 November 1894 the Horners' agents, Hippisleys, wrote to the company – "If you can only pay the half year to Michaelmas £24 Mr Horner cannot but fall in with this arrangement." They pointed out the Horners had allowed £60 for the installation of new machinery. The fixed plant at time of closure comprised a shovel-plating hammer, two lathe frames, two waterwheels and a boiler.

16 Wright to Hippisley & Co. 16 February 1895 (Mells Muniments).

17 Hippisley & Co. to the manager of Mells Ironworks, 12 July 1895 (Mells Muniments).

18 By 1901, following the closure of the Wadbury Works, Jordan was back in Hagley working as an edge-tool manufacturer's manager, possibly for Isaac Nash.

19 The auctioneers acted under the instructions of the firm of Beechcroft and Thompson, in which Edward Vaughan Thompson was by now a partner.

20 *Somerset Standard*, 19 October 1895.

21 The lot (25) comprised "Mells Iron Works, cottages, yards, premises, rocks, mill pond, roadway, sheds". The works was said to have an area of 5 acres, 2 rods, and 26 perches.

22 In the the 1901 census of Belbroughton, Sidney Rossiter (47) is described as an "Edge Tool Worker" born in Great Elm and William Rossiter (41) as a "Reap Hook Handler" born in Elm.

23 The Fussell trademarks acquired by Isaac Nash were Nos 11543, 11544, 11545 and 11546.

Epilogue

1   *Glasgow Herald*, 25 April 1899.

2   Tylee, Op. Cit., p64.

3   *Bristol Times & Mirror*, 6 August 1903.

Appendix A: The Postman and the Grinder's Wife

1   The Vincents were also recent arrivals from the Midlands and the laudanum may have been for her husband Benjamin, a spade finisher, who died a few months later.

Index